Explaining Violence
against Women in Canada

Explaining Violence against Women in Canada

Douglas A. Brownridge
and Shiva S. Halli

LEXINGTON BOOKS
Lanham • Boulder • New York • Oxford

LEXINGTON BOOKS

Published in the United States of America
by Lexington Books
4720 Boston Way, Lanham, Maryland 20706

12 Hid's Copse Road
Cumnor Hill, Oxford OX2 9JJ, England

British Library Cataloguing in Publication Information Available

Library of Congress Cataloging-in-Publication Data

Brownridge, Douglas A., 1969–
  Explaining violence against women in Canada / Douglas A. Brownridge and Shiva S.
Halli.
    p. cm.
  Includes bibliographical references and index.
  ISBN 0-7391-0166-8 (cloth : alk. paper)
    1. Abused wives—Canada. 2. Abused women—Canada. 3. Conjugal violence—
Canada. 4. Family violence—Canada. I. Halli, Shivalingappa S., 1952– II. Title.

  HV6626.23.C2 B76 2000
  362.82'92'0971—dc21   00-042434

Printed in the United States of America

⊖™ The paper used in this publication meets the minimum requirements of American
National Standard for Information Sciences—Permanence of Paper for Printed Library
Materials, ANSI/NISO Z39.48–1992.

In loving memory of David Austin Brownridge

Contents

Figures

Tables

Acknowledgments

A debt of gratitude is owed to the federal Department of Health who, in a forward thinking and somewhat controversial move, provided substantial funds for a large-scale survey of violence against women in Canada. We also wish to thank Statistics Canada for supplying data from the *Violence against Women Survey*. The academic community and the public will continue to bear the fruits of this commitment to understanding and reducing the prevalence of violence against women well into the future. We are also indebted to Dr. Carol Harvey, Dr. Rick Linden, Dr. G. N. Ramu, and Dr. Bali Ram for their helpful comments and suggestions. Finally, we wish to acknowledge the debt we owe to our families for all the support they provided us throughout the completion of this book.

Chapter 1

Introduction

Over the past three decades there have been hundreds of studies on wife abuse. These investigations have raised awareness of the extent, severity, and consequences of the problem of violence in marital unions. There has been an implicit assumption among most researchers in the area of family violence that those in common-law unions are sufficiently similar to married persons to be subsumed within the latter category. In fact, it might be assumed that rates of violence against women would be lower among common-law than marital unions since common-law unions can be seen as liberating from "ideological notions of subordination and dependence" associated with a marriage license (Freeman and Lyon, 1983:34). However, the relatively few studies that have separated these two marital status categories have consistently found violence against women to occur at higher rates in common-law than in marital unions. These findings, along with those of demographic studies that show that common-law unions are a family form on the rise in western Europe and North America, have recently led to concerns that rates of violence against women will increase. Dobash and Dobash (1995:469) write, "If the relationship between the type of union and differentials in rates of violence is substantiated by future research and current demographic patterns continue, these are further indicators of the need for urgent and careful attention to this issue." Furthermore, there has been a recognition

1

in recent literature on family violence that research is needed to explain higher reported rates of violence in specific groups, in particular among cohabitors (Anderson, 1997; Jackson, 1996). The present work addresses this issue by investigating the relationship between marital status and violence against women in Canada.[1]

Statement of Problem

DeKeseredy and Hinch (1991) have argued that married and cohabiting women should be combined to define a "wife." Noting that others have identified important differences between these two groups, DeKeseredy and Hinch (1991) cite several reasons for their position. First, the two groups should be combined simply to be consistent with other studies that have done so. Second, there are few differences between the two groups. For example, both groups adhere to the same patriarchal gender norms. Third, they argue that cohabitors are treated the same as marrieds by the legal system when they have children and/or when they have been living together for a sufficient amount of time. Finally, they write that cohabitors report comparable levels of satisfaction and closeness as well as similar conflicts and problems. DeKeseredy and Hinch (1991:8-9) conclude, "Our view is that it is difficult to differentiate between cohabitors and legally married women. Thus, our definition includes both groups."

DeKeseredy and Hinch's (1991) view is reflected in most of the research that has been conducted on violence against women. While many investigations into violence against women have been conducted since the 1970s, the vast majority of those that include a measure of cohabitation subsume these respondents within marrieds. The present work argues that, to achieve a better understanding of the causes of violence against women, it is important to disaggregate these groups, especially in view of increasing numbers of common-law unions. While most scholars assume that the increasing acceptance of common-law unions, as evidenced by their increasing numbers, and their increasingly similar treatment by the legal system means that marriage and cohabitation are sufficiently similar to be combined, the present work points to the differential occurrence of male partner violence against women as an indication that these two groups should not be treated as one.

Studies that do separate marrieds and cohabitors have found that cohabitors have far higher rates of violence than do marrieds. This suggests that something different may be operating for cohabitors than marrieds.

Combining these two groups in analyses, then, may confound findings related to causes. For instance, age is the variable that is most consistently associated with violence against women. In a descriptive comparison of age by marital status, Johnson (1996:151) concludes that "the overall decline in rates of violence according to the man's age is due primarily to cohabiting men." As well, Johnson (1996:154) conjectures that "The importance of low socioeconomic status cited in many studies of wife beating may actually be a combined effect of socioeconomic status, age, and common-law marital status, all of which are highly correlated." Similarly, Boba (1996:81), having contradicted the findings of previous studies, concludes that, "This may be because prior studies that found support for these variables did not control for all of the predictors found to be significant in this model—particularly not marital-cohabitation status." Hence, in addition to cohabitors having higher rates of violence, the findings of these researchers also suggest that it is important to separate marrieds from cohabitors to derive a more accurate understanding of the causes of violence against women. In this connection the present work outlines and tests a number of different explanatory frameworks for understanding marital status differences in violence. If, as Dobash and Dobash (1995:469) suggest, the "social revolution in the nature of family structure" as reflected in the increasing rate of common-law unions translates into an increase in the real rate of violence against women, then a big social problem will become bigger and an understanding of the dynamics of violence against women in common-law unions will become even more important.

Scope of the Book

While chapters 1 and 3 show that there is some support for the argument of the present study from those researchers who have separated cohabitors from marrieds in analyses of violence, there are a number of flaws that need to be overcome and gaps that need filling to allow one to make a more conclusive statement regarding the separation of cohabitors and marrieds in analyses of violence. The present study employs a large-scale survey to test explanations for marital status differences in violence. In so doing the findings can be judged to be more reliable than the vast majority of studies of marital status and violence. As well, this study is the only one of its kind based on a representative sample of Canadian women. Not only are the results much more generalizable than those of past studies, but also this is the only study of this type that is geared toward understanding the Canadian situation.

Note

1. While rates of violence vary by other marital status categories (e.g., single, separated, divorced), our interest lies in making a distinction between marrieds and cohabitors and, thus, it is beyond the scope of this book to investigate other marital status categories. In the present work, then, marital status will refer to marrieds, cohabitors, and, as will be discussed later, marrieds who have lived in a common-law union in the past with someone other than their husband.

Chapter 2

The Prevalence and Incidence of Violence against Women

Prior to discussing rates of violence it is necessary to clarify what is meant by prevalence and incidence rates of violence. Following this discussion, the prevalence and severity of violence against women in cohabiting and marital unions is examined. It is important to begin, however, with a brief overview of some key aspects surrounding cohabitation and marriage in Canada.

Common-Law and Marital Unions in Canada

It was not until 1981 that the Canadian Census began to distinguish between registered and common-law unions. Figure 2.1 graphically presents changes in the rate of couples living in common-law unions in Canada. In 1981, 6 percent of coresiding couples were living common-law. This figure rose to 8 percent in 1986 and 11 percent in 1991 (Che-Alford, Allan, and Butlin, 1994; Statistics Canada, 1992; Turcotte, 1988). Recent data indicate that this trend toward more common-law relationships continues. According to the 1996 Census, in that year 14 percent of couples in Canada were living in common-law unions (Statistics Canada, 1997). In other words, within a decade and a half, the number of cohabiting couples in Canada had more than doubled. The increase in the percentage of married couple families from 1991 to 1996, on the other hand, was under 2 percent (Statistics Canada, 1997). The impact of this trend toward increasing common-law unions in Canada is illustrated by Dumas (1997:130) who writes "consider that if the relative growth rates

5

were maintained for the two groups, by the year 2022 there would be as many common-law couples as married couples. Thus, in half a century . . . marriage would have relinquished its place as the conjugal norm in Canada."

Figure 2.1. *Rate of Couples Living in Common-Law Unions in Canada, 1981-1996.*

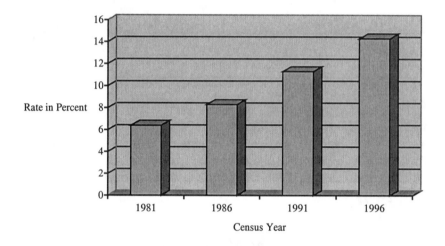

Census Year

Note: This is an original graph based on Statistics Canada Census data.

The dramatic rise in cohabitation relationships in Canada has been attributed to both social and economic factors. For some, common-law unions are either a stepping-stone or an alternative to marriage while economic and legal advantages are attractions for others (Che-Alford, Allan, and Butlin, 1994; Larrivée and Parent, 1993; Stout, 1991).[1] It has been posited (Che-Alford, Allan, and Butlin, 1994; Stout, 1991) that not only do common-law unions provide parallel economic and social support to marital relationships, but also they do so without the emotional, economic, and legal costs of divorce. Indeed, Cunningham and Antill (1995) have noted that, while it is natural to liken cohabitation to marriage, one can immediately see divergence when examining motives for entering into these unions. These researchers report that cohabitors rarely view their relationships as a type of marriage. One indication of this, according to Cunningham and Antill (1995), is that cohabitors typically do not expect to have children out of wedlock.

In terms of their demographic characteristics, cohabitors in Canada tend to be young, though their median age is increasing due to greater numbers of cohabitors 35 years of age and older (Che-Alford, Allan, and Butlin, 1994; Stout, 1991). Common-law unions were most prevalent among Canadians aged 20-24 in 1981. Since that time, they have been most prevalent among those aged 25-29 (Statistics Canada, 1997). While most cohabitors are never-married (63 percent in 1991), more than one-third of Canadian cohabitors have previously been married (38 percent of men and 33 percent of women) (Stout, 1991). From 1991 to 1996, there was also an increase in the number of common-law couple families with children, up 52 percent (Statistics Canada, 1997). Among common-law couple families in 1996, nearly 50 percent included children (Statistics Canada, 1997). Many of these children are from previous marital or common-law unions (1997). According to the 1995 General Social Survey, women who had given birth before their first conjugal union had a 50 percent greater chance than women without children to choose to live common law (Turcotte and Bélanger, 1997). Despite the increase in the number of children living in common-law unions, 73 percent of children in Canada in 1996 lived in families of married couples (Statistics Canada, 1997). As well, the number of Canadians entering multiple common-law unions is on the rise. In the early 1980s, 2 percent of men and women aged 18-64 had lived in two or more common-law unions. This figure had risen to 8 percent of men and 7 percent of women by 1990 (Stout, 1991). Common-law relationships have long been more prevalent in Quebec than in the rest of Canada. The 1996 Census confirms that this is still the case. Quebecers claim 43 percent of all common-law unions in Canada and one in four couples in Quebec live common-law (Statistics Canada, 1997).

Thus, cohabitation is a relatively new area of demographic study in Canada that seems to be rapidly expanding and changing. There are many topics in family sociology that should be investigated in light of this phenomenon. One such area of interest is the occurrence of violence against women in common-law unions.

The Conceptualization of Prevalence and Incidence Rates of Violence

Many methodological problems hinder our understanding of the scope of the problem of violence against women. One such difficulty is the choice of how to measure violence. In the quantitative research on family violence, most efforts at counting the rate of violence in the population are

Table 2.1. *Definitions of Incidence Employed in the Violence Literature*

Source	Definition
Straus et al. (1980:258)	"the percentage of the sample (or groups within the sample) who carried out one or more violent acts during the twelve months preceding the interview."
Hornung et al. (1981:681)	"whether or not one or more acts of the various types of spouse abuse occurred during the 12 months preceding the time of the interview."
Straus and Gelles (1986:468)	"the percentage of...spouses who used *any* of the violent acts included in the CTS during the year covered by the study."
Smith (1987:179)	"the percentage of women who reported having been abused one or more times in the past 12 months."
Rosenbaum (1988:95)	"whether each of the behaviors has occurred...with a time frame of the previous 12 months."
Brinkerhoff and Lupri (1988:419-420)	"the percentage of the total sample who reported having committed at least *one* of the eight violent acts against their respective partners during the twelve months preceding the interview."
Koss (1992:62)	"the number of separate criminal incidents that occurred during a fixed period of time—often a one year period."
DeKeseredy and Kelly (1993:35)	"the percentage of women who stated that they were abused and the number of men who indicated that they were abusive in the past 12 months."
Sommer (1994:9;161)	"abuse which has occurred within a specific time-frame." The percentage of respondents who "perpetrated some form of partner abuse against their intimate partners...during the past year."
Grandin and Lupri (1997:428)	"...(percentage), which reflects whether any violent acts occurred during the 12 months preceding the survey."
Barnett et al. (1997:37)	"frequency of a behavior over the past year."
Hilton et al. (1998:59)	"frequency of occurrences."

based on the traditional "crime survey" method (Dobash and Dobash, 1995; Smith, 1994), which has been viewed as measuring incidence. There has also been an increasing trend in recent years to collect what have been referred to as prevalence rates. Fekete (1994:45) has noted that the 1980s were witness to an "explosion" in the study of prevalence rates, which, he adds, are five to ten times higher than incidence rates. Brownridge and Halli (1999) have reviewed the family violence literature and concluded that there is tremendous inconsistency in the conceptualization of both prevalence and incidence rates of violence.

Confusion within Incidence Measures

There are two main sources of variation in definitions of incidence. The first refers to the dimension of violence a given researcher intends to tap with her/his measure. In other words, the meaning of the rate needs to be understood. An inspection of table 2.1 shows that incidence has been used in the family violence literature to refer to either the extent or the frequency to which violence occurs. More specifically, nine of the definitions of incidence tap the extent of violent behavior (Grandin and Lupri, 1997; Sommer, 1994; DeKeseredy and Kelly, 1993; Brinkerhoff and Lupri, 1988; Rosenbaum, 1988; Smith, 1987; Straus and Gelles, 1986; Hornung et al., 1981; Straus et al., 1980). These definitions give the percentage of the sample that reported the occurrence of violence. The remaining three definitions refer to the frequency of occurrence of violent behavior (Hilton et al., 1998; Barnett et al., 1997; Koss, 1992). Clearly, asking how many times violence has occurred has a very different meaning from asking whether or not violence has occurred.

Barnett et al. (1997:37) claim that "family violence researchers appear to have commonly used incidence to describe frequency of a behavior over the past year." However, our review of the violence literature suggests it is not the frequency of occurrences that most studies measure but, rather, the extent to which violence is occurring or not occurring in the sample.

The second source of variation in definitions of incidence refers to the assignment of limits on how long ago the violent behavior may have taken place. In other words, the time frame for the occurrence of violent incidents must be specified. Table 2.1 shows that the most common

Table 2.2. *Definitions of Prevalence Employed in the Violence Literature*

Source	Definition
Hornung et al. (1981:681)	Define "period prevalence" as "the total number of psychologically abusive acts, the total number of physically aggressive acts, and the total number of acts that were life threatening per couple year at-risk."
Smith (1987:179)	"the percentage of women who reported having ever been abused."
Rosenbaum (1988:95)	"whether each of the behaviors has occurred over the course of the relationship."
Koss (1992:62-63)	"the percentage of persons who have been victimized during their entire lifetime."
DeKeseredy Kelly (1993:35)	"the proportion of men who reported having been abusive and the percentage of women who indicated having been abused, since leaving high school."
Verburg (1993:37)	"how often...violence is a present and ongoing occurrence for women."
Smith (1994:112)	"the proportion of women in the sample who have ever been victimized, if not in their entire lifetime, in their adult lifetime, or within marriage or some other unbounded period of time."
Fekete (1994:45)	assaults that occur "over a lifetime, or some other lengthy time period."
Sommer (1994:9;161)	"abuse which has 'ever' occurred." The percentage of respondents who "perpetrated some form of partner abuse against their intimate partners at some point during their relationships."
Aldarondo (1996:145)	"the frequency of physical violence over the course of a year...i.e., the probability that the men would assault their female partners in a given year."
Barnett et al. (1997:37)	"frequency of a behavior over the lifetime of a relationship."
Magdol et al. (1998:49)	"if any physical abuse had been performed by the study member during the past 12 months."
Hilton et al. (1998:59)	"number of cases."

specification in incidence rates is a one-year period prior to the study. However, Koss's (1992) definition indicates that time frame need not be limited to one year and the definition of Hilton et al. (1998) does not place any restriction on time frame.

While a generalization can be made that incidence most often has referred to the occurrence/nonoccurrence of violence with a twelve-month time frame, it is, nevertheless, evident that conceptualizations of incidence vary in the family violence literature. The result of this inconsistency is that when we read about an incidence rate, it is not immediately clear what it means. Consequently, the impact of the statistic is lost in an often tedious, and sometimes futile, search for an operational definition of incidence.

Confusion within Prevalence Measures

A review of the definitions of prevalence provided in table 2.2 shows that, as with incidence rates, there is variation in the conceptualization of prevalence. There appears to be about the same level of inconsistency in the aspect of violence being tapped in definitions of prevalence as exists among those of incidence. As we have already shown, the majority of definitions of incidence refer to the occurrence/nonoccurrence of violence. On might be surprised to find, then, that this is also the case with definitions of prevalence. That is, eight of the thirteen definitions in table 2.2 clearly refer to the occurrence or nonoccurrence of violence (Hilton et al., 1998; Magdol et al., 1998; Sommer, 1994; Smith, 1994; DeKeseredy and Kelly, 1993; Koss, 1992; Rosenbaum, 1988; Smith, 1987).

While less evident from their definitions, two of the five remaining definitions also refer to the occurrence or nonoccurrence of violent behavior. In this discussion, Fekete (1994) implies that this is also the meaning of his use of prevalence. While Aldarondo (1996) uses the word frequency to describe prevalence, the additional description indicates that it is the probability of occurrence or nonoccurrence to which prevalence is referring.

On the other hand, Hornung and coworkers' (1981) definition of prevalence refers to the number of acts. For each type of violence Hornung et al. (1981:684) calculate prevalence as the mean number of acts based on either all couples in their study or on only those couples experiencing a given type abuse. Verburg (1993), in an article critiquing Statistics Canada's Violence against Women Survey, clearly uses prevalence to refer to the frequency of violence. Barnett et al. (1997) assert that prevalence is most commonly used by family violence researchers to refer to the frequency of violence. However, our review of the literature indicates most definitions refer not to the frequency of violence but the extent to which violence occurs.

With respect to time frame, an inspection of the definitions of prevalence in table 2.2 indicates that there are at least five time frames employed in conceptualizations of prevalence. Rosenbaum (1988), Sommer (1994), and Barnett et al. (1997) refer to the lifetime of a relationship. Smith (1987) and Koss (1992) use a time frame of an entire lifetime. DeKeseredy and Kelly (1993) employ "since leaving high school." Both Smith (1994) and Fekete (1994) note the potential use of more than one time frame. Smith's (1994) definition also includes "adult lifetime" as a possible time frame. Hornung et al. (1981), Aldarondo (1996), and Magdol et al. (1998) refer to a one-year period. Finally, Hilton et al. (1998) and Verburg (1993) do not specify any time frame.

Confusion across Prevalence and Incidence Measures

So far we have shown that definitions of incidence and prevalence used in the family violence literature vary in two respects. The first, the meaning of the definition, is crucial because a statistic based on the occurrence of violence cannot be compared to one referring to the frequency of violence; they have two completely different interpretations. The second, time frame, is also important. Even if the meaning of two rates is the same, the use of different time frames renders the rates incomparable. The magnitude of the rate will differ depending on the time frame used. It stands to reason that a rate with a time frame that spans many years will be significantly larger than one with a twelve-month reference period.

Since the consequence of using different time frames only increases the size of the rate, it seems logical that researchers would place more emphasis on the meaning of the definition to distinguish between prevalence and incidence. A comparison of the definitions of incidence and prevalence in tables 2.1 and 2.2, however, shows that this is not the case.

Of the eight sources that supply definitions of both incidence and prevalence, three vary in meaning between incidence and prevalence. Hornung and coworkers' (1981) definition of incidence refers to occurrence, while their definition of prevalence refers to frequency. Koss's (1992) and Hilton and coworkers' (1981) definition of incidence refers to frequency while their definitions of prevalence refer to occurrence. The remaining five sources employ the same meanings across incidence and prevalence. Four of these refer to the occurrence of violence across both incidence and prevalence (Smith 1987; Rosenbaum, 1988; DeKeseredy and Kelly, 1993; Sommer, 1994; Barnett et al., 1997). Barnett and co-workers' definitions, which they base on the family violence field in general, refer to frequency in their definitions of both incidence and prevalence.

Unlike the meaning of the definitions, in all definitions where a time frame is specified it varies between incidence and prevalence. In fact, in the majority of the sources reviewed in the present work, time frame is the distinguishing characteristic between incidence and prevalence. Each of the sources uses a one-year time frame for incidence and some longer time frame for prevalence. Thus, it appears that many researchers distinguish between incidence and prevalence not on the bases of what aspect of violence they measure, but in terms of how far in the past the reference period spans.

Overall, then, there is much conceptual confusion with respect to definitions of incidence and prevalence. This is particularly perplexing when it becomes apparent that some conceptualizations of incidence and prevalence measure the same phenomenon. For instance, all other things being equal, Rosenbaum's (1988) incidence rate would yield the same results as the prevalence rates of Aldarondo (1996) and Magdol et al. (1998). To avoid such quagmires resulting from multiple conceptualizations, clearly there is a need for a standard conceptualization of incidence and prevalence rates of violence.

A Proposed "Gold Standard"

Along with noting how prevalence and incidence have been commonly defined, Barnett et al. (1997) have also compiled more general scientific definitions of these rates. Barnett et al. (1997:37) write, "Incidence is the 'frequency with which a condition or event occurs within a given time and population ...' Prevalence is the 'percentage of the population that is affected with a particular disease [i.e., condition] at a given time." Hilton and coworkers' (1998) recent definitions of incidence as the frequency of occurrences and prevalence as the number of cases fit into this conceptualization. We agree with this distinction between prevalence and incidence such that prevalence should always refer to the

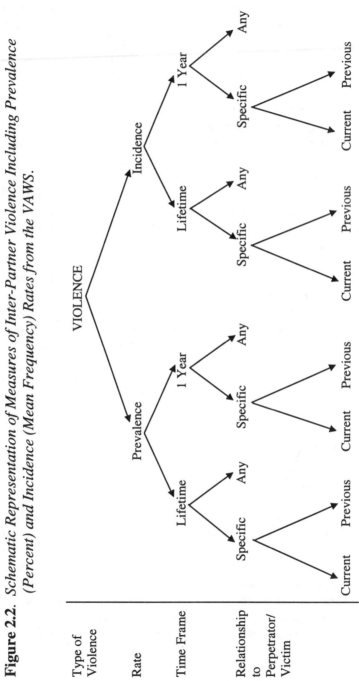

Figure 2.2. *Schematic Representation of Measures of Inter-Partner Violence Including Prevalence (Percent) and Incidence (Mean Frequency) Rates from the VAWS.*

occurrence or nonoccurrence of violence while incidence should always refer to the frequency of violence. More specifically, our view is that prevalence is the extent to which the violent behavior is distributed in the population, while incidence refers to the amount of violent behavior that occurs among those in the population who experience violence. These definitions also make sense semantically. Prevalence indicates how prevalent violence is in the population and incidence informs us of how many incidents are occurring. Thus, according to our definitions, a low rate of prevalence in conjunction with a high rate of incidence indicates that violence is occurring among relatively few couples who are experiencing repeated violence. On the other hand, a high prevalence rate in conjunction with a low rate of incidence indicates that violence is common in the population but it is not a behavior that is often repeated.

As we have shown, many family violence researchers make the distinction between incidence and prevalence solely on the basis of time frame. This appears to have been a main thrust leading to the confusion in the conceptualization of these two types of rates. Making the distinction between incidence and prevalence on the basis of time frame detracts from other distinctions that are even more fundamental to conceptual clarity. Differences in time frame will change the magnitude of the rate, but differences in the aspect of violence being tapped changes the entire meaning of the term. It is therefore on the more fundamental basis of meaning that we believe the distinction between incidence and prevalence should be drawn. As a result, we exclude time frame from the definition of incidence and prevalence rates.

There are, of course, many areas of study within the rubric of family violence. Since the present work deals with partner violence, the following illustration focuses on partner violence. Figure 2.2 contains a schematic representation of measures of interpartner violence. This figure shows that, as we have already outlined, there are several conceptual distinctions that will affect the rates of interpartner violence. Of course, there are also several methodological distinctions that will affect the rates achieved in a given study. These include the type and size of the sample, the method of administration, and the preamble to the questions.

The first conceptual distinction is the type of violence being investigated and the specific measures used to tap violence. Types of interpartner violence can range from emotional and psychological abuse to minor and severe physical and sexual violence. Next is the distinction between prevalence and incidence that we have defined above. Each type of rate can then vary by time frame. Since our focus is partner violence, we have identified two time frames: lifetime and one-year. Within each of these

Table 2.3. *Prevalence and Incidence Rates of Interpartner Violence as Described in the Literature*

Source	Type of Violence	Perpetrator	Location	Prevalence	Incidence
Straus et al. (1980)	Physical	Male	U.S.	----	12.1%[a]
Schulman (1981)	Physical	Male	Kentucky	21.0%[b]	10.0%[a]
Hornung et al. (1981)	Physical Aggression	Couple	Kentucky	1.75[c]	15.7%[a]
Smith (1985)	Physical	Male	Toronto	18.0%[d]	10.8%[e]
Straus and Gelles (1986)	Physical	Male	U.S.	----	11.3%[a]
Hotaling and Sugarman (1986)	Physical	Male	----	20.0-30.0%[b]	11.0-12.0%[a]
Smith (1987)	Physical	Male	Toronto	36.4%[d]	14.4%[e]
Dutton (1988)	Physical	Male	----	----	8.0-12.0%[a]
Brinkerhoff and Lupri (1988)	Physical	Male	Calgary	----	10.3%[a]
Kennedy and Dutton (1989)	Physical	Male	Alberta	----	11.2%[a]
Lupri (1989)	Physical	Male	Canada	----	18.0%[a]
Lupri et al. (1994)	Physical	Male	Canada	----	13.0%[a]
Sommer (1994) (wave II)	Physical	Male	Winnipeg	17.3%[b]	7.1%[a]
Grandin and Lupri (1997)	Physical	Male	Canada	----	18.3%[a]

[a] Current one year prevalence
[b] Current lifetime prevalence
[c] Current one year incidence
[d] Any lifetime prevalence
[e] Any one year prevalence

time frame categories, rates can vary depending on the respondent's relationship to the perpetrator or victim. The relationship can be specific, referring to violence by either a current partner or by a previous partner(s). The rate can also refer to violence by/toward any partner.

Conceptual Illustration

To illustrate the utility of a standard conceptualization of incidence and prevalence, we have applied our conceptualization to studies of interpartner violence conducted in the past. Table 2.3 contains prevalence and incidence rates as reported in a number of sources on interpartner violence.

As we have shown, the most common conceptualizations in the family violence literature make a distinction between prevalence and incidence on the basis of time frame alone. From an inspection of table 2.3, then, one may be tempted to conclude that reports of violence by current partners range from 2 to 36 percent at some time in the relationship and 7 to 18 percent in the past year. However, considering the notes at the bottom of the table which indicate the terminology for these rates in our conceptualization, an inspection of table 2.3 shows that the fourteen sources on interpartner violence in fact refer to five different rates.

All of the selected rates measure physical violence, though Hornung and coworkers' (1981) measure of "physical aggression" encompassed the nonlife-threatening items of the Conflict Tactics Scales (CTS). Table 2.3 shows that what twelve of the fourteen sources refer to as incidence, which we argue should be conceptualized as the frequency of violence among victims, really refer to one-year prevalence by a current partner. In other words, the figures indicate that across city, regional, and national studies in the United States and Canada, from 7 to 18 percent of women are victimized by their current partner in the twelve months prior to data collection. The two studies of Toronto women conducted by Smith (1985, 1987) refer to neither incidence nor one-year prevalence by a current partner. Rather, these figures refer to one-year prevalence by any partner. In Smith's definition, this encompasses any romantic relationship including boyfriends and dates.

Table 2.3 also shows that, of the six sources that present prevalence rates, three refer specifically to lifetime prevalence by a current partner. Thus, referring to these simply as prevalence rates does not provide enough information to make an adequate judgment about their interpretation. Not only must one indicate whether the rate refers to incidence or prevalence, but also one should specify the time frame in the terminology. The current lifetime prevalence rates range from 16 to 30 percent.

Hence, these figures suggest that from 16 to 30 percent of women are victimized by their current partner at some point in their relationship.

In all but one of these sources, a discussion of incidence and prevalence does not provide information on the actual amount of abuse that is occurring. That is, they do not provide information on our conceptualization of incidence. In the only case that does, that of Hornung et al. (1981), this information is provided as prevalence data. This figure suggests that the sampled Kentucky women reported experiencing violence by their current partner an average of 1.75 times in the past year. It is important to add that Hornung et al. (1981) calculate this figure based upon all couples in the study rather than only those who experience physical aggression. Calculated in the latter manner, the figure changes to more than eleven acts of physical aggression.

Finally, the two prevalence rates cited by Smith (1985, 1987) refer to lifetime prevalence of violence by any romantic partner. Thus, 18 to 36 percent of Toronto women report having suffered physical violence by a romantic partner at some time in their life.

In sum, it is evident that family violence scholars conceptualize what they refer to as prevalence and incidence quite differently. These differences can lead to confusion in terms of what is meant by prevalence and incidence. Clearly, a "gold standard" is desperately needed in the family violence field. While a standard will not solve all problems in comparing rates of violence across studies, it will certainly facilitate comparisons and ease of understanding for consumers of family violence research. The present study follows this "gold standard" conceptualization of prevalence and incidence.

The Prevalence and Severity of Violence against Women in Cohabiting and Marital Unions

American, Canadian, and New Zealand researchers have investigated marital status differences in violence against women.[2] While some of these studies have been specifically conducted to investigate differences in violence across marital status categories, for others the inclusion of common-law as a category is merely a reflection of the increasing recognition of this type of union. As a result, little attention is given to the differences between marrieds and cohabitors aside from noting differences

Table 2.4. *Rates of Violence for Marital and Cohabiting Relationships Reported in American, Canadian, and New Zealand Studies.*

Study	Married		Cohabiting	
	Rate in %	n	Rate in %	n
American				
Yllö and Straus (1981)[a]	3.6	2,049	13.5	37
Schulman (1981)[b]	6.1	1,729	11.7	20
Lane and Gwartney-Gibbs (1985)[c]	41.3	31	83.3	11
Stets and Straus (1989)[d]	15.0	5,005	35.0	237
Stets (1991)[e]	4.9	5,000	13.5	500
Jackson (1996)[f]	—	4,910	—	249
Boba (1996)[d]	9.6	5,811	26.5	355
Anderson (1997)[f]	—	—	—	—
Canadian				
Brinkerhoff and Lupri (1988)[d]	13.1	518	27.9	43
Smith (1986)[g]	14.1	192	34.0	47
Kennedy and Dutton (1989)[b]	8.7	631	24.4	48
Statistics Canada (1993)[b]	2.0	7,396	9.0	1,022
Sommer (1994)[b]	5.1	334	22.2	27
New Zealand				
Magdol et al. (1998)[h]	41.0	27	48.0	219

[a] Rates refer to one-year prevalence of male-to-female severe violence.
[b] Rates refer to one-year prevalence of male-to female overall violence.
[c] Rates refer to lifetime prevalence of physical violence experienced by male and female subjects from acquaintances, friends, partners, or dates.
[d] Rates refer to one-year prevalence of physical violence by either partner.
[e] Rates refer to one-year prevalence of physical violence perpetrated by respondent.
[f] Actual rates not reported but cohabitors found to be more violent.
[g] Rates refer to lifetime prevalence of physical assault by female respondent's current partner.
[h] Rates refer to one-year prevalence of physical violence perpetrated by respondent against a current or most recent partner in a cohort of young adults.

in their rates of violence. Rates from these studies are presented in table 2.4.

Table 2.4 demonstrates that a consistently higher proportion of co-habitors than marrieds report violence in past studies. Moreover, the difference in rates of violence for cohabitors is quite dramatic. Typically, the rate of violence for cohabitors exceeds that of marrieds by two times, but the difference can be higher than four times.

The large differences in the percentages of samples reporting violence reflect a number of methodological differences. As the notes at the bottom of table 2.4 show, rates vary in terms of time frame, violent acts that are being included, whether the male or both partners are perpetrating violence, and whether only current or past relationships are included. As well, populations being studied range from national samples (Anderson, 1997; Boba, 1996; Jackson, 1996; Johnson, 1996; Stets, 1991; Stets and Straus, 1989; Yllö and Straus, 1981), state- or province-wide samples (Kennedy and Dutton, 1989; Schulman, 1981), metropolitan samples (Brinkerhoff and Lupri, 1988; Magdol et al., 1998; Smith, 1986; Sommer, 1994), to student samples (Lane and Gwartney-Gibbs, 1985).

An inspection of table 2.4 also reveals that more than half of the studies reviewed in this work are based upon samples of less than fifty cohabitors. Use of small samples has had two implications. First, the small subsamples of cohabitors raises questions of representativeness and, therefore, limits the extent to which the findings of these studies can be generalized. Second, researchers studying small subsamples of cohabitors have been unable to reliably use regression-based multivariate statistical techniques to test explanations for differential rates of violence between cohabitors and marrieds. However, the five large-scale surveys provide reliable evidence that cohabiting unions are indeed more likely to be violent than marital unions.

The Severity of Violence in Cohabiting and Marital Unions

Finding that cohabiting unions are more likely to involve violence does not necessarily mean that they also are more likely to encompass severe violence. Some authors (Ellis, 1989; Ellis and DeKeseredy, 1989; Stets and Straus, 1989; Yllö and Straus, 1981) report that the gap between marrieds and cohabitors widens when only severe violence is analyzed. Indeed, Yllö and Straus (1981) found that cohabiting couples have twice the rate of overall physical violence as marrieds. However, when looking at only severe violence, cohabitors had more than four times the rate of marrieds.

Stets and Straus (1989) compared cohabitors and marrieds across a number of violent couple combinations and found that cohabiting couples have double the rate of mutual minor violence and six times the rate of mutual severe violence as marrieds. Among violent couples, more cohabiting (22 percent) than married couples (10.5 percent) reported both members of the couple using severe violence. These findings led Stets and Straus (1989:170) to conclude, "not only are cohabiting couples at greatest risk for violence, but, in addition, the most dangerous forms of violence occur when individuals cohabit."

Having divided the CTS into components of verbal aggression, minor violence, and severe violence, Jackson (1996:200) "found cohabitors to be more violent than spouses even at various levels ranging from minor to severe violence." Using the variety of abusive behaviours employed as an indicator of severity, Magdol et al. (1998) found that abusive young cohabitors employ a significantly greater variety of violent behaviours ($M = 2.78$) than do young marrieds ($M = 2.08$).

Boba (1996) compared marital and cohabiting unions on a measure of reported injury. The injury measure is based on "who has been cut, bruised, or seriously injured in a fight at any time in the relationship" (1996:54). Boba (1996) found that more cohabiting (5.6 percent of men and 13.8 percent of women) than married couples (1.3 percent of men and 5.7 percent of women) had experienced serious injury in their current relationship. Upon inspection of the subsample of violent cohabiting and married couples, however, more married than cohabiting women reported injury (59.2 percent versus 52.1 percent, respectively). Conversely, more cohabiting than married men reported injury (21.3 percent versus 13.6 percent, respectively). Based on these results, Boba (1996) concluded that married men are more severely violent than cohabiting men, and cohabiting women are more violent than married women.

Figure 2.3. *Intimate Femicide Rate by Union Type, 1974-1992.*

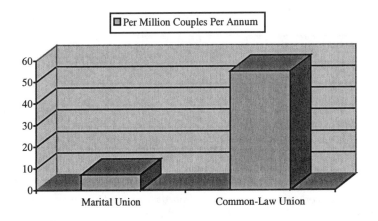

Source: Adapted from Wilson and Daly (1994)

The potential severity of violence against women in intimate relationships is disturbingly exposed when it escalates to the point where a woman loses her life. It is evident that women in common-law unions stand a much greater chance of being killed by their partner. The Canadian Centre for Justice Statistics (1994) reports that from 1974 to 1992, the rate[3] of intimate femicide[4] per million couples per annum has been almost eight times higher in common-law unions (55.1) than in married unions (7.2).[5] Figure 2.3 graphically represents the disproportionate risk of intimate femicide between married and cohabiting couples. This is clearly in keeping with and, in fact, exceeds the differences in rates of violence against women found in self-report studies.

Not only do intimate femicide rates encompass the most serious violence, but the fact that they are not based on representative sample surveys also indicates that marital status differences in violence are not due to research biases. Michael Johnson (1995) has written a provocative article that suggests that contradictions between "feminist" and "family violence" research are not due to theoretical misunderstandings of either group but, rather, to each perspective tapping different phenomena. Johnson (1995:288,291) argues that the differences that are found between shelter research and random sample studies are due to the fact that they are reaching two distinct, "largely nonoverlapping populations, experiencing different forms of violence." Random sample studies tap "com-

Table 2.5. *Marital Status (in Percent) of Couples in Partner Violence Cases Heard by the Winnipeg Family Violence Court, 1990-1997.*

Marital Status

Year	Cohab.	Ex-Cohab.	Spouse	Ex-Spouse	Dating	Ex-Dating	Other[a]
1990-92	35	12	20	10	12	7	4
1992-93	38	10	20	8	15	6	5
1993-94	36	11	19	6	18	9	2
1994-95	35	11	18	7	20	7	2
1995-96	38	9	16	7	21	6	3
1996-97	36	8	17	7	22	7	2

Note: This is an original table constructed from data provided by *Research and Education for Solutions to Violence and Abuse* (RESOLVE).
[a] Includes third party, homosexual partners, involvement of more than two family members, acquaintance, neighbour, stranger, friend, other and missing information.

mon-couple violence," which usually consists of minor violence, only "rarely escalating into serious, sometimes lifethreatening, forms of violence" (1995:285).[6] "Patriarchal terrorism," on the other hand, results from a man's "more general need to be in charge of the relationship" and is associated with families where "the beatings occur on average more than once a week, and escalate in seriousness over time" (1995:286,287). Straus (1993) has referred to this problem in terms of representative and clinical sample fallacies. The clinical fallacy occurs when findings based on police statistics and shelters are used for policy development to handle relatively minor and infrequent violence in the general population. The representative sample fallacy occurs when findings from community surveys are used to create policy to deal with the most severe cases, too few of which are contained in the data to be analyzed separately.

In addition to intimate femicide rates, another nonrepresentative sample indicator that can be used to get an idea of the seriousness of violence in different marital status categories is court records. Since its inception in 1990, the Winnipeg Family Violence Court (FVC) has dealt with "first appearances, remands, guilty pleas and trials for spousal abuse, child abuse and elder abuse" (Ursel, 1995:170). Table 2.5 presents the percentages of partner violence cases by the marital status of the couples involved for each year that data are available.[7]

As shown in table 2.5, from 1990 to 1997 men and women in an ongoing common-law union comprised the most frequent number of partner violence cases (M = 36 percent) heard by the FVC. Among expartners, former common-law couples also show the highest representation (M = 10 percent). On average, taken together nearly half (46 percent) of all partner violence cases heard by the FVC from 1990 to 1997 involved couples who were currently, or had been previously, living together in a common-law union. This is compared to a figure of 26 percent for married couples and 25 percent for dating couples. It is clear, then, that the relationship between common-law unions and interpartner violence shown in representative sample studies is also reflected in homicide statistics and the FVC data.[8]

Summary

Common-law relationships are increasing rapidly in Canada. Cohabitors and their relationships have different demographic characteristics than marrieds and their unions. It seems possible that these differences are linked to the finding that several studies using different methodologies have demonstrated that violence is more common in cohabiting than marital unions. Of course, since there are many more married than cohabiting people, a higher rate of violence among cohabitors does not mean that violence among this group is a bigger problem in terms of real numbers than is violence among marrieds. However, Statistics Canada's Violence against Women Survey shows that 38.4 percent of all women reporting violence in the twelve months prior to the survey were living common-law. If we can generalize these findings to other years it can be inferred that in a given year in Canada more than one-third of all violent victimizations among "spouses" are taking place in cohabiting unions. While there is some variation in the severity of violence across union types, cohabiting relationships also appear to be more likely to include severe violent behaviour. Cohabitors are also overrepresented in terms of the most severe violence, murder. The differential rates of murder along with a higher representation of cohabitors in the Winnipeg Family Violence Court buttress the findings of representative sample surveys. The fact that cohabitors are more likely to be violent, and perhaps more severely violent, is indicative that something different may be operating in the production of violence against women in these unions. We turn now to a discussion of some potential explanatory frameworks for understanding why cohabitors are more likely to be violent.

Notes

1. It is important to note that both partners entering a common-law union are not necessarily similarly motivated (Holland, 1995).

2. A detailed description of these studies is presented in table A.1 of appendix A.

3. This rate is calculated from the average annual number of homicides divided by the weighted average of population-at-large numbers of coresiding couples (Wilson and Daly, 1994).

4. Since uxoricide refers to "the killing of one's wife" (Funk and Wagnalls, 1982), the term intimate femicide, which refers to "the killing of women by their current or former partners" (Crawford and Gartner, 1992:iii), has been chosen. It is important, though, to note that the present discussion refers only to homicide perpetrated by a current partner.

5. The rate of men killed by their female partners is even more disproportionate among common-law unions; fifteen times higher in unregistered unions. It is important to add that former common-law partners and "estranged lovers" are not included in the analysis. Hence, the fact that separation is associated with

intimate femicide does not confound the results (Canadian Centre for Justice Statistics, 1994; Wilson, Daly, and Wright, 1993).

6. Grandin and Lupri (1997:440) have criticized Johnson's conceptualization of common-couple violence, arguing that "to lump together minor-only and severe violence into the category of common-couple violence tends to trivialize the potentially devastating physical and psychological consequences that some of the life-threatening violent acts may have on the victims."

7. Separate data for the years 1990-1991 and 1991-1992 are unavailable.

8. One may argue the possibility of a class bias in the FVC data. Previous research points to married persons having a greater likelihood of possessing a high socioeconomic status (Ellis, 1989; Ellis and DeKeseredy, 1989; Stets, 1991). It is arguable that persons of higher status are less likely to use services due to social stigmatization and that marrieds may therefore be underreported in the FVC data. However, the findings of the FVC are consistent with those of the surveys based upon self-reports and homicide surveys. Moreover, when past studies have controlled for socioeconomic status, higher rates of violence among cohabitors persist (Boba, 1996; Stets and Straus, 1989; Yllö and Straus, 1981).

Chapter 3

Explanatory Frameworks

Understanding the higher rates of violence in common-law than in marital unions is the subject of a good deal of speculation but relatively little actual theorizing and even less empirical testing. The following identifies and discusses explanatory frameworks that have either been applied to this issue or that may apply but remain untested.[1]

Feminist Theory

Sociological approaches to violence against women make a distinction between family violence and feminist approaches (Kurz, 1993a, 1993b). The main difference between the two approaches is that while family violence theorists see patriarchy as *one* cause of intimate violence among many, feminist theorists view it as *the* cause, or at least the "ultimate root," of violence among intimates.[2] The implications of marital status differences in violence for feminist theory are unclear in the literature. To the extent that one focuses on male dominance within marriage, marital status differences can be seen as undermining the feminist argument. Yllö and Straus (1990:384) write "Societal tolerance of wife beating is a reflection of patriarchal norms that, more generally, support male dominance in marriage. Traditional marriage, in turn, is a central element of patriarchal society." Pearson (1997:132), in critiquing feminist theory, writes "That men have used a patriarchal vocabulary to account for themselves doesn't mean that patriarchy *causes* their violence, any more than being patriarchs prevents them from being victimized. Studies of

27

male batterers have failed to confirm that these men are more conservative or sexist about marriage than nonviolent men. To the contrary, some of the highest rates of violence are found in the least orthodox partnerships—dating or cohabiting lovers." However, if the focus is removed from the institution of marriage to a more general focus on the influence of patriarchal norms then feminist theory is back in the equation as an explanation. Pearson's (1997) assertion misses the point that men who choose to cohabit are not necessarily any less subject to the patriarchal norms of society. In fact, Ellis (1989) argues that cohabiting men are more committed than married men to patriarchal norms and values that legitimate male violence against female intimates.

Lenton (1995a) makes a connection between feminist theory of violence against women and marital status. Using Statistics Canada's Violence against Women Survey data, Lenton (1995b) found a statistically significant association between marital status and a patriarchy index. Lenton (1995a:319) concludes, "common-law, low-income males are more likely to adhere to a patriarchy ideology than are legally married men from a higher income household." The effect of patriarchy, then, may actually be exacerbated in common-law unions. For instance, common-law husbands may engage in conflict and violence because they lack a sense of ownership that a marriage license might provide.[3]

Lenton (1995a:324) notes that "additional support for the feminist theory comes from research on the relationship between marital status and wife abuse." The research Lenton (1995a) cites in support of this contention is based on "family violence" theories, particularly resource theory. Indeed, violence that occurs as a result of a man having fewer resources than his wife is indicative of an underlying dimension of patriarchy. Similarly, men with low levels of education, low-status jobs and low incomes are also more likely to espouse a familial patriarchal ideology (Smith, 1990b). Thus, the association between socioeconomic status and violence against women may also operate through patriarchal ideology. If cohabiting men are more likely to be low in SES and gender-status inconsistent then they may also be more likely to subscribe to a patriarchal ideology that is linked to violence.

Resource Theory

The basic premise of resource theory is that the powerful will dominate the less powerful (Blood and Wolfe, 1960; Johnson, 1996). The balance of power between two partners depends on which partner contributes the greater number of resources to the family, which, in turn, depends on their relative resourcefulness and life circumstances (Bersani and Chen, 1988). Men have traditionally held more power than women because of their greater income, social standing outside the family, and knowledge and expertise due to their employment (Johnson, 1996). Goode (1971) added a central proposition to resource theory. According to Goode, possessing more resources than another provides an individual with the ability to use force. Alternatively, men who do not have access to resources that will allow them to dominate their partner, such as money or occupational status, may use violence, the "ultimate resource," to keep their partners in line.

Ellis and DeKeseredy (1989) argue that cohabiting men are more likely than married men to be dependent on their female partner because they tend to have fewer resources (i.e., less education, more unemployment, and lower income) than their female partners. In an effort to restore gender-status consistency these men resort to violence. However, Dobash and Dobash (1995) point out that there is little evidence of difference between marrieds and cohabitors in terms of potential conflicts over allocation of resources.

Anderson (1997) tested educational status incompatibility to see to what extent it would explain the effect of sociodemographic factors including cohabiting status. Anderson's (1997) results show that, while male cohabitors may lack educational resources relative to their female partners, educational incompatibilities do not account for the marital status-violence relationship. Boba (1996) also tested status incompatibility in terms of education and found it not to have a significant effect on violence.

Anderson (1997) also tested the effect of income incompatibility on cohabiting status and found that a lack of income resources relative to their female partner does not account for the higher levels of violence among cohabiting men. Anderson (1997:664) concludes, "status incompatibility is not a central mechanism through which race, education, age, and cohabiting status are associated with domestic violence."

Routine Activities Theory

Routine activities (RA) theory focuses on the lifestyles people lead and the extent to which their lifestyles relate to their probability of victimization. For instance, according to this theory, young single women "are vulnerable to assault because they frequent places, such as bars, parties, and fraternity houses, also frequented by young single males, who are the group with the highest rates of offending" (Johnson, 1996:16).

In a test of RA theory on stranger violence, Rodgers and Roberts (1995) do not include marrieds and cohabitors citing the difficulty of applying RA theory to these groups. Rodgers and Roberts (1995:370) state that "According to RA theory, activities outside the home increase contact with strangers, thereby decreasing guardianship and increasing risk of stranger victimization, but these same activities may in fact decrease risk of wife assault because contact with potential offenders is actually decreased." In a critique of Rodgers and Roberts's (1995) study, Dobash and Dobash (1995:474) write, "By excluding from analysis the violence women experienced from intimates in a private setting, RA theory has not been put to the most stringent test where one would expect it to have even less applicability." Similarly, Felson (1997) suggests: "Activities that draw people away from their home are not likely to increase violence in the home. If anything, they would have the opposite effect, because going out at night reduces the frequency of contact between family members."

Considering, however, that violence among common-law unions is often grouped within "spousal" violence, and given that the prevalence of violence in these couples exceeds that of marrieds, it may be that RA theory is applicable to understanding "spousal" violence. To date there has not been an application of RA theory to understanding differences in violence between marrieds and cohabitors.[4] However, one indication of the different lifestyles of marrieds and cohabitors is their respective rate of stranger violence. Johnson (1996) reports that women in common-law unions have three times the rate of stranger violence compared to married women. This is indicative that there is something about the lifestyles of common-law women that places them in a position of being more susceptible to violence by strangers.

Rodgers and Roberts (1995) do note that marital status affects lifestyle; a central component of RA theory. It may be that cohabitors' lifestyle takes them to places and leads them to engage in activities that increase the risk of violence. For instance, given that cohabitors tend to be young (Ellis, 1989; Johnson, 1996; Stets and Straus, 1989) and are more likely to be childless (Boba, 1996; Wilson, Johnson, and Daly, 1995), they may be more likely to have an active "night life." Violence among cohabitors may be precipitated to the extent that this includes activities such as going to the bar, which, given the increased likelihood of sexual advances mixed with alcohol consumption, is conducive to conflict. Wilson et al. (1995:343) argue, "There is reason to suppose that husbands may be less secure in their proprietary claims over wives in common-law unions than in registered unions." As well, research has shown that cohabitors are more likely than marrieds to exhibit drunkenness (Stets, 1991) and to report more alcohol problems (Horwitz and White, 1998). The fact that the couple is living in the same residence means that they are more available for the conflict arising from these outside activities to be translated into violence in the home. Thus, while going out at night may reduce the frequency of contact between a couple, it also may increase the frequency of contact with potential sexual rivals, thereby exacerbating insecurities over a lack of formal commitment. Felson (1997:210) argues, "A positive relationship between night life and domestic violence cannot be attributed to differences in opportunity." However, if by "opportunity" one means a favorable or advantageous circumstance or combination of circumstances, a positive relationship between nightlife and violence could be attributed in part to opportunity, particularly for cohabitors.

Subculture of Violence Theory

The originators of subculture of violence theory, Wolfgang and Ferracuti (1967), began with the observation, much like resource theory, that violence tends to be more prevalent within particular sections of the social structure and particularly among low socioeconomic status people. Through socialization, members of a subculture learn that culture's norms and values, including those involving violence. With respect to interpartner violence, Bowker (1983) found that the extent to which an abusive husband is a member of certain male peer subcultures, patriarchal subcultures encouraging gender and age domination, is positively related to the extent to which he beats his wife. Recent research on dating violence has provided some support for subculture of violence theory. Based on a representative sample of Canadian university and college dating relationships, DeKeseredy and Kelly (1995:47) have found that "male peer support is one of the most important predictors of sexual victimization in university/college dating relationships."

Ellis (1989) has applied the logic of subculture of violence theory to understanding higher rates of violence among cohabitors. Ellis (1989) notes that cohabiting men spend more time interacting with their peers than do married men. Moreover, due to the demographic characteristics of cohabitors, their peers are deemed more likely than married men's peers to subscribe to patriarchal subcultural values and norms. Ellis

(1989) suggests that the combination of spending more time with peers and the characteristics of these peers increases the probability that cohabiting men are violent toward their partners. This theory, however, remains to be empirically tested.

Social Learning Theory

According to social learning theory, behavior is learned through modeling (Bandura, 1971). Observing or experiencing violence by influential people reinforces the use of violence for children and teaches them how to be violent (Barnett, Miller-Perrin, and Perrin, 1997). Girls who witness or experience violence may learn to expect violence in relationships and are therefore more likely to find themselves in a violent adult relationship. Indeed, Statistics Canada's (1993) Violence against Women Survey found that women who had witnessed their father being violent toward their mother were almost twice as likely as women who had not witnessed violence to be in a violent relationship.

Jackson (1996) used data from the National (U.S.) Family Violence Resurvey to test whether higher rates of violence among cohabitors relative to marrieds is due to social learning variables. In line with social learning theory, Jackson (1996) found that experiencing violence in childhood significantly predicts future violence. In terms of marital status, however, Jackson (1996) found that, of cohabitors and marrieds who had been physically abused by a parent, cohabitors were more likely to engage in violence. Similarly, while frequency of childhood victimization is positively related to violence, when the frequency of childhood victimization is controlled the marital status-violence relationship persists. Jackson (1996) also found that observing parental violence during childhood does not account for the higher levels of violence among cohabitors.

Of all theories of violence against women, social learning theory has received the most consistent support in empirical tests. Yet, Jackson's (1996) test indicates that differential learning does not account for the differences between marrieds and cohabitors. As Kaufman and Zigler (1987:199) have stated with respect to social learning and violence, "Being maltreated as a child puts one at risk for becoming abusive but the path between these two points is far from direct or inevitable." As with the etiology of violence in general, based on Jackson's (1996) analysis it would appear that the marital status-violence relationship is more complex than simply differential modeling of behavior.

Sex-Role Theory

Sex-role theory focuses on the sex-role socialization of boys and girls. The sex-role socialization of boys is viewed as teaching them to be dominant in relationships, to be the breadwinner, to be the king of his castle, and to use force if deemed necessary. On the other hand, girls are taught to be passive to men and to perform the roles of wife and mother. In studies of wife abuse, however, there has been little empirical support for sex-role theory (Mihalic and Elliott, 1997).

The only test of sex-role theory in terms of marital status and violence is that of Boba (1996). Boba (1996) found that marrieds and cohabitors are not significantly different in terms of views on the sharing of tasks. However, cohabitors were significantly more egalitarian in responding to questions about the man being the sole breadwinner and preschool children suffering if their mother is employed. In terms of violence, Boba's (1996) descriptive analysis showed that both women and men who are more egalitarian are more likely to be in a violent relationship. The logistic regression showed that men are more likely to be violent when they are traditional and their partner is egalitarian. These differences, however, did not account for the different rates of men's violence across marital status categories.

Social Isolation

A number of studies (Cazenave and Straus, 1979; Stets, 1991; Stets and Straus, 1989; Yllö and Straus, 1981) have pointed to social isolation as being responsible for higher assault rates among cohabitors. Yllö and Straus (1981:346) note that married couples that are young and poor are less violent than their cohabiting counterparts, and they suggest that the superior coping of the marrieds may be due to "the greater social support and integration in the kin network of the married couple." Stets and Straus (1989) have also postulated the importance of being isolated from one's network of kin in determining rates of violence. They argue that cohabitors' greater isolation from their networks of kin, either by choice or due to stigma attached to cohabitation relationships, may make physical violence "less likely to be recognized or challenged" (Stets and Straus, 1989:176). Ellis (1989) has also noted that married men have attachments that cohabiting men do not posses. According to Ellis (1989), by virtue of marriage, men are more likely to be surrounded by family who will both support the woman if she decides to break her silence and act as inside observers that are potential sources of punishment.

Stets (1991) has tested the social isolation hypothesis. Among Stets's (1991) findings we see that, while cohabitors are less likely to be tied to groups/organizations and their partner, they are more likely than married couples to have ties to family and friends. Stets explains cohabitors' greater attachments to informal networks as their attempt to compensate for their isolation from formal networks and their partner. According to Stets (1991:677), "the less integrated cohabitors are, the more likely they are to engage in aggressive behavior."

A close examination of Stets's (1991) article, however, reveals some problems. For instance, measurement seems to be problematic. Stets (1991) does not have a direct measure of social isolation. Instead, hypothesized effects of social isolation, namely social support and social control, are used as indicators. Level of commitment, measured by perceived probability of separation, is used as an indicator of social control. Stets's (1991) finding that cohabitors are less likely to be tied to their partner derives from this variable. Elsewhere in the article, Stets (1991, endnote 4) recognizes that by definition cohabiting unions are less committed relationships. It is not surprising, then, that Stets (1991) finds cohabitors to be less tied to their partner. But it is a very limited measure of social control and an even more limited measure of social isolation. Similarly, Stets (1991) seems surprised to find that cohabitors are actually more tied to family and friends than are marrieds and, hence, on this measure, are less socially isolated. However, when one considers the measures of ties to family and friends in light of some of the other explanatory frameworks discussed in the present work, this finding is not surprising. Stets (1991) operationalizes ties to family and friends by constructing an index based on the frequency of spending a social evening (a) with relatives, (b) with a neighbor, (c) with people you work with, (d) with friends who live outside your neighborhood, (e) by going to a bar or tavern, and (f) participating in a group recreational activity, such as bowling, golf, or square dancing. In light of the previous discussion, it seems reasonable to expect that cohabitors would score higher than marrieds on these measures. Rather than accounting for greater ties to family and friends *post facto* as a compensation for isolation from formal networks and one's partner, subculture of violence theory and routine activities theory would predict cohabitors to be more likely to spend time with friends and go to the bar. Moreover, as will be discussed shortly, an application of Berger and Kellner's (1994) work would also predict cohabitors to be less individuated from their respective family.

The DAD Model

Ellis and DeKeseredy (1989) have synthesized some of the above explanations and risk factors in an attempt to construct a model of marital status differences in woman abuse.

Figure 3.1. *The DAD Model of Woman Abuse.*

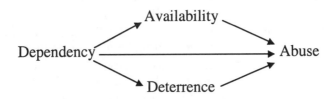

Source: Ellis and DeKeseredy (1989). Copyright 1989 by M. D. Publications Pvt. Ltd.

This model, as displayed in figure 3.1, suggests that higher rates of violence against cohabiting women are due to variations in three domains: Dependency, Availability, and Deterrence (DAD).[5] The first component of the model, dependency, corresponds to resource theory with the additional risk markers of drug and alcohol dependence. Dependency in relation to woman abuse has two facets; dependency of women on men and dependency of men on women. Ellis and DeKeseredy (1989) suggest that married women are more likely to be economically dependent on their partner than cohabiting women, since cohabiting women are more likely to be employed. However, men in cohabiting relationships are less well educated, have lower rates of employment, and tend to earn less than their partners. This is inconsistent with patriarchal cultural norms in which male status is based upon dominance. As a result, these males may resort to violence to achieve their status of dominance. As already discussed, however, Anderson's (1997) test of resource theory did not account for higher rates of violence among common-law unions.

Ellis and DeKeseredy (1989) further note that dependence on alcohol and drugs may play a role in higher rates of abuse among cohabitors. Men whose previous marriages have failed due to their alcohol and drug problems are more likely to be overrepresented among cohabitors, which, in turn, increases the likelihood of abuse directed toward their cohabiting partner.

Holding constant the time-at-risk or availability of cohabitors and marrieds for abuse, cohabitors have higher rates of woman abuse.[6] Ellis and DeKeseredy (1989) assert that this may be due to the time cohabitors spend together being more "risky." That is, cohabiting men's dependency leads them to be jealous and concerned with the fidelity of their partner, whereas married men have some assurance of their wives' fidelity. Thus, Ellis and DeKeseredy (1989:80) posit, "violence, in threat and in use, is one way in which jealous cohabiting men may attempt to keep their mates faithful and loyal to them, and/or, to stop the 'jealous nagging' of mates who voice their own suspicions of them."

Drawing on social control theory, Ellis and DeKeseredy (1989) explain that male cohabitors' social isolation, youthfulness, and low income means that they are less deterred from being abusive than are married men. Since cohabiting men have less to lose by being abusive they are not as deterred as married men by threat of legal and/or social punishment. Ellis and DeKeseredy (1989) also argue that cohabiting men's tendency to have a past history of woman abuse leads them to possess higher "aggressive habit strength," which, in turn, renders them less likely than married men to be deterred by legal and/or social norms.

Sherman (1992) has also argued that unmarried persons are less deterred by arrest than married persons. Miller and Krull (1997) have tested this argument on two data sets. In one data set, based on 1,078 victims of spouse assault in Colorado Springs, Miller and Krull (1997) found that those victims who were married to the suspect reported experiencing more recidivistic violence than victims not married to the suspect. In the other data set, collected on 470 victims in Omaha, Miller and Krull (1997) arrived at exactly the opposite findings. As a result, Miller and Krull (1997) conclude that they have no definitive findings about marital status and revictimization.

Ellis and DeKeseredy's (1989) DAD model is clearly a step in the right direction in terms of drawing on theory and making connections between various risk markers of violence among common-law unions.[7] However, the model itself omits a number of causal linkages among concepts hypothesized to explain marital status differences in violence. As well, testing of this model alone would not allow a key distinction to be made. This distinction involves the extent to which marital status differences in violence are due to the type of people who cohabit or to their current type of relationship itself. The discussion now turns to this subject.

Selection versus Relationship

Studies attempting to understand the effect of premarital cohabitation on marital stability have typically made a distinction between two explanations. Nock (1995:73) writes that "the unanswered question raised repeatedly in...research is whether cohabitation attracts a different type of person initially or whether the experience itself should be credited with producing observed differences between cohabitation and marriage." Several researchers have reported differences in the type of people who cohabit. These include maturity (Yelsma, 1986), being more nonconventional (Booth and Johnson, 1988; Newcomb, 1986), and more risk-taking (Booth and Johnson, 1988; Newcomb, 1986). Cohabitors have also been found to differ from marrieds in terms of relationship characteristics. These include lower levels of happiness (Nock, 1995; Stack and Eshleman, 1998), lower degrees of commitment (Booth and Johnson, 1988; Nock, 1995; Wu, 1999), and poor quality relationships with parents (Nock, 1995; Newcomb, 1986) and friends (Newcomb, 1986).

One method of investigating the relative contribution of selection and relationship factors is to control for them by running regression models with only selection factors, only relationship factors, and selection and relationship factors combined. Stets (1991) tested the effect of demographic factors (age, race, and education), which can be conceived as selection factors, and social factors (measures of social isolation, depression, and alcohol), which can be conceived more as relationship factors, on marital status differences in violence. Stets (1991) found that only the combination of both demographic and social factors accounted for the marital status differences in violence. This indicates that a combination of both selection and relationship factors are operating in the production of marital status differences in violence.

In an investigation of the quality of marital and cohabitation relationships, Nock (1995) identified another method for studying the selection-relationship dichotomy. Nock argues that separating marrieds into two groups, those who cohabited with their partner before marriage and those who did not, would allow an assessment of selection versus relationship factors. Nock (1995:63) reasons

> Should consistent differences be found between the relationships of the two groups of married individuals, this would support prior research suggesting that those who cohabit prior to marriage differ from those who do not. On the other hand, if both married groups differ from cohabitors, this would suggest

that the nature of the relationships is important in explaining differences between married and cohabiting individuals.

Nock (1995) finds that previously cohabiting marrieds are more similar to nonpreviously cohabiting marrieds than to cohabitors. Based on this finding, Nock concludes that the differences are largely due to the lack of institutionalization in cohabitation relationships. In other words, Nock finds that the poorer quality of cohabiting unions is due more to relationship than selection factors.

The only study of violence to apply Nock's (1995) method of separating marrieds into previous and nonpreviously cohabiting is that of Boba (1996). Boba (1996:21) reasons "if PC[8] married couples are more violent than non-PC married couples, the argument that the current type of relationship explains an increased likelihood of violence would not be supported since PC married couples are now married." Boba (1996) found that violence among marrieds is more likely to occur among those who cohabited with their partner prior to marriage ($n = 766$) than those who did not premaritally cohabit ($n = 5,034$).[9] Logistic regression showed that, controlling for a number of variables, those who cohabited with their partner prior to marriage have 54 percent greater odds of being violent than non-PC marrieds and those who are currently cohabiting have 116 percent greater odds of being violent than non-PC marrieds. Furthermore, cohabitors have 41 percent greater odds than previously cohabiting marrieds of being violent. The fact that there is a significant difference in rates between previously and nonpreviously cohabiting marrieds indicates that current relationship status, that is, simply being married or cohabiting, does not account for different rates of violence. Boba (1996:124) writes, "the current relationship of a couple does not explain the increased likelihood of PC marrieds to be violent" and concludes, "cohabitation itself has a negative influence on the quality of later marriages."

These methods of investigating selection and relationship factors are important developments for understanding marital status differences in violence. If, following Nock's (1995) method, the two groups of marrieds are different, one can conclude that the differences between cohabitors and marrieds are not due to the type of relationship per se. That is to say, the current status of the relationship does not make a difference to rates of violence. However, this does not necessarily mean that the differences are due solely to the type of people who cohabit. Relationship factors may still be playing a role. Indeed, Stets's (1991) analysis indicates that some combination of selection and relationship factors account for marital status differences in violence. The discussion of the theoretical synthesis in the next chapter provides some insights into how this may be the case.

Summary

The general failure to recognize the importance of separating cohabiting from marital unions in analyses of violence has led to a paucity of theorizing about marital status differences in violence. However, several different frameworks can be applied to explain marital status differences in violence. On the face of it, each of these approaches has some merit. However, the lack of empirical research means that the majority of the propositions from these explanations remain untested. We turn next to a general theoretical frame of reference to guide the present investigation. However, it is important to note that insights about most of the aforementioned explanations are gleaned from the present study.

Notes

1. See also Brownridge and Halli (2000).

2. Of course, to group all feminists into one category is an oversimplification. For a review of radical feminist, socialist feminist and Marxist feminist positions on violence against women see DeKeseredy and MacLeod (1997). However, Lenton (1995a:567) has concluded, "Most feminist research in the area of wife abuse is consistent with a radical feminist position because it focuses exclusively on patriarchy as the explanation for wife abuse."

3. In their study, Yllö and Straus (1981:345) mention the possibility that, in the absence of a marriage license, "for *some* cohabitors physical violence toward one's partner serves as a symbol of closeness and ownership."

4. Felson (1997) does include a measure of marital status, but does not separate marrieds from cohabitors. Felson found that night life increases the probability of nondomestic but not domestic violence. However, among the limitations of this study is its sample size ($n = 245$).

5. While the model attempts to explain higher rates of woman abuse relative to marrieds among those who are cohabiting, separated, and divorced, the discussion of the model is restricted to cohabitors.

6. Ellis and DeKeseredy (1989) are referring here to the use of one-year prevalence instead of lifetime prevalence rates.

7. Ellis (1989) has also synthesized sociological theory and research findings regarding marital status differences in violence into several submodels. However, this synthesis does not form a cogent, testable model. Wherever relevant, Ellis's (1989) insights are included in the present work.

8. PC and non-PC refer to previously and nonpreviously cohabiting, respectively.

9. Boba (1996) notes that the study is limited by the measurement of cohabitation only with the current partner. Thus, persons who had cohabited with someone other than their partner were counted as non-PC marrieds, "blurring the PC/non-PC distinction" (1996:138).

Chapter 4

Toward the Development of a Synthesis

Cunningham and Antill (1995) have noted that an understanding of the processes that take place in cohabitation is missing from our knowledge of these unions. These researchers write, "we know far more about the demographics and attitudes of those who cohabit than about the ways they weave their lives together, define the meaning of their relationship, and, in general, go about the business of enacting connection" (1995: 150). What follows draws on Berger and Kellner's (1994) phenomenological thesis to theorize about the process of reality construction for cohabitors. In addition, the variables linked to various explanations for violence among cohabitors can be included within this theoretical synthesis. Moreover, an application of Berger and Kellner's (1994) thesis is instructive in understanding how the status of the relationship itself may not make a difference to rates of violence, but how relationship factors may nevertheless play a role. This chapter concludes with a summary of the general purposes of the study and a specification of the hypotheses to be tested.

Basic Structure of Berger and Kellner's Thesis

Berger and Kellner (1994) begin with Durkheim's observation that marriage protects the individual from anomic states. They argue that it makes more sense to direct our attention toward the nomic processes that prevent anomic states.

According to Berger and Kellner (1994), all societies have their own way of perceiving and defining reality, and they transmit this reality to individuals through language. Through invocation of this reality, all individuals in the society share a system of ready-made typifications. Typifications refer to "typical actions for typical situations" and are used in situations where individuals have learned them to be appropriate behaviors (Ritzer, 1988:214). Since all members of the society share these typifications, they become objectivized. That is, though their meanings are subjectively experienced, they become objective to the individual and, through interaction with others, become common to everyone and hence, "massively objective." As a result, this reality is taken for granted as the only possible world; the world *tout court*. However, while the individual is given this reality, by virtue of living in it she or he continually modifies it. Not only does one's reality become objectivized through interaction, but also it is through interaction with others that an individual sustains or validates her or his reality. According to Berger and Kellner (1994), everyone in an individual's world serves a validating function for that person, but it is significant others, those who are closest to an individual, that provide the best validations. This validation occurs through an individual's ongoing conversation with her or his significant others. For Berger and Kellner (1994), marriage is the most significant of all validating relationships.

The Marital Conversation

Berger and Kellner (1994) argue that marriage is a nomos-building instrumentality; through marriage individuals unwittingly construct a new reality that gives them greater stability in their lives.[1] According to these researchers, marriage constitutes a nomic rupture for both individuals in the relationship since with the event of marriage a new nomic process commences. When two persons get married, Berger and Kellner (1994) observe, they are essentially two strangers uniting and redefining themselves. Because the marital partners tend to be homogamous in terms of region, class, and ethnic affiliations, these individuals have accumulated a similar stock of experience. That is, the reality they have internalized, including definitions and expectations of marriage, is similar. Nevertheless, each individual comes from a different area of conversation; their pasts are not shared. However, Berger and Kellner (1994:22) state, "With the dramatic redefinition of the situation brought about by the marriage . . . all significant conversation for the two new partners is now centered in their relationship with each other; in fact, it was precisely with this intention that they entered upon their relationship." The marital partner thus becomes the most significant of the significant others.

While each partner in the new marriage comes from a different area of conversation, with the event of marriage

> most of each partner's actions must now be projected in conjunction with those of the other. Each partner's definitions of reality must be continually correlated with the definitions of the other. The other is present in nearly all horizons of everyday conduct. Furthermore, the identity of each now takes on a new character, having to be constantly matched with that of the other, indeed being typically perceived by people at large as being symbiotically conjoined with the identity of the other. (1994:25)

According to Berger and Kellner (1994), the reconstruction that takes place in the marriage results from the marital conversation. It is essential that a common overall definition be worked out between the two individuals so that the conversation and the relationship can continue. The process is as follows: In the course of the marital conversation, both partners contribute to their realities. Their realities are continually "talked through" and as a result become objectivized. As the marital conversation continues, these objectivations are confirmed and reconfirmed and become more "massively real." As these objectivations become stronger and more massively real, the married couple's world, which consists of these objectivations, becomes more stable.

The content of the marital conversation, Berger and Kellner (1994) assert, is not limited to the present but is also concerned with the past. Through the marital conversation, each partner's past is reconstructed in a way that is congruent with his or her self-definitions objectivated in marriage thereby creating a common memory. Moreover, through sharing "future horizons" in the marital conversation, each partner's future projections are narrowed. The whole process of reality construction in marriage is typically unapprehended.

For Berger and Kellner (1994), then, the entire process of reconstructing reality in marriage stabilizes their common objectivated reality, the total reality of the partners. Berger and Kellner (1994:29) state, "In the most far-reaching sense of the word, the married individual 'settles down,' and must do so, if the marriage is to be viable."

Conversing with Violence: The Construction of Violence in Cohabiting Unions

Similar to marriage, it would seem reasonable to argue that cohabitation also constitutes a nomic rupture. Handel and Whitchurch (1994) have commented that cohabitation may be a nomos-building instrumentality of equal stature to that of marriage and which, *ipso facto*, creates as much stability for the members of the couple as does marriage. However, while the process of reality construction can be seen as being essentially the same in both the cohabiting and marital relationship, the research already discussed indicates differences between the two groups that might render the content of the process, and hence the outcome, quite different.

Figure 4.1. *Model of Reality Construction Process Leading to Violence for Cohabitors.*

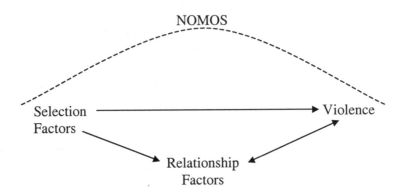

Figure 4.1 provides a pictorial depiction of the process of reality construction leading to violence for cohabitors. Based on past research it appears possible that factors such as youth, low socioeconomic status, status inconsistency, histories of having witnessed or experienced violence, previous marriage, region of residence, greater independence, and less willingness to invest in a relationship may select such individuals into a less committed type of union; cohabitation. Cunningham and Antill (1995) assert that the key concept in understanding differences between marriage and cohabitation is commitment. These researchers write, "Uneasiness about a lifetime commitment to the present partner or to the institution of marriage arises continually in surveys of cohabitors" (1995:167). It is argued here that focusing only on a lower level of commitment as a concept is too simple and too general. We need to under-

stand why cohabitors are less committed and what effect this has on their relationship. It is the differing processes that lead cohabitors to have a lower commitment and the consequent relationship processes that are key.

Bearing Berger and Kellner's (1994) thesis in mind, it is reasonable to argue that selection factors may render cohabitors less likely than marrieds to project actions in conjunction with their partner and less amenable to have their identity take on a new character. That is, it would seem possible that the cohabiting individual is less likely to "settle down" to the same extent as the married individual. This, in turn, may affect the relationship. For instance, the lower security in such unions may lead to higher levels of compensatory domineering behavior, more sexually proprietary behavior, greater social isolation, more alcohol consumption, and a higher probability of depression. Some combination of these selection and relationship characteristics may then result in more disagreements, conflict, and violence.

In effect, then, cohabitors may unwittingly establish a less stable nomos than do marrieds. It is reasonable to suggest that for those who have premaritally cohabited a second nomic rupture through marriage may be insufficient in reconstructing a stable world for the couple. That is, once the couple has established a reality in the context of living together unmarried, the more nomos-building changes that accompany marriage may not be enough to overcome the couple's already existing, and less stable, reality. This may explain how the status of the relationship may not make a difference to rates of violence but how relationship factors may still play a role. That is, while the PC married couple has the relationship status of married, their nomos has been affected by their previous cohabitation.

It is also possible that there is a carry-over effect from a previous cohabitation relationship(s) to persons other than one's marital partner. Nomos becomes *sui generis*. It thus reflects on each individual in the couple to shape her or his subjective reality. In the case of a break-up, one's subjective reality carries over to a new relationship. After one's first serious relationship, one can never start with a completely clean slate because we are all products of our past interactions. In the new relationship, each partner's subjective reality affects the development of a new objective reality. This new objective reality, in turn, reflects on their subjective reality. Due to their past experiences with cohabitation, then, PC marrieds are expected to be different from non-PC marrieds in the direction of current cohabitors.[2]

Purposes

There are several general purposes of the present study. First, the likelihood of experiencing violence by marital status will be identified. This will provide an accurate account of marital status differences in levels of violence in Canada. Second, levels of each form of violence will be compared across marital status groups. These comparisons will enrich our understanding of the experiences of violence by marital status through the identification of underlying patterns. Third, the various explanatory frameworks for understanding marital status differences in violence will be tested. These tests will allow an evaluation of different explanations and hence provide insights into the causes of marital status differences in violence. Finally, post-violence comparisons across marital status will be conducted. These analyses will provide some context for the violence experienced by each marital status group.

Hypotheses

In addition to the propositions linked to each of the explanatory frameworks discussed in chapter 3, the overall hypotheses of the study are:

- Cohabitors and PC marrieds will report higher rates of violence than will non-PC marrieds.

- Cohabitors and PC marrieds will be more likely than non-PC marrieds to report severe violence.

- Cohabitors and PC marrieds will differ from non-PC marrieds on selection characteristics.

- Cohabitors and PC marrieds will differ from non-PC marrieds on relationship characteristics.

- Cohabitors' and PC marrieds' differential selection and relationship characteristics will be linked to their greater likelihood of violence.

- Cohabitors and PC marrieds will be more likely to experience injury as a result of physical violence at the hands of their male partner.

Notes

1. Safilios-Rothschild (1969) and Bernard (1982) have argued that women and men have different experiences in marriage, such that there is not one reality in marriage but two very different realities. However, the two perspectives are not necessarily incompatible. There is no doubt that men and women have different perceptions, but this does not preclude the existence of an objective reality of interaction (nomos) between the couple. Just as when individuals in a society come together to form an entity *sui generis*, so does a couple in a marriage or common-law union. One might say that there is "her reality," "his reality," and "couple's reality," which simultaneously exist and interact nonrecursively.

2. Ideally, then, the most effective application of Nock's (1995) method would involve dividing marrieds into those who did not cohabit premaritally, those who cohabited with their current marital partner, and those who cohabited with someone other than their current marital partner.

Chapter 5

Materials and Methods

In a major attempt to overcome the relative lack of national data in Canada, Statistics Canada, with funding from Health and Welfare Canada through the Federal government's Family Violence Initiative, conducted the Violence against Women Survey (VAWS). These data are employed in the present study of marital status differences in violence against women.

The Data Set: Statistics Canada's Violence against Women Survey

In 1993 Statistics Canada conducted a unique national telephone survey. A random sample of 12,300 women 18 years of age and older completed in-depth telephone interviews concerning their experiences of physical and sexual violence since reaching the age of 16 (Statistics Canada, 1993). While there have been national victimization surveys in Canada, the Canadian Urban Victimization Survey (CUVS) and the General Social Survey (GSS), these projects were not specifically designed to understand women's victimization (DeKeseredy and Hinch, 1991; Johnson, 1995b). The VAWS was conducted "to provide reliable estimates of the nature and extent of male violence against women in Canada" (Rodgers, 1994a:4).[1]

Reliability of the Data

The accuracy of survey data on violence against women is an important issue because this is a highly sensitive topic of investigation. Indeed, the problem of violence against women is still largely viewed as a private matter in our society. Past surveys have been characterized by several weaknesses that led to underreporting (Johnson, 1996). Reasons for women's underreporting of violence include embarrassment or shame, feeling that the violence is too minor, forgetting and repressing the violence (Smith, 1987). The VAWS effectively deals with many problems of previous surveys via extensive pretesting of the survey, use of multiple measures, innovative selection and training of interviewers, large-scale sampling, and use of lifetime victimization rates (Johnson, 1995b).

Statistics Canada drew from victims and survivors of violence, community groups, federal and provincial government representatives, academics, and other experts in the development of the survey (Rodgers, 1994a). This consultation process provided "sensitive question wording into which respondents could fit their experiences" (Johnson, 1995b: 127). Multiple measures were used to improve respondent recall and to give respondents more than one opportunity to divulge painful experiences (Johnson, 1995b). Interviewers were trained to be sensitive to the needs of respondents such as recognizing respondent's concerns about being overheard. Among the innovations in this regard, respondents were provided with a toll-free telephone number. This allowed respondents to call if they had questions about the survey and/or if they needed to complete the survey at a time when it was safe for them to do so (Rodgers, 1994b).

Unlike past studies that tend to have very small samples of common-law couples, the VAWS contains a sub-sample of 1,022 women living in a common-law union at the time of the survey.[2] As a result, meaningful and more generalizable regression-based multivariate analyses can be conducted on these data to aid in our understanding of the causal dynamics of violence against women.

Recognizing that rates with a one-year time frame may undercount victimization, the VAWS also measured lifetime rates of violence. As mentioned above, respondents were asked about their experiences of violence since becoming 16 years old.[3]

Finally, while the CTS measures ways of addressing *conflict*, the questions asked about women's partners in the VAWS are phrased to elicit responses about women's experiences of *violence* (Johnson, 1995a:151; Johnson, 1995b:131).[4]

Despite the aforementioned improvements, based on the public use microdata file, one cannot be certain of the reliability of the VAWS.[5] Therefore, one must be cautious in the interpretation of the data.

Naming and Defining Violence

Before discussing how violence is measured in the present study, it is essential to discuss and identify the terminology and definitions that are used.

Terminology

There has been much debate in the literature concerning what terms to use to describe violence against women. Terms that have been employed include "wife beating," "wife battering," "woman abuse," "family violence," "domestic violence," "wife assault," "woman assault," "male violence against women," "spousal abuse," "intimate violence," "wife abuse," "marital violence," "spousal violence," and "woman battering." Whether or not one regards it as appropriate, the terminology one uses is often closely connected to their beliefs concerning the roots of the problem and, consequently, the measures to be taken in dealing with it.

DeKeseredy and MacLeod (1997) have traced the tides of usage for several of these terms. They note that the initial terms, "wife beating" and "wife battering," were borrowed from the criminal justice system. Recent terminologies, "wife assault" and "woman assault," have also emphasized the criminal aspect of violence. DeKeseredy and MacLeod (1997) assert that a focus on only that to which the justice system can respond narrows the definition too much. Some prefer the term "wife" because it focuses on the institution of marriage while others reject it because it restricts attention to legal marriages (Ratner, 1995).

While terms like "domestic violence" are broader, they also have their problems. DeKeseredy and Hinch (1991) argue that such gender-neutral terms ignore several points. They ignore that women are primarily on the receiving end of violence, who initiates violence, who is more physically and mentally empowered for violence, the purpose of the violence, and the implications for treatment. To deal with this, some researchers used the term "male violence against women." DeKeseredy and MacLeod (1997) assert that this term does not draw attention to systematic power imbalances that lead to women's inequality and power imbalances.

According to DeKeseredy and MacLeod (1997), the term "woman abuse" came into use for two main reasons. First, "male violence against women" was seen by aboriginal, immigrant, and refugee women as not reflecting the oppression experienced by their male partners. DeKeseredy and MacLeod (1997) argue that the term "abuse" more adequately represents these women's concerns. Second, "woman" is preferred to "wife" because it communicates "the breadth of violence experienced by women related to gender inequities" (1997:20) and, more understandably, it prevents the definition of women in terms of marital roles. Ratner (1995) notes that some have rejected this term because it ignores what they believe to be the foundation of the problem, legal marriage.

DeKeseredy and MacLeod (1997) have noted that since the 1970s social workers, counselors, health professionals, and governments have used the term "family violence," and the mid-1990s have seen a resurgence of this term among governments and community groups to recognize all parties involved and all forms of abuse. DeKeseredy and MacLeod (1997:29) also note that aboriginal, immigrant, and minority women prefer this terminology "because it emphasizes the need for family healing and points out the systematic, institutionalized roots of the problem."

Since the purpose of the present study is to distinguish common-law from marital unions, "wife" is considered to be an inappropriate term. "Beating" and "battering" imply only a physical component so, as will be elaborated shortly, they too are inappropriate for use as an overall term in the present study. Similarly, "assault" is too legalistic as it excludes acts such as verbal abuse. Terms like "domestic" or "interpartner" are not appropriate because the subject matter of the present study deals only with male perpetration and female victimization. For the same reason, it is also unnecessary to use "male violence against women."

Adams (1986:322) has noted that a distinction can be made between abuse and violence "with violence referring to all forms of physical aggression, while abuse refers to aggression that causes injury and also to nonphysical acts of maltreatment that cause harm…. But abuse and violence are employed almost synonymously in much of the literature." Given these definitions, it is little wonder that the two terms are used interchangeably. Violence refers to physical acts, but abuse refers to acts that at once cause injury and are therefore more severe than some "minor" physical acts, and at the same time to nonphysical acts that cause harm! A more clear distinction could be drawn such that violence refers only to physical acts at all levels of severity while abuse includes violence as well as nonphysical acts. However, it is likely that their synonymous use will continue. Moreover, whether one terms it "woman *abuse*" or "male *violence* against women," the phenomenon still falls under the rubric of "family *violence*." Therefore, all acts of abuse or violence in the present study are considered to be components of "violence against women." Thus, the term that will be used throughout this work is "violence." However, as will be outlined later, each subcomponent of violence in the present study has been carefully named based on its content.

Nominal Definitions

Researchers have observed that one of the most controversial areas of inquiry in terms of family violence is defining family violence (Barnett, Miller-Perrin and Perrin, 1997; Hamberger, 1994). There is wide variation in definitions of violence in the literature. Perhaps the most common definition in the past has defined violence as an act carried out with the intention or perceived intention of causing physical pain or injury to another person (Lupri, Grandin, and Brinkerhoff, 1994; Straus, Gelles, and Steinmetz, 1980). However, some researchers have argued that this definition is too restrictive. These researchers variously argue that violence not only includes physical acts, but can also encompass psychological abuse, emotional abuse, neglect, financial or economic abuse, verbal abuse, spiritual abuse, and sexual abuse or coercion.[6] It has been widely reported that psychological and emotional abuse tend to have more detrimental consequences for women than does physical violence (Aguilar and Nightingale, 1994; Follingstad et al., 1990; Hoglund and Nicholas, 1995; Kasian and Painter, 1992; Straus, 1993).

Duffy and Momirov (1997) have pointed out that how we define family violence affects how we as a society both view and respond to it. According to these researchers, a balance must be found between definitions that are too wide and those that are too narrow. Duffy and Momirov (1997:14;15) caution that sweeping definitions "may result in a breakdown of interactions between people as they label each other's actions 'abusive'" while a narrow definition "makes it appear that only certain (usually extreme) actions qualify as abusive." Violence against women in the present study includes acts of physical assault, psychological aggression, verbal abuse, and sexual coercion perpetrated by a woman's current marital or common-law partner.[7] We will now turn to a discussion of how these components of violence are operationalized in the present study.

Measurement of Violence Variables

At this juncture it is necessary to engage in a brief discussion of the way in which the VAWS measures violence and the manner in which this work uses these measures. The designers of the VAWS restricted their conceptualization of violence to legal definitions of physical and sexual assault as contained in the Canadian Criminal Code. Johnson (1996:48) writes, "Ten specific questions were used to measure *violence* by a spouse ranging from threats of physical harm to use of a gun or knife" (emphasis added). These ten items were based on the most widely used instrument for measuring violence, the CTS (Straus, 1979). It is conventional with the CTS to divide the items into minor and severe categories of violence. While the VAWS items do not replicate the CTS items exactly,[8] the minor-severe distinction can be made on the same basis. However, both the CTS and its division into minor and severe subscales have been the subject of much criticism (Brush, 1990; Dobash et al., 1992). Subsequently, Straus and his colleagues (1996) have revised the original scale terming the new instrument the CTS2.[9] The main changes to the instrument are the addition of two new scales, one tapping sexual coercion and the other tapping the physical injuries from partner assaults. Changes in nomenclature comprise the other major improvements. The verbal aggression subscale is now called psychological aggression to reflect the fact that some of the acts on the new scale are nonverbal. The violence scale is changed to physical assault because "it avoids confusion with the use of violence as a much broader concept" (1996:290).

The distinction between minor and severe for each scale of the CTS1 remains, however, in the CTS2. Ratner (1995, 1998) criticizes the approaches provided by Straus and his colleagues for determining the severity of acts of physical assault that are "based on conceptualizations of physical aggression that underlie both versions of the CTS." Using "the most promising" method provided by Straus (1990) for scoring severity of the CTS1 items, Ratner (1998:455) assigned severity weights to each of the acts of physical aggression. Ratner hypothesized that, if Straus's severity weights were correct, her severity weighted variables representing acts of physical aggression would not require the addition of directed effects between these acts and measures of physical injury. Ratner's (1998:459) analysis of the VAWS data found, however, that "the model required additional directed effects" leading her to conclude that "it is apparent that the severity weights hypothesized by Straus...were incorrect." Based on the revision by Straus and his colleagues (1996) as well as the severity weights calculated by Ratner (1995, 1998), then, the decision was made to divide the physical assault items into three categories encompassing minor physical assault, moderate physical assault, and severe physical assault.

Physical Assault. In the VAWS, the items adapted from the CTS1 were prefaced with the following statement: *We are particularly interested in learning more about women's experiences of violence in their homes. I'd like you to tell me if your husband/partner has ever done any of the following to you. This includes incidents that may have occurred while you were dating.*[10] To prevent respondent fatigue, after every three questions respondents who answered "no" to all three questions were asked if their husband/partner had ever been violent in any other way. If not, the remainder of these questions were skipped.[11] The authors of the survey reasoned that, since the ten physical violence items increase in severity, respondents who say no to all three items in a set are unlikely to endorse any of the subsequent items. Less than 1 percent of respondents refused to answer any of these questions (Wilson, Johnson and Daly, 1995).

One-year and lifetime time frames are determined by a question that asks when the most recent incident happened (J22).[12] Since this variable asks only about the timing of the most recent incident of any type of "physical" assault, and since close to half (41 percent) of respondents reporting an incident reported more than one incident, it is not possible to determine the one-year time frame on each act for every respondent in the sample. Rather, the one-year time frame can only be used when all the acts are combined into one variable because it is only this variable that contains all possible "most recent incidents."

It is important to note that time frame has consequences for the interpretation of analyses. Brownridge and Halli (1999) found that the time frame employed in analyses of interpartner violence can have a major impact on the results. Unlike rates with a lifetime time frame, rates with a one-year time frame, by definition, have a built-in control for time-at-risk for violence. Nevertheless, this still does not take into account duration of relationship, which is probably more important with respect to marital status differences. Since common-law unions are of a much shorter average duration than marital unions, it is crucial to control for duration of relationship when comparing the two groups. For example, given an inverse relationship between violence and duration of relationship, a woman together with her partner for twenty years will be less likely to report violence in the past year than will a woman who has been together with her partner for two years. It is therefore still important to compare reports of violence in the past year for married and cohabiting women who have been together with their partner for one year, two years, three years, and so forth. Since rates with lifetime time frames refer to the duration of the entire relationship to the time of the survey, time-at-risk is controlled simply by controlling for duration of relationship.

Taken independently of controls for duration of relationship, then, rates with one-year time frames probably operate more accurately than those with lifetime time frames because they have some built-in control for time-at-risk. Moreover, since the independent variables in studies of violence against women tend to refer to current characteristics (in the absence of controls), rates with a one-year time frame may provide greater clarity in analyses. For bivariate comparisons with variables other than duration of relationship it is thus preferable, though not perfect, to use a rate that employs a one-year time frame. However, since this is not possible with all tests in the present study, those tests of risk markers on dependent variables with a lifetime time frame and that do not control for duration of relationship will have to be considered tentative.

It is important to add that, even with controls for duration of relationship in analyses of rates with a one-year or a lifetime time frame, one should still expect some differences in the operation, and hence interpretation, of the results of comparisons with time-dependent independent variables. Let us say that we select respondents from a sample of marrieds and cohabitors who have been together for five years. A prevalence rate based on a one-year time frame will give us the percentages of marrieds and cohabitors who have experienced violence in the past year, that is, in the fifth year of the relationship. We would expect this rate to decrease with increasing duration. The percentage of respondents reporting violence in the past year should tend to decrease when looking at relationships of increasingly longer durations for a number of potential reasons. Relationships that have lasted should be less likely to include violent persons than those of short durations who have had less time to terminate their relationships. Age could also be a factor. Relationships of longer durations tend to include older people, and age is inversely related to violence. Now, let us again take the same couples that have been together for five years. A prevalence rate based on a lifetime time frame will give us the percentage of marrieds and cohabitors who have experienced violence during their relationship. We would expect this rate to tend to increase with increasing duration because it is cumulative. Relationships that experience at least one episode at any time during the relationship are included. Therefore, in a longitudinal study, all other things being equal, such a rate can never decrease with the passage of time. In a cross-sectional study we would still expect to see an increase with increasing duration. However, some decrease in the older age groups may occur due to recall bias or some other circumstance such as a cohort effect in which people born in earlier cohorts were less likely to experience violence in the lifetime of their relationship. As Brownridge and Halli (1999) point out, it is important for researchers to bear in mind the manner in which their risk markers will be affected by the time frame of their dependent variable.

Minor Physical Assault. Minor physical assault is measured by two items. The first item (J4) asks respondents *Has he ever pushed, grabbed, or shoved you?* The second measure of minor physical assault (J7) asks *Has he ever slapped you?* These dichotomous variables were recoded (*J4A* and *J7A*) so that the higher value indicates a positive response.[13] Where necessary for analysis, these variables are combined into one dichotomous variable (*MINORPA*).

Moderate Physical Assault. The concept of moderate physical assault is measured by three items. The first question (J13) asks the respondent *Has he ever choked you?* The second item (J3) asks the respondent *Has he ever THROWN anything at you that could hurt you?* The third question (J9) asks *Has he ever hit you with something that could hurt you?* Each of these dichotomous items were recoded (*J13A, J3A,* and *J9A*) so that the higher value indicates a positive response. Where necessary for analysis, these variables are combined into one dichotomous variable (*MODPA*).

Severe Physical Assault. Severe physical assault is measured by three items. The first item (J14) asks *Has he ever threatened to or used a gun or knife on you?* Ratner (1995, 1998) suggests that items that involve threats of harm should be distinguished from physical aggression because there is no potential for physical injury. However, the present item is double-barreled because it also refers to an actual act of physical aggression. Since a distinction cannot be made and the use of a gun or knife is severe physical violence, it was decided to include this variable under physical aggression.[14] The second item (J8) asks *Has he ever kicked, bit, or hit you with his fist?* The third item (J12) asks *Has he ever beaten you up?* Each of these dichotomous items were recoded (*J14A, J8A,* and *J12A*) so that the higher value indicates a positive response. Where necessary for analysis, these variables are combined into one dichotomous variable (*SEVPA*).

Verbal Abuse. Name-calling has been specifically identified as a component of verbal abuse (Kasian and Painter, 1992). The concept of verbal
abuse in the present study is measured by a variable (H5) derived from a
question that asks the respondent if the following statement describes her
current husband/partner: *He calls you names to put you down or make
you feel bad.* This dichotomous variable was recoded into a new variable
(*H51*) so that a positive response takes a higher value.

Psychological Aggression. The concept of psychological aggression is
measured with one variable. Consistent with a similar item on the CTS2,
the item on the VAWS (J2) that asks *Has your husband/partner ever
THREATENED to hit you with his fist or anything else that could hurt
you?* is deemed to represent psychological aggression. This dichotomous
variable was recoded into a new variable (*J2A*) so that a positive response takes a higher value.

Sexual Coercion. Sexual coercion is measured with a question (J15) that
asks *Has he ever forced you into any sexual activity when you did not
want to, by threatening you, holding you down, or hurting you in some
way?* This dichotomous variable was recoded (*J15A*) so that a positive
response takes a higher value.

Violence. To determine the prevalence rates of all forms of violence
taken together two variables were constructed. Lifetime prevalence is
constructed by simply combining each violence variable into a new variable (*ZALLV*). Lifetime prevalence, then, gives the percentage of the
sample who experienced at least one type of violence by their current
partner since they have become married or began living common-law.
One-year prevalence (*ZALLV1YR*) is based on only those incidents that
occurred in the twelve months prior to the survey. For all but the verbal
abuse item, a respondent falls into the one-year category if she experienced any of the violence variables within the past twelve months. With
respect to the verbal abuse variable, since the question refers to current
behavior, any respondent reporting verbal abuse is included in the one-
year category.

Measurement of Independent Variables in Etiological Model

Several variables are included in the etiological model. These are measured as follows:

Selection Variables

Age. Respondents were asked for their year and month of birth. The age variable is a derived variable (AGE) from this question such that age 75 includes women age 75 and older.[15] For the descriptive analyses, the age variable was recoded (*RAGE*) into the following categories: 18-24; 25-29; 30-34; 35-39; 40-44; 45-54; 55 and over. These categories provide a fairly even distribution of cases across categories with the exception of the 18-24 category which comprises only 5.6 percent of the sample. However, this category is retained as it is because it is this age group that is expected to be most likely to report experiencing violence.

Age Heterogamy. Age heterogamy is measured with age difference (DVAGEDIF). This variable is derived by Statistics Canada from respondent and spouse's age. Age difference was recoded (*DVAGED*) into the following categories: spouse 6 or more years older; spouse 1-5 years older; spouse and respondent same age; spouse 1-5 years younger; spouse 6 or more years younger. For the multivariate analyses, four dummy variables were created with the reference category being "spouse and respondent same age."

Socioeconomic Status. Information exists for both the respondents' and their partners' socioeconomic status. Variables in the study that tap SES are education, employment, and income.

Education. Respondents were asked about their own (DVEDUC) as well as their current husband/partner's (DVEDUCSP) highest level of education attained. For the multivariate analyses the values for each category of the education variables were recoded to reflect their meaning in terms of years of education (*DVEDUCR* and *DVEDUCSR*). "Less than high school" was given a value of 6, "high school diploma" was given a value of 12, "some post secondary"[16] was given a value of 14, and "university degree" was given a value of 15.

Employment. Respondents were asked whether they (E2) and their current husband/partner (G2) had worked at a business or paid job in the twelve months prior to the survey. For women being employed is expected to increase the probability of experiencing violence, so having worked is assigned a value of 1 (*E21*). Since partner's unemployment is hypothesized to lead to greater likelihood of violence, this variable was recoded (*G21*) so that the higher value reflected being unemployed.

Income. Respondents were asked about their "best estimate" of both their personal income before deductions and their household income in the twelve months prior to the interview. To calculate spouse's income, it was first necessary to recode the two original income variables (DV-

PERS3 and DVHHOLD3) so that the values for each category of income
would represent actual income values. This was accomplished by taking
the midpoint of each income category on the original variable. Spouse's
income (*SPINC*) was then calculated by subtracting the respondent's income (*DVPERS3R*) from the household income (*DVHHOLDR*). A limitation of the spouse's income variable is that, in households that contained more than two people earning an income, spouse's income may be
confounded with others in the household. However, an inspection of the
"total number of persons in the household receiving income" variable
(DVE25) showed that in only 12.6 percent of households were there
more than two people receiving income. Moreover, a cross-tabulation of
with whom the respondent lives (DVLVGRGR) by the total number of
persons in the household receiving income shows that 70 percent of
households where three people earned income consisted of the respondent, her spouse, and a single child less than age 25. Eighty-three percent
of households where four or more people earned an income fell into the
latter category. Thus, it would appear that where there are more than two
incomes, they are most likely to be from the respondent's children. Unfortunately, given the coding in the VAWS, it is impossible to determine
the exact age of the children. Since the children are living with their parents, however, it is reasonable to argue that the majority of these children
have a relatively low income.

For the descriptive analyses, the respondent's (*DVPERSRC*) and
spouse's (*SPINCR*) incomes are recoded into the following categories:
less than $15,000; $15,000-$29,999; $30,000-$59,999; $60,000 or more.
These categories were selected because they are consistent with those
used by the main architect of the survey (Johnson, 1996).

Status Inconsistency. This concept reflects the differences between partners in terms of educational and income resources. To create the variable
representing income status incompatibility, the ratio of the respondent's
income to her partner's income was calculated (*DVPERS3R/SPINC* =
INCDIFF2).[17] Anderson (1997:659-661), noting that ratio variables assume a linear relationship with the dependent variable, employs dummy
variables to represent status inconsistency. Since the assumption of linearity does not apply to dichotomous independent variables one can use
dummy variables to deal with the assumption of linearity. However, this
method has two major problems. First, because one is taking a ratio variable and collapsing it into categories, information is being lost. This is
because all we can say is that the cases corresponding to a given category
fall within that category. Following Anderson (1997), if one takes all of
the respondents with a ratio of female to couple's income of less than .31

and refers to all of these respondents as being "woman earns much less income," then all one knows is that the cases corresponding to that category fall somewhere within that category. It is much more informative to know the income ratio for each case. Second, the interpretation of results becomes limited because one has to interpret the dummy variables with respect to the reference category. If the relationship is nonlinear, it is preferable, then, to employ another method such as squaring the original variable. While the ratio variable is used for the multivariate analyses, a categorical variable (*INCDIFFX*) was created for use in the descriptive analyses. To be comparable with Anderson (1997), the categories for the descriptive analysis are based on the ratio of the respondent's share of the couple's total household income (*DVPERS3R/DVHHOLDR = INCDIFFR*). The categories are: the woman earns much less income (ratio < .31); the woman earns less income (ratio = .31-.45); the woman earns levels of income similar to her male partner's income (ratio = .46-.54); the woman earns more income (ratio = .55-.69); and the woman earns much more income (ratio > .69).

To create the variable representing educational status incompatibility the respondent's education was divided by her partner's education (*DVEDUCR/DVEDUCSR = DVEDURR2*). For the descriptive analyses, categories comparable to Anderson (1997) were calculated. This was accomplished by first creating a variable that represents the couples total years of education (*DVEDUCR + DVEDUCSR = DVCPLEDU*). Then the ratio of the woman's share of the couple's total years of education was calculated (*DVEDUCR/DVCPLEDU = DVEDURR*) and made into a new variable (*DVEDIFFX*) with the following categories: the woman has much less education (ratio < .46); the woman has less education (ratio = .46-.49); the woman has the same years of education as her partner (ratio = .50); the woman has more education (ratio = .51-.54); and the woman has much more education (ratio > .54).

Social Learning. The VAWS includes two measures of social learning, one for the respondent (M2) and the other for her current partner (M4). Respondents were asked if, to the best of their knowledge, their father/father-in-law was ever violent toward their mother/mother-in-law. For the multivariate analyses, two dummy variables were created to represent a positive response (*M2A* and *M4A*) and no father/father-in-law being present, do not know, and not stated (*M2B* and *M4B*).[18] The reference category is the response category indicating no or do not think that her father/father-in-law was ever violent toward his wife.

Dating Violence. To measure dating violence a question (J23) is employed that asks respondents who had reported violence with their current partner whether this had also happened before living married/common-law. This variable was recoded (*J23a*) so that a positive response takes the highest value.

Previous Partner Violence. Previous partner violence is a derived variable that refers to whether or not a respondent was ever threatened and/or physically or sexually attacked by a previous husband/common-law partner (ALLVPSP). For the multivariate analyses two dummy variables were created with the first representing previous partner violence (*ALLVPSPA*) and the second representing respondents who did not give a response and for whom this variable was not applicable (*ALLVPSPB*). The reference category refers to those who had a previous partner who was not violent.

Previous Marriage. Previous marriage is derived from a question (F7) which asks: *(Including your current husband), how many times have you been married?* The coding employed for this variable by Statistics Canada was insufficient for the task at hand. Since a code of 1 for marrieds means no previous marriage while a code of 1 for cohabitors means 1 previous marriage, it was necessary to recode the values on F7 to account for this discrepancy. The resulting variable (*PREVMARR*) is a dichotomous variable with 0 representing no previous marriage and 1 representing previous marriage.

Region. Region is measured by identifying the respondent's region of residence. To construct this variable (*REGION*) the variable in the VAWS indicating province (PROV) was recoded. Respondents from Newfoundland, Prince Edward Island, Nova Scotia, and New Brunswick were combined to represent the Atlantic region. Respondents from Quebec and Ontario represent the Quebec and Ontario regions respectively. Respondents from Manitoba, Saskatchewan, and Alberta represent the prairies. Like Quebec and Ontario, the province of British Columbia represents a unique region unto itself.[19] For the multivariate analyses, four dummy variables were created with Ontario as the reference category.

Marital Status

Marital status is a derived variable (DVMS1) from a series of questions. Only those currently married or living common-law are included in the study. The marital status variable was recoded such that the new variable (M_STATUS) represents three marital status categories: non-previously cohabiting married, previously cohabiting married, and cohabitor. The previously cohabiting marrieds (PC marrieds) were selected from married respondents who indicated having lived with a man in a common-law relationship not followed by marriage (F8) at least once. Boba (1996) indicated that measuring premarital cohabitation only with a current partner blurs the distinction between PC and non-PC marrieds. Booth and Johnson (1988:255) have indeed suggested that "cohabiting with individuals other than the person they eventually marry may affect marital quality." The measure in the proposed study overcomes this problem. However, it is limited in that premarital cohabitation with the current marital partner cannot be determined.

For the purpose of multivariate analyses, two dummy variables were created representing PC marrieds (*M_STAT_A*) and cohabitors (*M_STAT_B*). The category expected to have the lowest rate of violence, non-PC marrieds, is the reference category.

Relationship Variables

Duration. Duration is measured by a variable (DVF6YR) derived from a question that simply asks how long in years and months the couple has been married or living together.[20] For the purposes of descriptive analyses, the duration variable is recoded (*RDURAT*) into three categories: less than 4 years; 4-9 years; and 10 or more years. These categories were selected to be consistent with those of the main architect of the survey (Johnson, 1996).

Sexual Proprietariness. Sexual proprietariness is measured by the respondents' answers to two questions. The first (H2) asks if the following statement describes their current husband/partner: *He is jealous and doesn't want you to talk to other men.* In the same manner, the second (H4) statement reads: *He insists on knowing who you are with and where you are at all times.* These variables were recoded into new dichotomous variables (*H21* and *H41*) such that a positive response holds the higher value.

Partner's Alcohol Consumption. Alcohol consumption by the respondent's partner is measured by variables from two questions. The first (G11) refers to frequency of drinking and asks: *In the past month, how often did your husband/partner drink alcoholic beverages?* The second question (G12) encompasses heavy drinking. This item asks: *How many times in the past month has your husband/partner had five or more drinks on one occasion?* For the descriptive analyses, the frequency of drinking variable was recoded so that the more frequent the drinking the higher the value associated with it (*G11RX*). For the multivariate analyses, the frequency of drinking variable was recoded (*G11R*) so that the values on the variable would reflect a count of the number of times per month that the respondent's partner had consumed alcoholic beverages.[21] For the multivariate analyses, the variable representing the number of times in the past month the respondent's partner had consumed five or more drinks was recoded into a new variable (*G1A*) so that the "not applicable" is included with those who did not drink heavily in the month prior to the survey. For the descriptive analyses, this variable was recoded into a new variable (*G1AX*) with the following categories: didn't drink five or more drinks on one occasion in the past month, once in past month, two to four times in past month, and five or more times in past month. These categories were selected because of the time frame of the item. That is, with these categories one can identify those who tend not to drink heavily, those who drink heavily relatively infrequently, those who drink heavily weekly or biweekly, and those who drink heavily an average of more than once a week.

Social Isolation. Social isolation is measured with a variable (H3) derived from an item that asks a respondent if the following statement describes her current husband/partner: *He tries to limit your contact with family or friends.* This dichotomous variable was recoded into a new variable (*H31*) so that a positive response takes the higher value.

Dominance. Dominance is measured with a variable (H6) derived from a question asking the respondent if the following statement describes her current husband/partner: *He prevents you from knowing about or having access to the family income, even if you ask.* This dichotomous variable was recoded into a new variable (*H61*) so that a positive response takes a higher value.

Children. The presence of children is computed from a derived variable (DVLVGR) that includes a categorization of respondents in terms of currently living with their spouse only or living with their spouse and a single child less than 25 years of age. For the multivariate analyses, two dummy variables were created. The first dummy variable (*DVLVGRGA*) represents a couple living with a single child less than age 25. The second dummy variable (*DVLVGRGB*) represents several other categories of living arrangements that are not of interest but that must nevertheless be accounted for in the analysis. The reference category is those respondents who live only with their spouse.

Depression. Respondents' depression is measured with a variable (E15C) derived from a question that asks: *During the past month, have you used drugs or medication to help you get out of depression?* This variable was recoded into a new variable (*E15C1*) so that a positive response takes a higher value.

Measurement of Post-Violence Variables

To acquire a fuller understanding of the differing experiences of violence against women in cohabiting, PC married and non-PC married unions, several post-violence variables are also explored. An intimate abuse report was recorded in the VAWS for a randomly selected incident experienced by the respondent (if there was more than one). Variables analyzed from this section of the VAWS are organized as follows:[22]

Consequences

Several different dimensions of the consequences of violence are tapped in the present study. These are physical injury, psychopathology, altered psyche, anger, alcohol/drug use, and time off everyday activities.
Physical Injury. Victims were asked first if they were physically hurt in any way (W6). Those who indicated that they were physically hurt were asked: *What were your injuries?* (W7). Types of injuries include bruises, cuts/scratches/burns, fractures/broken bones, and miscarriage/internal injuries.
Psychopathology. The three marital status groups are compared in terms of psychopathology following the conceptualization of Ratner (1998). Ratner (1995:455) defines psychopathology as "a psychologically, mentally, or behaviorally disordered state." To be consistent with Ratner (1998), the same variables were used to measure psychopathology. Respondents in the VAWS who answered the intimate abuse report were asked how the experience of violence affected them (W9). The response categories representing psychopathology are: depression/anxiety attacks, fear, caution/weariness, sleep problems, shock/disbelief, hurt/disappointment, upset/confused/frustrated.
Altered Psyche. The extent to which the victim's psyche is altered is also a point of comparison for each marital status group. Ratner (1998:455) defines alterations to the psyche as "changes to a woman's sense of her soul, spirit, or mind; how she values herself, including how she values herself in relation to others." Again, the same variables used by Ratner (1998) are employed in the present study to represent alterations to the

psyche. The response categories from the VAWS (W9) representing alterations to the psyche are ashamed/guilty, lowered self-esteem, problems relating to men, and increased self-reliance.

Anger. Victims' anger as a consequence of violence is measured with the response category from the VAWS (W9) which simply read "Angry."

Alcohol/Drug Use. Alcohol and drug use as a consequence of violence is measured with a question (W10) that asks victims: *Have you ever used alcohol, drugs or medication to help you cope with this experience?*

Time Off Everyday Activities. Victims were also asked the question (W11): *Did you ever take time off from your everyday activities because of what happened to you?*

Help-Seeking

Victims were also asked a number of questions about if and how they sought help for the violent incident. This encompasses seeking medical treatment, confiding in others, the use/failure to use services, and spousal counseling.

Medical Treatment. Victims were asked: *Did you ever see a doctor or nurse for your injuries?* (W8)

Confiding. Victims in the VAWS were asked: *Did you ever talk to anyone about what happened, such as...?* (W12) Response categories are "family," "friend/neighbour," "doctor," "minister, priest or clergy."

Services. Victims were asked: *Did you ever contact any of the following services for help?* (W13). Response categories are "shelter or transition house," "crisis center/crisis line," "another counsellor," "women's center," "community/family center."

Reasons Services Not Used. Finally, with respect to help-seeking, respondents were asked: *Is there any reason why you didn't use these services?* (W14). Response categories include: "Didn't know of any services," "none available," "waiting list," "too minor," "shame/embarrassment," "wouldn't be believed," "he prevented me," "distance," "fear of losing financial support," "fear of losing the children," "didn't want relationship to end," "didn't want/need help."

Spousal Counseling. Finally with respect to services, respondents were also asked if their husband/partner ever received counseling for his violent behavior (W41).

Leaving and Returning

Victims in the VAWS were also asked questions involving leaving and returning to the relationship.

Leaving. Victims were asked: *Did you ever leave or stay apart from your current (or previous) husband/partner because he was abusive or threatening?* (W21). Response categories include "yes/she left," "yes/he left," and "no." If victims responded that they had left, they were asked: *Did you ever stay at a transition house or a shelter?* (W22). If victims did not do so they were asked: *Where did you stay?* (W23). Response categories for the latter question include: "friends or relatives," "hotel, motel, etc.," "hostel (Salvation Army, church)," and "got her own place."

Returning. Victims who left their partner were also asked: *Did you eventually return home?* (W24). Those who responded positively were then asked: *What was the main reason you returned home?* (W25). Response categories include: "spouse left," "spouse promised to change," "court ordered him away," "resolved problems," "no money," "no where to go," "sake of children," "shame of divorce," "lack of housing," "wanted to give relationship another try."

Police Response

Victims were asked several questions about the police response to the incident. They were asked: *Did the police ever find out about the (an) incident?* (W26); *Did they respond by seeing you?* (W27); *Did the police take your husband/partner away?* (W28); *Did they tell you about or put you in touch with any services in your community?* (W30). To measure victims' satisfaction with the police, they were asked: *How satisfied were you with the way the police handled the case?* (W31). Response categories for the latter question ranged from "very satisfied" to "very dissatisfied." In addition to asking a scale question regarding police satisfaction, victims were also asked: *Is there anything (else) they should have done to help you?* (W33). Response categories for this question include: "no/nothing," "take him out of house," "charge/arrest him," "respond more quickly," "refer/take you to service," "relocate you," "take you to hospital," and "be more supportive/sympathetic." Victims were also asked about violence following the police response to the incident. More specifically, victims were asked: *After the police were involved, did your husband's/partner's violent or threatening behavior toward you . . .*

(W32). Response categories for this variable include: "increase," "decrease," and "stay the same." Finally, victims who did not contact the police were asked why they chose not to do so (W39). Response categories for this question include: "wouldn't be believed," "didn't think police could do anything," "fear of husband/partner," "too minor," "keep incident private," "shame/embarrassment," "didn't want involvement with police/courts," and "didn't want him arrested/jailed."

Methodological Considerations

In this section the methods of data analysis are outlined, the weighting scheme employed in the analysis is discussed, and some methodological advances of the present study over previous research are put forth.

Methods of Data Analysis

The analysis of the data was conducted in two stages. The first stage consisted of a descriptive analysis in which a simple chi square test of significance is used for examining bivariate relationships. More elaborate analyses were conducted using multivariate analyses to verify the hypotheses. The multivariate technique used for this purpose is logistic multiple regression. Logistic regression is an appropriate technique for predicting a dichotomous dependent variable, in this case a variable having the categories "violence" or "no violence," from a set of independent variables. This technique also has a very simple interpretation. For a given variable, it simply provides a ratio of the odds of violence occurring. If the value of the odds is greater than one, the variable is positively related to violence. If the value is less than one, the variable is negatively related to violence. Logistic regression is used in the present study to assess the effects of each independent variable net of all other independent variables in each marital status model as well as to test the effects of the block of selection variables and the block of relationship variables in explaining violence.

Weighting

The VAWS used a stratified sampling design. Statistics Canada employed the Elimination of Non-Working Banks (ENWB) sampling technique. Each household falling within a stratum had an equal probability of selection. Because the VAWS does not consist of a simple random sample, it is necessary to weight the data so that the population is adequately represented. Statistics Canada assigned each respondent a "case weight." This was accomplished by first assigning a weight to each responding and nonresponding household in the sample of telephone numbers.[23] This weight for a given household is equal to the inverse of that household's probability of selection. Next, within each stratum weights were adjusted to represent nonresponding households. Households that had more than one residential or nonbusiness telephone number then had their weights adjusted downward to account for their higher probability of selection. From this a person weight was calculated for each respondent in the sample. The person weight was calculated by multiplying the household weight by the number of women in the household who met the eligibility criteria for the survey. The final person weight (PERWGHT) was calculated by making further adjustments to make population estimates consistent with census projected population counts and with census projected province-age group-sex distributions for June of 1993 (Statistics Canada, 1994).

Weights were also assigned for the respondents' reports of violent incidents (INCWGHT). Adjustments were made to the person weight to account for the selection of only one type of violence (e.g., physical or sexual assault by a current partner), for nonresponse to detailed questions about the incident, and for the fact that some respondents experienced the incident in more than one of their relationships (Statistics Canada, 1994).

Statistics Canada points out that many types of analyses calculate variance estimates that depend on the scale of the weights.[24] Since for many variables in the VAWS much of the variance comes for the variability of the weights, one wants to preserve this variability in their analysis while at the same time avoiding the erroneous answers that come from a given statistic's dependence on scale. To avoid this problem, the weights employed with the data must be rescaled in a manner that preserves the variability of the original weights but that has an average value of one. This is accomplished by first calculating the average weight for those respondents in the analysis and then dividing each respondent's weight by this average. The resulting "working weight" is the weighting factor to be used in the analysis.

Methodological Advances

There are a number of methodological advances in the present study. In addition to utilizing a new conceptualization of prevalence and incidence rates of violence and arriving at a new conceptualization of violence, the extensive review of the literature and the theoretical synthesis identify more precisely than ever before the manner through which we can arrive at an understanding of differences between cohabitors and marrieds in terms of violence. Another major methodological advance of the present study is its holistic approach. Previous studies typically only test variables corresponding to one theory. But each of the explanatory frameworks for understanding marital status differences in violence seems to have some merit *prima facie*. By only testing variables pertinent to one theory, previous studies do not control for the effects of other potentially important variables linked to other theories. Testing all of the theories in one model, as in the present study, allows one to make a much more comprehensive assessment of each theory's ability to account for marital status differences in violence.

Summary

The present study employs a large-scale national survey of Canadian women to bring a new level of understanding to the relationship between marital status and violence against women. Among the advantages of this survey is its large subsample of 1,022 Canadian cohabitors, which allows a much more representative, reliable, and, thus, generalizable test than ever before in Canada. Several aspects of violence against women are investigated in the present study including physical assault, psychological aggression, verbal abuse and sexual coercion. Having precisely operationalized the variables to be employed, identified the methods of statistical analyses to be used, namely, cross-tabulation and logistic multiple regression, discussed the weighting scheme to be employed as well as methodological advances of the study, we can now embark on the odyssey of data analysis.

Notes

1. The survey did not include the Yukon and the Northwest Territories for primarily practical reasons (Doob, 1995). With respect to the present work, inclusion of the Northwest Territories would have been particularly desirable since it is in this jurisdiction, along with Quebec, where cohabitation relationships are most prevalent (Holland, 1995).

2. The married subsample of the VAWS consists of 7,396 women. Wilson et al. (1995) reduced the married subsample to 7,363 as a result of excluding women not residing with their husbands at the time of the interview due to employment or other reasons. However, the present work retains these cases because it is possible that the violence variables could be experienced while living apart. This is particularly the case with verbal abuse, psychological aggression and the item that taps threats to use a knife or gun since these acts can take place by telephone or, though less likely, in writing.

3. By using random digit dialing (RDD) telephone procedures, women forced to live on the streets and women who have homes but cannot afford telephones are excluded. Smith (1989) and DeKeseredy and Hinch (1991) have criticized this method as leading to conservative estimates of woman abuse because many of these women were abused. However, while homeless women remain unrepresented, the weighting scheme devised by Statistics Canada adjusts for undersampling so that all estimates incorporate women who do not have telephone service in their residence (Ratner, 1995).

4. For further discussion of modifications to the CTS in the VAWS see Johnson (1995b).

5. Some inconsistencies emerge when lifetime prevalence of violence is cross-tabulated with respondent's age. One would expect this rate to increase with age. But, in fact, it declines for women in the 45-54 and the 55+ age groups. Although these results may be theoretically possible due to the use of synthetic cohorts, they are unlikely because this is contradictory to what one sees in reality. There is no way to identify the source of these results in the public use microdata file. Alternatively, it would have been useful to triangulate with other studies that compare lifetime and one-year prevalence rates by age. However, the author was unable to find another study that makes these comparisons.

6. For example, see Lupri, Grandin, and Brinkerhoff (1994).

7. It would have been possible to include an item as a measure of financial abuse. However, bearing in mind Duffy and Momirov's (1997) remarks regarding a balanced definition and the fact that this item embodies the partner's desire to control the respondent, it was decided to use this item to represent the concept of Dominance.

8. The VAWS includes two items that are not usually included in the violence indexes of the CTS (Straus, 1979). The first involves the item: *Threatened*

to hit you with his fist or anything else that could hurt you. The second is designed to account for forced sexual activity.

9. For clarity, the original CTS is henceforth referred to as the CTS1.

10. An analysis of the variable indicating whether the only or the most recent incident had occurred while living married or common-law (DVJ25) shows that 12 percent of these incidents occurred only while the respondents were dating their current marital/common-law partner. Since the purpose of the present investigation is to understand the etiology of violence within marital or common-law relationships, the relevant dependent variables were recoded so that they refer only to incidents that occurred while married or living common-law. In the present study, then, the lifetime time frame spans from the time of the survey to when the respondent and her partner became married or began to live common-law. Unfortunately, as a result of computing new variables that are contingent on values of other variables, the number of missing cases also increased for some of the dependent variables. That is, some women who reported incidents did not state whether the (most recent) incident occurred during dating or during marriage/common-law. As a result, the number of missing cases for variables *J4A* and *J7A* increased by a value of one.

11. As a result of the skip questions, several of the variables in this set of questions contain "Not Applicable" categories. Since the assumption of skipping is that these respondents would not have experienced the remaining types of "violence," it was deemed reasonable in the present study to combine the "Not Applicable" and "No" categories.

12. All caps text in parentheses refer to variable names in the VAWS and italicized all caps text in parentheses refer to names of variables created by the author.

13. All dichotomous variables are converted into dummy variables by coding them into categories of 0 and 1. This allows these variables to be used in regression type techniques that require interval level measurement. For the violence variables a 1 indicates a positive response. For the independent variables a 1 indicates the category that is expected to be associated with a higher likelihood of violence.

14. Ratner (1998:455), including this variable under "Threats of Harm," emphasizes the threatening aspect of this item noting that "the act included incidents in which a man threatened to use a knife or gun but did not."

15. Statistics Canada is not releasing the data on partner's age (Wilson, Johnson, and Daly, 1995).

16. This category includes those with "some trade, technical or vocational," "some community college, CEGEP," "some university," "trade, technical, vocational diploma," and "community college, CEGEP diploma" (Statistics Canada, 1994).

17. Since the denominator contained some zero values (respondents who reported their partner having no income) the spouse income variable was recoded (*SPINC2*) with the category representing no income having a value of 1.

18. Since the logistic regression procedure in SPSS allows only listwise deletion of missing cases, for some variables additional dummy variables were created to prevent the cases they represent from being excluded from the analysis. These additional variables are simply entered and left out of the interpretation. In addition to the extra dummy variables for social learning (*M2B* and *M4B*), such variables are added for previous spousal violence (*ALLVPSPB*) and presence of children (*DVLVGRGB*).

19. Persons from the Yukon and Northwest Territories were not surveyed in the VAWS.

20. Trussell and Rao (1989) have discussed the analysis of duration in logistic regression. These researchers note that "the probability of experiencing an event increases with duration of exposure to risk" and, as a result, in logistic regression "one must account for the fact that two persons who have identical covariates except that one was exposed for 10 years and the other for only 1 year must somehow be treated differently" (1989:537). Since, in the present analysis, duration is not a measure of elapsed time from relationship commencement to an event of abuse, but, rather elapsed time from relationship commencement to the time of the survey regardless of whether the event occurred, this does not pose a problem.

21. For categories representing a range of values, the midpoint was used.

22. The variables in this section of the VAWS are applicable to violence experienced by both current and previous partners. It was necessary, then, to make adjustments so that only incidents with current husbands or common-law partners are included and, second, to include incidents that occurred while living married or common-law. Since these variables are analyzed separately from the etiological model, and because these changes must be made uniformly across all variables included in this analysis, these adjustments were accomplished by simply selecting cases involving a husband or common-law partner (QUESTID = 12) and in which the incident occurred while living married/common-law (DVJ25 = 1). The resulting subsample consists of 702 women. It is also important to note that all variables analyzed in this section of the book are dichotomous. They are simply coded yes = 1 and no = 0.

23. For more information on the calculation of the weights, see Statistics Canada (1994).

24. Personal communication with David Paton at Statistics Canada, June 25, 1998.

Chapter 6

Descriptive Results

The sample from the VAWS used in this study consists of 8,418 women representing a total of 6,642,558 women 18 years of age or older, living married or common-law in one of ten Canadian provinces in 1993. Seven thousand three hundred and ninety-six respondents represent 5,811,610 married women and 1,022 respondents represent 830,949 women living in common-law unions at the time of the survey. Among married respondents, 6,837 had not lived common-law prior to their marriage (non-PC married) leaving 552 respondents who had lived in a common-law union prior to their marriage (PC-married).

The Prevalence of Violence and Marital Status Differences

Employing a lifetime time frame, 16.3 percent of women reported experiencing at least one form of violence since beginning to live common-law or married with their current partner. This represents more than one million women in Canada. Roughly half of these women, or 8.4 percent, reported experiencing at least one type of violence in the twelve months prior to the survey.

Table 6.1 provides the prevalence of each component of violence cross-tabulated with the selection variables. An inspection of table 6.1 shows, somewhat surprisingly, that the most common component of violence is minor physical assault. Intuitively, one might expect the less

Table 6.1. *Lifetime Prevalence of Each Component of Violence by Selection Variables (in Percent).*

	Verbal Abuse	Psych. Aggression	Minor Physical Assault			Moderate Physical Assault				Severe Physical Assault				Sexual Coercion
	Name Calling	Threat	Push	Slap	Total	Choke	Throw	Hit	Total	T.Gun	Kick	Beat	Total	Forced Sex
Total F Experience	6.8	6.2	10.8	4.0	11.3	1.1	3.3	1.2	4.0	0.6	2.2	1.3	2.7	1.5
Marital Status														
Common-Law	6.5	6.6	12.2	3.9	13.1	1.5	5.2	2.6	5.8	—	3.2	1.7	3.5	—
Married	6.8	6.2	10.6	4.0	11.0†	1.0	3.0‡	1.0†	3.7†	0.6	2.1†	1.3	2.6*	1.6*
Non PC	6.6	5.9	10.4	4.0	10.8	1.0	2.9	1.0	3.6	0.6	2.0	1.2	2.5	1.6
PC M	9.5†	10.1‡	14.5‡	4.0	14.7†	—	5.0†	—	5.6†	—*	—	—	3.2	—
Age														
18-24	7.7	7.2	11.6	4.1	13.3	—	5.6	4.1	7.2	—	3.6	—	3.6	—
25-29	6.7	6.6	10.6	2.4	10.7	—	4.1	—	4.6	—	2.1	—	2.4	—
30-34	7.1	7.2	12.0	4.0	12.3	—	3.7	1.3	4.0	—	2.4	—	2.7	—
35-39	6.0	6.8	10.6	4.2	11.4	—	3.3	1.3	4.0	1.3	2.4	2.2	3.0	1.7
40-44	6.4	6.5	12.3	3.5	12.6	—	2.8	1.1	3.4	—	1.6	—	2.0	—
45-54	6.4	6.4	12.9	5.7	13.1	1.3	3.3	1.1	4.3	0.9	2.5	1.4	3.3	1.5
55+	7.4	4.8*	8.0‡	3.5‡	8.4‡	1.0	2.5†	0.7†	3.1‡	—†	1.8	1.1	2.3	2.3†
Age Difference														
6+ Older	7.6	6.7	11.2	4.8	11.8	—	2.9	1.5	3.9	1.1	2.2	1.5	2.8	1.8
1-5 Older	6.7	6.5	11.1	4.3	11.6	1.3	3.6	1.1	4.3	0.6	2.2	1.1	2.7	1.8
Same Age	7.1	5.0	10.4	2.9	10.5	—	2.7	—	3.7	—	2.4	1.5	2.5	—
1-5 Younger	5.1	5.7	9.5	2.7	9.8	—	3.0	—	3.2	—	1.8	—	2.3	—
6+ Younger	11.9‡	7.0	13.2	6.1‡	13.6	—	—	—†	—	—†	—	—†	—*	—*
Resp.'s Education														
<High school	9.2	7.7	11.7	5.7	12.9	1.9	4.6	1.8	5.7	1.4	3.2	2.2	4.1	2.5
High school	7.2	6.7	10.7	3.8	10.9	0.9	3.7	1.0	4.0	—	1.8	1.2	2.3	1.4
Some post sec.	5.8	5.9	10.5	3.6	10.9	0.9	2.6	1.1	3.5	—	2.1	1.0	2.2	1.5
Univers. degree	4.0‡	3.8‡	10.2	2.7‡	10.2*	—†	1.9‡	—†	2.1‡	—†	1.6†	—†	2.0‡	—†

‡ p < 0.01; † p < 0.05; * p ≤ 0.10; — not statistically reliable

Table 6.1 continued.

	Verbal Abuse	Psych. Aggression	Minor Physical Assault			Moderate Physical Assault					Severe Physical Assault			Sexual Coercion
	Name Calling	Threat	Push	Slap	Total	Choke	Throw	Hit	Total	T.Gun	Kick	Beat	Total	Forced Sex
Partner's Educ.														
< High school	9.5	8.6	13.2	6.1	14.1	1.8	5.0	1.9	6.1	1.4	3.2	2.2	4.1	3.0
High school	5.5	6.1	9.8	3.9	10.1	0.9	3.2	1.1	3.5	—	2.0	1.1	2.4	1.0
Some post sec.	7.3	6.4	11.3	3.3	11.5	1.0	2.7	1.1	3.8	—	1.9	1.2	2.1	1.0
Univers. degree	3.1‡	2.7‡	8.0‡	2.2‡	8.2‡	—‡	1.3‡	—‡	1.5‡	—‡	1.4‡	—‡	1.6‡	—‡
Resp. Employed														
Yes	6.5	6.6	11.3	4.2	11.8	1.0	3.6	1.2	4.1	0.5	2.3	1.2	2.7	1.5
No	7.3	5.5‡	9.9‡	3.7	10.3‡	1.3	2.8*	1.0	3.9	0.9‡	2.1	1.6	2.8	1.7
Partner Employed														
Yes	6.4	6.4	11.3	4.1	11.7	1.1	3.3	1.1	4.0	0.6	2.3	1.3	2.7	1.3
No	8.0†	5.7	9.2†	3.7	9.7†	1.2	3.3	1.3	3.8	—	1.9	1.5	2.6	2.3‡
Resp. Income														
<$15000	7.4	6.5	11.6	4.2	12.2	1.4	3.4	1.3	4.5	0.9	2.4	1.7	3.2	2.0
$15000-$29999	8.0	6.4	10.9	4.0	11.1	0.7	3.6	1.2	4.0	—	2.2	1.4	2.6	1.2
$30000-$59999	4.3	5.9	10.6	3.7	10.9	0.9	3.1	0.9	3.4	—	1.7	0.9	2.0	1.4
$60000+	—‡	—	13.8	—	14.2	—*	—	—	—	—	—	—*	—*	—‡
Partner Income														
<$15000	8.8	6.9	12.3	4.4	12.7	1.4	3.9	1.5	4.8	0.9	2.4	1.3	3.0	2.1
$15000-$29999	6.4	7.3	11.3	5.1	11.6	1.1	3.8	1.6	4.2	—	2.5	1.9	3.0	1.0
$30000-$59999	6.2	5.9	11.7	3.7	12.1	0.9	2.7	0.9	3.7	0.6	1.9	1.1	2.5	1.6
$60000+	—‡	5.6	12.1	—*	12.4	—	—*	—‡	4.4	—	—	—*	—	—‡
Educ. Consistency														
F much less	7.5	5.5	11.4	4.7	11.7	—	3.5	—	4.1	—	2.5	—	2.7	—
F less	4.5	3.2	7.3	2.2	7.5	—	1.8	—	2.0	—	—	—	—	—
F similar	6.8	7.0	11.0	4.3	11.6	1.2	3.2	1.2	4.2	0.9	2.8	1.6	3.5	1.6
F more	5.1	4.4	9.1	2.4	9.5	—	2.6	—	2.8	—	—	—	—	—
F much more	8.4‡	8.1‡	14.2‡	5.5‡	14.4‡	1.4‡	4.8‡	1.6‡	5.4‡	—‡	2.6‡	1.7‡	3.1‡	2.6‡

Table 6.1 continued.

	Verbal Abuse	Psych. Aggression	Minor Physical Assault			Moderate Physical Assault				Severe Physical Assault				Sexual Coercion
	Name Calling	Threat	Push	Slap	Total	Choke	Throw	Hit	Total	T.Gun	Kick	Beat	Total	Forced Sex
Inc. Consistency														
F much less	6.7	6.7	11.5	4.4	12.1	1.3	3.2	1.0	4.3	0.8	2.4	1.5	3.1	1.7
F less	7.1	5.8	11.1	3.7	11.1	1.0	3.1	1.2	4.0	—	2.9	1.6	3.3	1.0
F similar	7.5	8.1	13.7	3.8	13.8	—	4.7	—	5.3	—	—	—	2.6	2.6
F more	4.2	6.0	10.9	3.8	11.1	—	2.5	—	2.9	—	—	—	1.6	—
F much more	8.2‡	6.4	11.9	4.8	12.3	1.4	3.9*	1.2	4.5	—	2.0†	1.2	2.4*	1.6†
Partner Fath. Viol.														
Yes, think so	16.0	18.6	26.4	12.3	26.9	4.4	11.3	4.1	12.8	2.6	9.0	6.1	11.3	4.6
No, not think so	5.1‡	4.4‡	8.3‡	2.8‡	8.7‡	0.5‡	2.3‡	0.8‡	2.7‡	0.4‡	1.3‡	0.7‡	1.5‡	1.1‡
Father Violent														
Yes, think so	9.3	10.9	17.5	6.8	18.3	2.2	6.2	2.3	7.1	1.4	4.2	2.6	5.2	3.0
No, not think so	6.0‡	5.0‡	9.1‡	3.2‡	9.4‡	0.9‡	2.6‡	0.8‡	3.1‡	0.4‡	1.8‡	1.0‡	2.1‡	1.2‡
Dating Violence														
Yes	26.7	25.9	27.5	20.8	31.7	8.3	15.8	8.8	21.7	6.7	12.5	10.4	16.2	4.2
No	6.2‡	5.7‡	10.3‡	3.5‡	10.7‡	0.9‡	2.9‡	0.9‡	3.5‡	0.5‡	1.9‡	1.1‡	2.3‡	1.5‡
Previous Marriage														
Yes	8.0	7.5	11.1	5.0	11.4	1.7	4.3	1.7	4.7	—	4.2	2.6	4.4	1.3
No	6.6*	6.1*	10.8	3.9*	11.3	1.0†	3.1*	1.1*	3.9	0.6	1.9‡	1.1‡	2.4‡	1.6
Prev. Partner Viol.														
Yes	9.2	10.1	15.3	6.0	15.8	2.5	6.1	1.9	7.0	—	5.1	3.2	5.6	1.8
No	6.6*	6.1‡	8.4‡	3.0‡	8.5‡	—†	3.0‡	—*	3.4‡	—	—†	1.3‡	2.1‡	—†
Region														
Atlantic	7.0	7.0	10.8	3.9	11.1	—	3.5	—	3.9	—	2.1	—	2.7	—
Quebec	4.7	4.5	7.9	2.4	8.7	1.1	2.7	1.4	3.6	—	1.4	1.3	2.0	1.6
Ontario	7.4	5.8	10.9	3.9	11.2	0.8	3.3	1.0	3.9	0.7	2.2	1.2	2.7	1.4
Prairies	7.4	8.1	12.4	5.3	12.9	1.2	3.3	—	3.9	—	2.4	1.5	2.8	1.4
British C.	8.3‡	8.2‡	14.6‡	5.9‡	15.0‡	1.9‡	4.4	—	5.3	—	3.7‡	1.8	4.1†	1.9

overt and physically consequential verbally abusive and psychologically aggressive behaviors to be the most common. However, 11 percent of respondents have experienced minor physical assault during their current common-law or marital relationship with the most common occurrence of this form of violence involving pushing, grabbing, or shoving. Nearly 11 percent of married and cohabiting women in the sample report that their partner had pushed, grabbed, or shoved them since becoming married/common-law. The next most common type of violence is verbal abuse. Nearly 7 percent of women in the sample report that their current partner has called them names to put them down or make them feel bad since becoming married/common-law. Psychological aggression is reported at similar levels to verbal abuse. Slightly more than 6 percent of respondents report that their partner has threatened to hit them with his fist or anything else that could hurt them. As one would expect, the more severe the physical assault the less likely it is to occur in the population. Four percent of respondents report having experienced moderate physical assault. The most common form of moderate physical assault by a factor of about 3 is having something thrown at the respondent that could hurt her. Nearly 3 percent of respondents report experiencing one or more of the most severe forms of physical assault. The most common form of severe physical assault is being kicked, bit, or hit with a fist. The least common form of violence experienced by the respondents involves being threatened with or having a knife or gun used on them by their partner. While the percentage of the sample reporting this component of violence seems small, these respondents represent 42,268 women in Canada. Put in this context one may see the substantive significance of such a "small" number. Finally, 1.5 percent of respondents report that in the course of their current marital or common-law relationship they have been forced into some sexual activity when they did not want to, by being threatened, held down, or hurt in some way.

The Prevalence of Violence by Marital Status

An examination of the prevalence rates for each marital status category in table 6.2 shows that, as expected, cohabitors and PC marrieds report higher rates of violence than do non-PC marrieds. The hypothesis that cohabitors and PC marrieds will report higher rates of violence than will non-PC marrieds is supported by the data. This result, which is based on a larger subsample of cohabitors than most previous studies,

Table 6.2. *Lifetime and One-Year Prevalence Rates by Marital Status (in Percent).*

Marital Status	Time Frame	
	Lifetime	One-Year
Common-Law	17.3	11.8
Married	16.1	7.9
PC-Married	21.2	12.5
Non-PC Married	15.8	7.5

buttresses the findings of past research that consistently shows cohabitors to have higher rates of violence.

With respect to lifetime prevalence rates, the data reveal that women in common-law unions are slightly more likely than married women to experience violence at some point during their relationship.[1] Among marrieds,[2] those that did not live with a man other than their husband have the lowest lifetime prevalence rate. Interestingly, PC marrieds have the highest lifetime prevalence rate of violence. Reports by women who had cohabited prior to getting married exceed those of currently cohabiting and non-PC married women by more than 5 percent.

An examination of the one-year prevalence rates in table 6.2 reveals the same pattern. Again, women in common-law unions are more likely to report experiencing violence than are married women as a whole. A comparison of the two married categories shows that PC married women are more likely to experience violence in the past year than are non-PC married women. Examining all three estimates, it is evident that PC married women report higher rates of violence in the year prior to the study than do women currently living common-law and non-PC married women.[3] Though, with the one-year rate, there is less than 1 percent difference between cohabitors and PC marrieds.[4]

These findings are slightly contradictory to the only other study to make the PC/non-PC distinction. While non-PC marrieds report the lowest rates of violence in both samples, in Boba's (1996) study cohabitors were found to be more likely to report violence than PC marrieds. As the following discussion will show, this difference may be due to the way in which violence is defined in Boba's (1996) study. Boba (1996) restricted the operational definition of violence to arguments in the past year that became *physical*.

Figure 6.1 graphically represents the prevalence rates of each component of violence for the three marital status groups.[5] With respect to verbal abuse, the cross-tabulation analysis shows that there is no signifi-

Figure 6.1. *Lifetime Prevalence Rates of Each Component of Violence by Marital Status (in Percent).*

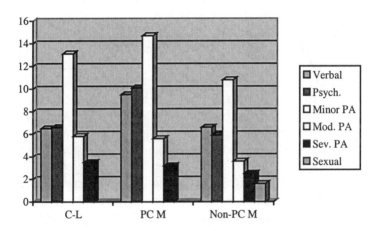

cant difference between cohabitors and marrieds as a whole. However, when examining the two married groups it is apparent that PC marrieds have a significantly higher prevalence of verbal abuse than non-PC marrieds. Cohabitors and non-PC marrieds have virtually identical rates of verbal abuse while PC-marrieds are nearly one-third more likely to experience verbal abuse.

A similar pattern to verbal abuse emerges in terms of psychological aggression. Unlike verbal abuse, the prevalence of psychological aggression is slightly higher among cohabitors than marrieds. Similar to verbal abuse, the differences in psychological aggression between marrieds as a whole and cohabitors is not significant. Examining PC and non-PC marrieds separately, however, reveals that non-PC marrieds are the least likely to report psychological aggression. PC marrieds are more than one-third as likely to report psychological aggression as non-PC marrieds and cohabitors.

It is only with the physical and sexual assault items that significant differences between cohabitors and marrieds as a whole can be seen. Cohabitors are significantly more likely to report minor physical assault in comparison to marrieds. Similar to verbal abuse and psychological aggression, however, when PC marrieds are examined separately it is apparent that they have the highest prevalence rate of minor physical assault. Since there are no significant differences between any of the marital status groups in terms of being slapped, it follows that the differences are primarily due to differential rates of being pushed, grabbed, or shoved.

Overall, then, with respect to the less physically consequential variables it is PC marrieds who have the highest lifetime prevalence rates. Contrary to the hypothesis that PC marrieds and cohabitors would be more alike than non-PC marrieds, in terms of these components of violence it is cohabitors and non-PC marrieds who appear to be more alike. While this finding is contrary to expectations, it remains indicative that marital status differences are not due to the type of relationship itself. Rather, there appears to be something about having lived with someone else before getting married that leads to a greater propensity to experience verbal abuse, psychological aggression, and minor physical assault in marriage.

A pattern like that which was hypothesized emerges when examining marital status differences in moderate physical assault. Common-law couples are more likely to report moderate physical assault than are marrieds as a whole. The significant differences remain when marrieds are examined separately with cohabitors followed closely by PC marrieds and then non-PC marrieds. With respect to the components of moderate physical assault, no significant differences are found between cohabitors and marrieds in terms of being choked. Although significant differences between non-PC and PC marrieds are found with respect to being choked, there are too few PC married cases to provide a reliable comparison on this variable.[6] Significant differences between cohabitors and marrieds are found for both having something thrown at the respondent that could hurt and being hit with something that could hurt. In both cases the pattern of differences follows that of the overall moderate physical assault variable. PC marrieds are also found to be significantly more likely than non-PC marrieds to report having something thrown at them that could hurt.

A similar pattern to moderate physical assault emerges with severe physical assault. Cohabitors are significantly more likely to report severe physical assault than are marrieds as a whole. Examining PC and non-PC marrieds separately, cohabitors still report the highest rates followed closely by PC marrieds and then non-PC marrieds. There are no significant marital status differences in terms of being beaten up. There are significant differences in terms of being kicked, bit, or hit with a fist between cohabitors and marrieds as a whole. The only other significant difference is between PC and non-PC marrieds in terms of being threatened with or having a knife or gun used.

Overall, the results for the moderate and severe physical assault variables are similar to the marital status differences in physical violence found in Boba's (1996) study. In keeping with the hypothesis of experiencing more severe violence, cohabitors and PC marrieds report higher rates of moderate and severe physical assault than do non-PC marrieds. While cohabitors do have higher rates than PC marrieds, they are nevertheless very similar to one another. Again, following Nock (1995) this suggests that the differences in violence between marrieds and cohabitors are not due to the relationship itself. Simply being married or cohabiting does not explain the differences in violence, since those who cohabited but are currently married are significantly different from those who did not cohabit before marriage.

There are too few cases in the cross-tabulation with sexual coercion to provide reliable estimates. It can nevertheless be noted that a significant difference is present between cohabitors and marrieds as a whole.

In sum, it is evident that there is a relationship between marital status and violence and that this relationship varies depending on what component of violence is being investigated. To begin to understand this relationship it is necessary to investigate how violence varies with the selection and relationship factors hypothesized to have an effect on violence and the extent to which the different marital status categories are represented on each selection and relationship factor. Before doing this, however, we will very briefly examine marital status and the incidence of violence.

The Incidence of Violence and Marital Status Differences

The incidence of violence provides an indication of how often violent incidents are occurring among those who experience violence. As shown in table 6.3[7], an examination of the incidence of violence in the present study shows that, of women who reported at least one incident of violence, victimization had occurred an average of 1.6 times in the year prior to the study and 3.1 times since beginning to live married/common-law to their partner.[8]

An examination of the lifetime and one-year incidence of violence

Table 6.3. *Lifetime and One-Year Incidence Rates of Violence.*

Time frame	Overall	non-PC Married	PC Married	Cohabitor
Lifetime	3.1	3.1	3.3	2.9
One-Year	1.6	1.3	1.5	1.8

by marital status in table 6.3 shows that the differences in the extent to which violence is repeated across marital status categories are small. These results indicate that, while cohabitors and PC marrieds are more likely to experience violence, when violence does occur it is likely to be repeated at similar levels, regardless of marital status.

Selection Factors, Marital Status, and Violence

Based on the theoretical synthesis, it is necessary to identify and study a number of risk markers of violence. Hotaling and Sugarman (1986:102) define a risk marker as "an attribute or characteristic that is associated with an increased probability to either the use of husband to wife violence, or the risk of being victimized by husband to wife violence." Of course, it should not be surprising that an argument is made in the present work that this definition should be altered such that the terms "husband" and "wife" are changed to "partner." Following the theoretical synthesis, risk markers of violence against women in common-law unions are divided in this study into selection and relationship factors. For this purpose, selection factors are those characteristics of the respondent and/or her partner that tend to be brought with the individual to the union.

Age, Marital Status, and Violence

Some researchers have argued that the higher rates of violence among cohabitors may be due to their youth (Johnson, 1996; Yelsma, 1986). Cohabitors have been found in previous research to be more likely than marrieds to be young (Ellis, 1989; Stets and Straus, 1989) and youth is generally strongly negatively associated with violence (Johnson,

Table 6.4. *Selection Variables by Marital Status (in Percent).*

Marital Status

Selection Var.	C-Law	Married	Non-PC	PC
Age				
18-24	22.7	2.4	2.3	3.6
25-29	22.6	8.6	8.0	16.0
30-34	20.0	13.5	12.8	23.9
35-39	10.6	14.6	14.1	21.7
40-44	8.7	12.8	12.6	17.0
45-54	11.2	20.1	20.6	13.0
55+	4.1	28.0‡	29.6	4.9‡
Age Difference				
6+ Older	22.9	18.1	17.9	21.7
1-5 Older	40.2	51.2	52.1	38.9
Same Age	11.2	12.3	12.5	8.9
1-5 Younger	19.3	16.3	15.5	26.1
6+ Younger	6.5	2.2‡	2.0	4.3‡
Resp.'s Education				
< High school	21.3	25.2	25.4	22.1
High school	27.7	28.9	28.7	31.0
Some post sec.	35.0	29.7	29.7	29.4
Univers. degree	16.0	16.2‡	16.2	17.4
Partner's Education				
< High school	28.1	29.8	30.3	23.5
High school	26.0	25.7	25.5	28.4
Some post sec.	29.9	24.5	24.2	27.6
Univers. degree	16.1	20.0‡	20.0	20.4†
Resp. Employed				
Yes	80.2	61.8	60.9	73.9
No	19.8	38.2‡	39.1	26.1‡
Partner Employed				
Yes	87.5	76.6	75.6	89.9
No	12.5	23.4‡	24.4	10.1‡
Resp. Income				
< $15000	40.7	49.9	50.4	43.0
$15000-$29999	31.6	27.0	27.0	26.7
$30000-$59999	26.1	20.5	20.1	24.9
$60000+	1.6	2.6‡	2.4	5.3‡

‡ $p < 0.01$; † $p < 0.05$; * $p \leq 0.10$; — not statistically reliable

Table 6.4 continued.

Marital Status

Selection Var.	C-Law	Married	Non-PC	PC
Partner Income				
< $15000	32.5	24.3	24.2	25.4
$15000-$29999	35.1	27.9	27.9	28.4
$30000-$59999	30.9	42.6	42.5	44.0
$60000+	—	5.2‡	5.4	—†
Educ. Consistency				
F much less ed.	8.9	10.5	10.3	12.7
F less ed.	12.6	13.1	13.2	12.1
F similar ed.	46.3	50.5	50.4	51.3
F more ed.	14.9	10.9	10.9	11.2
F much more ed.	17.2	15.1‡	15.3	12.7
Inc. Consistency				
F much less	22.1	39.3	39.6	35.1
F less	21.0	20.9	20.9	21.0
F similar	12.3	8.8	8.9	7.7
F more	19.9	14.2	14.2	14.8
F much more	24.7	16.8‡	16.4	21.4*
Partner's Fath. Viol.				
Yes, think so	13.6	9.5	9.4	11.0
No, not think so	86.4	90.5‡	90.6	89.0
Father Violent				
Yes, think so	24.2	16.1	15.1	29.0
No, not think so	75.8	83.9‡	84.9	71.0‡
Dating Violence				
Yes	5.0	2.6	2.3	6.3
No	95.0	97.4‡	97.7	93.7‡
Previous Marriage				
Yes	35.9	10.3	9.0	27.4
No	64.1	89.7‡	91.0	72.6‡
Prev. Partner Viol.				
Yes	61.5	49.2	48.9	49.5
No	38.5	50.8‡	51.1	50.5
Region				
Atlantic	6.5	8.9	9.0	6.3
Quebec	43.9	23.1	23.3	21.1
Ontario	27.0	38.1	38.3	35.4
Prairies	11.5	17.4	17.4	17.4
British Columbia	11.2	12.5‡	11.9	19.8‡

Table 6.5. *Lifetime and One-Year Prevalence Rates by Selection Variables (in Percent).*

Prevalence

Selection Variable	Lifetime	One-Year
Age		
18-24	16.9	13.8
25-29	15.5	9.3
30-34	16.6	8.8
35-39	16.3	7.3
40-44	18.2	7.9
45-54	17.0	7.8
55+	14.8	7.9‡
Age Difference		
6+ Older	17.0	9.2
1-5 Older	16.4	7.9
Same Age	16.2	9.0
1-5 Younger	14.2	6.8
6+ Younger	22.8†	17.1‡
Resp.'s Education		
< High school	18.2	10.3
High school	15.9	8.3
Some post sec.	16.1	7.5
Univers. degree	13.8‡	6.8‡
Partner's Education		
< High school	19.8	10.8
High school	14.3	7.1
Some post sec.	17.6	9.3
Univers. degree	11.3‡	4.7‡
Resp. Employed		
Yes	16.7	8.2
No	15.6	8.6
Partner Employed		
Yes	16.4	8.2
No	15.9	9.1
Resp. Income		
< $15000	17.1	8.9
$15000-$29999	17.4	9.4
$30000-$59999	14.7	6.4
$60000+	17.3*	9.7‡

‡ p < 0.01; † p < 0.05; * p ≤ 0.10

Table 6.5 continued.

Prevalence

Selection Variable	Lifetime	One-Year
Partner Income		
< $15000	18.5	10.9
$15000-$29999	15.6	8.2
$30000-$59999	17.1	7.5
$60000+	16.2	5.9‡
Educ. Consistency		
F much less ed.	16.2	9.0
F less ed.	12.1	5.2
F similar ed.	16.5	8.4
F more ed.	13.7	8.3
F much more ed.	20.5‡	10.1‡
Inc. Consistency		
F much less	17.1	8.1
F less	15.6	7.9
F similar	19.5	9.4
F more	14.1	6.5
F much more	18.9‡	10.8‡
Partner's Fath. Viol.		
Yes, think so	34.2	19.0
No, not think so	12.9‡	6.4‡
Father Violent		
Yes, think so	24.7	12.6
No, not think so	14.0‡	7.2‡
Dating Violence		
Yes	46.1	32.1
No	15.4‡	7.7‡
Previous Marriage		
Yes	16.5	11.2
No	16.2	7.9‡
Prev. Partner Viol.		
Yes	21.7	14.0
No	13.2‡	8.3‡
Region		
Atlantic	15.3	8.4
Quebec	13.0	6.5
Ontario	16.9	9.1
Prairies	17.7	8.7
British Columbia	20.1‡	9.6†

1996). It would seem possible, then, that there is a connection between being young, being selected into cohabitation, and experiencing violence.

Table 6.4 presents the results of the cross-tabulations of the selection variables by marital status. As shown in table 6.4, respondent's age is significantly related to marital status. Canadian women living in common-law relationships are much more likely to be young than are their married counterparts. Women living common-law are nine times more likely than married women to be between the ages of 18-24. In fact, it is not until one examines respondents in the sample age 35-39 that women are more likely to be married. Table 6.4 also suggests that PC marrieds are significantly more likely to be young in comparison to non-PC marrieds. The largest difference in favor of PC marrieds is in the 25-29 age group in which they are two times more likely than non-PC marrieds to fall. Consistent with past research, then, it is predominantly young women in Canada who cohabit.

The results of the cross-tabulations of violence by the selection variables are presented in tables 6.1 and 6.5. When taken together as one violence variable, the results in table 6.5 suggest that there is not a significant relationship between age and lifetime prevalence of violence. This may be due to the fact that woman's rather than man's age is being used. However, women do tend to be similar in age to their partner (Eshleman and Wilson, 1998). Moreover, it is not surprising that age would not be related to lifetime prevalence of violence, since the nature of this dependent variable is cumulative with age. Therefore, the fact that the lifetime prevalence is high in the youngest age groups and remains relatively stable as age increases is indicative of a negative relationship between age and violence. That is, many of the older women reporting violence during their relationship may well have experienced it when they were younger. Indeed, as shown in table 6.5, when age is cross-tabulated with one-year prevalence of violence a significant negative relationship emerges. If one subtracts the one-year rate from the lifetime rate for each age group one can see that with increasing age more and more women who were experiencing violence by their partner in the more distant past were not experiencing violence in the year prior to the survey. However, the reduction in reports of lifetime prevalence of violence for the oldest age groups requires explanation. There are a few potential explanations. It is possible that there is a cohort effect. That is, perhaps these women and their partners experienced some event in common that leads to a lower likelihood of violence. However, there is no theoretical reason to posit such an effect. As well, if one examines the one-year rates one can see that there is very little difference among those aged 35 and above.

This suggests that the low lifetime rate for women in the older age groups is not due to a cohort effect. One could also posit some reporting bias among older women. However, the fact that they are just as likely to report violence in the year prior to the study as women aged 35 and above suggests that there is no such bias. A more probable explanation involves recall bias. Since the duration of older persons' relationships is more likely to be long, it is possible that some of these women will have forgotten about violent incidents.[9]

In terms of the specific components of violence, age of respondent does not appear to have an effect on the lifetime prevalence of verbal abuse. As shown in table 6.1, the differences in rates of verbal abuse across each category of age are not significant. It appears that verbal abuse is approximately equally likely to be reported at all ages. There is, however, a significant difference in rates of psychological aggression across age groups. Respondents under age 30 report the highest rate of psychological aggression. However, there is little difference between most of the age categories with the exception of respondents age 55 or older who are less likely to report psychological aggression. A similar pattern emerges with respect to minor physical assault. That is, the majority of the age categories report similar rates of this form of violence with the exception of women age 55 or older. On the other hand, women age 18-24 have the highest lifetime prevalence of moderate physical assault with a fairly steady decline in rates to the oldest respondents. Though there are significant differences in terms of being threatened with or having a knife or gun used on a respondent, there are too few cases in most of the age groups to provide reliable estimates. Overall, there are no significant differences in severe physical assault across age groups. Significant age differences are present on the sexual coercion item but, again, there are too few cases in several of the age groups. Interestingly, of the three categories that do have enough cases to provide reliable estimates, it is the oldest group of respondents who have the highest rate. The fact that the lifetime prevalence gets higher as opposed to remaining stable is indicative that new occurrences of sexual coercion are taking place in the older age groups.

Consistent with past research, then, cohabiting women in Canada are more likely than marrieds to be young. PC married women are also more likely than non-PC marrieds to be young. Also consistent with previous studies, there appears to be a negative relationship between age and violence in the present study. Overall, it appears possible that there is a relationship between being young, being a cohabiting or a PC married woman, and experiencing violence.

Age Heterogamy, Marital Status, and Violence

Discrepancy between the partners' characteristics has been hypothesized to both decrease the chances of a couple getting married and increase the probability of union disruption (Wu and Balakrishnan, 1995). They have argued that age heterogamy is often the result of attempts to avoid the costs of spending more time searching for a partner that is a closer match. According to these researchers, the resulting differences tend to lead to conflict between the partners. Dobash and Dobash (1995) have noted how homicide data collected in several countries demonstrate that couples that are more heterogamous in age have higher uxoricide rates for both marital and common-law unions. This relationship between age heterogamy and uxoricide holds true in Canada as well (Wilson, Johnson, and Daly, 1995). Based on the work of these researchers, it would seem possible that a connection exists between couples of different ages being selected into cohabitation and those couples experiencing violence.

Table 6.4 shows that significant marital status differences are present across categories of age heterogamy. It is conventional in Canadian society for partners in a couple to be of the same age or for the male partner to be slightly older (Eshleman and Wilson, 1998; Martin-Matthews, 2000). The cross-tabulations show that people in the more conventional type of union are most likely to conform to this pattern. That is, married women are more likely to report that their partner is the same age or one to five years older than they. On the other hand, cohabiting women are more likely to report either that their partner is six or more years older or more than one year younger than they. Women living common-law are three times more likely than married women to report that their partner is six or more years younger than they. However, while cohabitors are more likely to report being in an age heterogamous union, it is important to note that the pattern of differences is the same for marrieds and cohabitors with the majority of cohabiting women having a partner who is either the same age or one to five years older. Examining PC versus non-PC marrieds it is evident that PC marrieds follow the same pattern of age differences as do cohabitors. PC married women are more likely to report that their husband is either six or more years older or more than one year younger than they. PC married women are twice as likely as non-PC married women to report that their husband is six or more years younger than they. Overall, cohabiting and PC married women in Canada are significantly more likely than non-PC married women to be marginal with respect to age heterogamy.

Unlike the age variable, with the age heterogamy variable there should not be a major difference in operation between the lifetime and one-year prevalence rates of violence since each category of age difference is stable over time. A comparison of prevalence rates with these two time frames in table 6.5 shows this to be the case. Significant differences in prevalence rates across age difference categories are present in both time frames. As expected, the greater the age heterogamy within a couple the higher the prevalence of violence. However, the largest difference in prevalence occurs when the respondent's partner is six or more years younger than she. It would appear that women with a partner much younger than they have a disproportionate risk of violence. As shown in table 6.1, there are only two components of violence in which there are significant differences and sufficient information to provide reliable estimates. Each of these variables follows the same pattern as the combined violence variables. That is, women with a partner who is six or more years younger than they have a disproportionate risk of being called names to make them feel bad and of being slapped.

Difference in age implies a greater potential for incompatibility. As already discussed, Wu and Balakrishnan (1995) have argued that age difference is indicative of an insufficient search for a more closely matching partner. While there does appear to be some support for the effect of age difference on violence in the present study, the fact that the highest prevalence rates occur when the woman's partner is much younger than she is indicative that there is something more to this relationship. First, as has already been established, younger men are more likely to commit violent acts. Second, in addition to differing characteristics of the much younger male from his older female partner, the fact that both partners in this category are engaging in socially marginal behavior may also be a factor. In today's society it remains much more socially acceptable for men to couple with women who are much younger than they rather than vice versa. Thus, it may also be that men and women who are willing to enter such relationships possess other characteristics that lead to violence.

Overall, violence is found to be most likely to occur among age heterogamous couples, especially where the man is six or more years younger than his partner. Cohabiting and PC married women are significantly more likely than non-PC married women to have a partner outside the typical range. This is particularly the case in the age heterogamy category that also has the highest rate of violence. That is, cohabiting and PC married women are more likely to have a partner that is six or more years younger than they. Based on the descriptive comparisons in the present study, then, it appears possible that there is a connection between being a cohabitor or PC married, choosing a partner that is six or more years younger, and violence.

Wilson et al. (1995) report that no relationship exists between age heterogamy and rates of nonlethal violence for either marital or common-law unions. This may appear surprising given that these researchers used the same data employed in the present study. However, the results of their study are not directly comparable to those in the present study. First, the measure of violence is different between the two studies. An examination of age heterogamy with one-year prevalence of violence as Wilson et al. (1995) have measured it, that is, excluding verbal abuse, does result in a significant relationship (p < 0.05). Second, Wilson et al. (1995) also code age heterogamy differently than in the present study. These researchers employ the following categories: "wife 6 or more years older," "wife 3-5 years older," "wife 1-2 years older," "same age," "wife 1-2 years younger," "wife 3-5 years younger," "wife 6-10 years younger," "wife 11 or more years younger." There is a problem with this coding because the age difference categories are not consistent, which confounds comparisons between each side of the age difference distribution. Furthermore, there is no theoretical reason to posit that differences of a few years will have an effect on violence. Rather, it is more probable that these effects will be seen in larger gaps of at least five years. Wilson et al. (1995) also only analyze the relationship between age heterogamy and violence for marrieds and cohabitors separately. As one would expect, a replication of Wilson et al.'s analyses in the present study produces the same results. Wilson et al. (1995) were expecting a curvilinear relationship between nonlethal violence and age. While this is not the case, regardless of which study's categorizations of violence and age heterogamy are employed, women with a partner six or more years younger are more likely to report violence. Therefore, rather than ruling out a relationship between nonlethal violence and age heterogamy, it would have instead been more accurate for Wilson et al. (1995) to conclude that, unlike lethal violence, there does not appear to be a curvilinear relationship between age heterogamy and nonlethal violence.

SES, Marital Status, and Violence

It is often conjectured in the violence literature that cohabitors tend to rank low in terms of socioeconomic status (SES) and that the links between SES variables and violence play a large role in understanding cohabitors' higher rate of violence. Given the amount of data to be discussed with respect to SES, education, employment, and income will be discussed in turn.

Education. Ellis (1989) reports that cohabitors are more likely to be represented in the low education categories than marrieds. Boba (1996) compared marrieds and cohabitors in terms of education and found that cohabitors had only slightly less education than marrieds. Finally, Thornton, Axinn, and Teachman's (1995:762) results suggest that "less educated individuals tend to substitute cohabitation for marriage, while those with a greater school accumulation are more likely to marry." The data in the present study run contrary to each of these researchers.

In terms of women's education, table 6.4 shows that there are significant differences between marrieds and cohabitors. While the pattern across categories of differences is the same for marrieds and cohabitors, married women are more likely to have less than a high school education or only a high school education. Cohabiting women are more likely to have some post-secondary education. Married and cohabiting women have roughly equal percentages who report having a university degree.

Since cohabiting women are most likely to be young, cohabiting women's higher representation in the "some post-secondary" category may be partially because many cohabiting women are currently in university but have yet to complete their degree. An examination of each original education category by marital status shows that cohabiting women are more likely to report having some university than are married women (8.5 versus 5.6 percent, respectively) (p < 0.01). However, a higher percentage of cohabiting than married women report having some community college or CEGEP (8.3 versus 5.3, respectively) as well as having a community college or CEGEP diploma (11.5 versus 9.9, respectively). Cohabiting women, then, show a tendency to be slightly more likely to have a community college level education. The comparison of women's education by the two married categories do not show significant differences. Overall, the relationship between a woman's education and her choice to live married or common-law does not appear to be very strong.[10]

A similar pattern of differences between marrieds and cohabitors exists with respect to partner's education. The results in table 6.4 indicate that married men are slightly more likely to have less than high school education. Almost identical percentages of married and cohabiting men report having a high school diploma. Men in a common-law union are more likely than married men to have some post-secondary education. However, married men are more likely to have a university degree than cohabiting men. It does not appear that the cohabiting men who have some post-secondary education are disproportionately working toward a university degree. A comparison of common-law with married men reporting some university education yielded virtually identical percentages (4.7 versus 4.6, respectively). Moreover, a higher percentage of common-law than married men reported having a community college or CEGEP diploma (9.6 versus 6.9, respectively). Married men, then, appear to be significantly more likely to be highly educated.

In terms of marrieds, the differences between non-PC and PC marrieds are significant with the largest difference consisting of non-PC married men being more likely to have less than high school education than PC married men. PC married men are more likely to have a high school diploma and some post-secondary education. However, the two married groups are almost equally likely to have a university degree. As with women, the relationship between partner's education and marital status does not appear to be very strong. There is, however, a more clear pattern for married men, particularly non-PC. They report having very low education levels while cohabiting men are likely to have a moderate education, and married men, regardless of PC or non-PC status, are likely to have the most years of education.

While the findings with respect to marital status and education are somewhat surprising, respondent's education is related to violence in the manner expected. Table 6.5 demonstrates that there is a significant negative relationship between a respondent's education and violence in both the lifetime and one-year time frames. Women with less than high school education are more likely to report having experienced violence at some time in their relationship and in the past year than are women with more education. Women with a university degree are the least likely to report having experienced violence by their partner. In terms of the different forms of violence, table 6.1 demonstrates that respondent's education is related to all but one component of violence, being pushed, grabbed, or shoved. In the remaining types of violence the differences across respondents' education tend to be highly significant and inverse.

Partner's education also appears to be significantly negatively related to violence. However, the relationship between partner's education and violence appears to be less strong. While men with less than high school education clearly have the highest rates of violence and men with a university degree have the lowest rates, in both the lifetime and one-year time frames in table 6.5 men with some post-secondary education have higher prevalence rates than those having only high school diplomas. Significant differences are present on every component of violence for partner's education. The data in table 6.1 show that the differences between men with a high school diploma only and men with some post-secondary education are more similar or in the expected negative direction on most of the physical assault and sexual coercion variables. It is on the nonphysical items of verbal abuse and psychological aggression, as well as the minor physical assault item involving being pushed, grabbed, or shoved, in which men with some post-secondary education most prominently outscore men with a high school diploma.[11] Perhaps the fact that some of these men have had to terminate their advanced educational goals is somehow connected to their exhibition of higher rates of violence against their female partner. In addition, it may also be precisely because these men have a slightly higher education that they tend to choose to use the less physically severe, and more psychologically damaging, acts of violence. Interestingly, the biggest difference as one moves from less than high school to high school education is on the sexual coercion variable. Women with a partner who has less than high school education are three times more likely to report being forced into any sexual activity when they did not want to by being threatened, held down, or hurt in some other way.

Overall, there are some surprising findings regarding education in the present study. The data that Boba (1996) and Thornton and his colleagues (1995) employ are based on American samples. It appears possible that cohabitors in Canada tend to be more highly educated relative to marrieds than are cohabitors in the United States. Ellis's (1989) discussion on social class and cohabitation is also based on American research. In addition, it seems possible that the characteristics of cohabitors have changed. The results of this study suggest that cohabitation is not related to level of education in Canada. While education is negatively related to violence, the descriptive findings with respect to marital status and education suggest that education is not a differentiating factor in understanding marital status differences in violence.

Employment. Turcotte and Bélanger (1997) found that employed women in Canada were twice as likely as unemployed women to choose cohabitation as their first "conjugal" union. This suggests that employed women may be selected into cohabitation. The only study to compare married and common-law unions in terms of employment and violence is that of Boba (1996). Boba's bivariate comparisons showed that both male and female cohabitors were more likely to be employed than marrieds. Further, it was found that violent couples were more likely to be employed. This suggests a connection among employment, cohabitation, and violence.

Consistent with Turcotte and Bélanger (1997), the results of the descriptive analysis in table 6.4 indicate that cohabiting women are significantly more likely than married women to have worked at a business or paid job in the twelve months prior to the survey. Interestingly, PC married women are also more likely than non-PC married women to have been employed in the year prior to the survey. With respect to partner's employment, non-PC married men are most likely to have not worked in the year prior to the study followed by cohabiting men and PC married men. One possible explanation for the high percentage of unemployed non-PC married men is that they are more likely than PC married and cohabiting men to include older and, therefore, retired men. To investigate this possibility, a cross-tabulation of partner's employment by marital status controlling for respondent's age was performed.[12] The results show a strong trend for common-law men to be more likely to be unemployed until reaching the respondents' age group of 55 or older. For instance, among women age 18-24, common-law partners are more than twice as likely to be unemployed than are married men. Overall, it appears that common-law and PC married women are more likely to work than non-PC married women, while nonretirement age cohabiting men are more likely than married men to be unemployed.

Kantor and Jasinski (1998:26) have recently suggested that, in terms of partner violence, "Education may be most important as it relates to the likelihood of finding employment in a stable and well-paying job." However, the overall results of the bivariate analysis in the present study do not appear to support this suggestion. For both respondent's and partner's employment, table 6.5 shows that there were no significant differences in either the lifetime or one-year prevalence rates of violence. As expected, on the individual components of violence in table 6.1, where a significant difference is present it tends to be higher for women who have worked at a business or paid job in the twelve months prior to the survey. Specifically, women who worked reported significantly higher lifetime prevalence rates of psychological aggression and being pushed, grabbed, or shoved. This is consistent with the feminist theory that men whose wives work are more likely to feel that their patriarchal authority is threatened. Similarly, there is also a tendency for men's employment to be related to individual components of violence in the expected direction. Women whose partner did not work in the twelve months prior to the survey report significantly higher lifetime prevalence rates of verbal abuse and being forced into sexual activity against their will. However, women whose partner worked in the past twelve months report a significantly higher lifetime prevalence rate of being pushed, grabbed, or shoved. It may be that men who are unemployed are more likely to vent their frustrations on their partner by humiliating them through verbal abuse and forced sexual activity. On the other hand, employed men who are violent may be doing so for different reasons with different manifestations. While employment is not significantly related to overall violence, then, it does appear to operate as expected with a few individual components of violence.

Overall, there does not appear to be a strong relationship between employment and violence in the present study. For individual components of violence, women who are employed are more likely to report violence, and common-law and PC married women are more likely to work than non-PC married women. This is consistent with Boba's (1996) results. The relationship between men's employment and violence is less clear. The overall violence variables indicate that employment is unrelated to violence. However, investigating separate components of violence shows that unemployed men are more likely to commit some acts of violence. Furthermore, nonretirement age cohabiting men are more likely than their married counterparts to be unemployed. Based on the descriptive analysis, then, it appears possible that there is some connection between being a cohabiting man, being unemployed, and being violent.

Income. Boba's (1996) data showed that cohabitors have significantly lower total incomes than do marrieds, and that violent couples also have significantly lower incomes. Again, this leads to the hypothesis that low-income people are selected into cohabitation and this in turn is linked to cohabitors' greater likelihood of violence.

The results of the cross-tabulation of respondent's income by marital- status presented in table 6.4 show that most women have incomes of less than $15,000. Of women who work, married women are significantly more likely to be low-income earners (below $15,000) and high-income earners ($60,000 or more). Women in common-law unions who work are more likely to earn from $15,000 to $59,999. Among marrieds, non-PC married women are more likely to earn less than $15,000. Virtually identical proportions of non-PC and PC married women earn $15,000 to $29,999. However, PC married women are more likely to earn more than $30,000 with these women being more than twice as likely to earn $60,000 or more in the year prior to the study.

There are also significant differences across marital status categories for men. Those in common-law unions are more likely than married men to earn $29,999 or less. More than two-thirds of common-law men earn less than $30,000 compared to just over half of married men. Non-PC and PC married men appear to be distributed across income categories in a very similar manner, with the largest difference favoring non-PC married men who are more likely to earn $60,000 or more.

In terms of violence by respondent's income, while there are significant differences across income categories for both lifetime and one-year prevalence rates as shown in table 6.5, it is difficult to determine the direction of the relationship. For both time frames women with incomes between $30,000 and $59,999 have the lowest rates of violence. Interestingly, women in the highest income range have slightly higher prevalence rates than women in the lowest income category. These results indicate that when a woman works her partner may see it as a threat regardless of how much she earns. There are no significant differences in lifetime prevalence of violence across categories of partner's income, and there does not appear to be a strong relationship between partner's income and one-year prevalence of violence.

The results of the descriptive analysis in the present study support Boba (1996) in finding that cohabiting men are more likely to have low incomes compared to married men. However, they add to Boba's (1996) couple data by showing that married women, at least in Canada, are most likely to be both low-income and very high-income earners. There does not appear to be a clear relationship between income, cohabitation, and violence.

The relationship among SES, marital status, and violence appears to be complex and, compared to other variables in the present study, not particularly strong. Based on the descriptive analyses there seems to be more than SES differences operating in the production of marital status differences in violence.

Status Consistency, Marital Status, and Violence

As discussed earlier, Ellis and DeKeseredy (1989) argued that cohabiting women are less likely than married women to be dependent, while cohabiting men are more likely than married men to be dependent. The disparity in status in cohabiting relationships is hypothesized to be inconsistent with patriarchal norms, which in turn leads to male violence in cohabiting relationships. Anderson (1997) found, however, that income and education inconsistency do not account for marital status differences in violence.

The results in table 6.4 indicate that there are significant differences in educational consistency between common-law and marital unions in the present study. While the pattern across categories is similar with the largest percentage in each group involving both members of the couple having similar levels of education, married women are more likely than cohabiting women to have similar education levels as well as less or much less education than their partner. Conversely, cohabiting women are more likely than married women to have more or much more education than their partner. With respect to the two marital groups, the differences are not significant. It appears, then, that currently cohabiting women stand out as being more likely than married women to be more educated than their partner.

The differences in income consistency are compatible with educational consistency, though they are much larger. In conjunction with married women's greater likelihood to have low levels of education, married women are more likely than cohabiting women to report that they earn much less income than their partner. Nearly 40 percent of married women earn less than their partner, compared to 22.1 percent of cohabiting women. Virtually identical percentages of married and cohabiting women report that they earn less income than their partner. However, more cohabiting than married women report that they earn either similar levels of income, more income, or much more income than their partner. With respect to the PC versus non-PC distinction, there are significant differences that appear to be in the most extremely inconsistent categories. That is, non-PC married women are more likely to report that they earn much less than their partner, while PC married women are more likely to report that they earn much more than their partner.

In terms of violence, the data in table 6.5 show that there is a significant relationship between a couple's education consistency and both lifetime and one-year prevalence of violence. A similar pattern emerges in both time frames with the highest rates among the most inconsistent categories as well as where both members of the couple have similar education. However, women most likely to report violence are those who have much more education than their partner. In terms of each component of violence, the results in table 6.1 demonstrate that every violence variable has significant differences across the education consistency categories. A similar pattern to the overall violence variables is also present for verbal abuse, psychological aggression, minor physical assault, and moderate physical assault. For severe physical assault and sexual coercion there were several categories in which there were insufficient cases to provide reliable comparisons.

Income consistency is also significantly related to violence. The distribution of women reporting violence in the past year in the income consistency categories, as shown in table 6.5, indicates that women earning much more income than their partner have the highest prevalence of violence followed by women with a similar income to their partner. However, with the lifetime prevalence rate it is women with a similar income level to their partner who report the highest prevalence of violence closely followed by women with much more income than their partner. Only four of the individual components of violence in table 6.1 have significant differences across income consistency categories. Women with much more income and with similar levels of income to their partner are most likely to report having been verbally abused. Women who have similar levels of income followed by women with much more income are most likely to have something thrown at them that could hurt. Conversely, it is women with less income and much less income than their partner who are most likely to report severe physical assault. Finally, forced sexual activity is most likely to be reported by women with similar levels of income to their partner.

Education consistency seems to be more consistently related to violence than income consistency. It appears that women who have much more education than their partner are the most likely to report violence. This finding is consistent with the theory that men with a partner who has more resources than they feel emasculated and use violence as an "ultimate resource" to recoup or maintain their sense of manhood. The findings related to income consistency are also very interesting. It appears that women with much more income or similar levels of income are most likely to experience less severe forms of violence. On the other hand, women with less income and much less income than their partner are most likely to be severely physically assaulted. It may be that men who are bothered by their partner earning more than they act out their dissatisfaction but do so with less severely violent means because their partner has greater independence and can therefore leave the relationship more easily. Also, it is possible that women in such relationships are more likely to leave the situation before the conflict escalates to the more severe levels of violence. On the other hand, men with a partner who earns less than they may nevertheless be bothered by some aspect of their partner working. That, combined with their partner's greater dependence on them for money, allows them to use more severe forms of violence to vent their frustrations.

Based on the descriptive analysis it appears that the first part of Ellis and DeKeseredy's (1989) argument has some merit. Common-law women are significantly more likely than married women to be more educated than their partner and to earn as much or more than their partner. Both education and income consistency are related to violence. With respect to education consistency, women with much more education than their partner are most likely to report violence. Based on the descriptive analysis, there may be a connection between being a cohabiting woman, being much more educated than a male partner, and experiencing violence.

In terms of income consistency, in addition to cohabiting women, PC married women are more likely than non-PC married women to have a higher income than their partner. Women earning as much or more than their partner are more likely to experience less severe forms of violence. There may be a connection between being a cohabiting or PC married woman, earning similar or more income than one's partner, and experiencing violence, albeit less severe forms of violence. Since non-PC married women are most likely to earn less than their partner, and women in this income category are most likely to report the most severe forms of violence, there may be a connection between being non-PC married, earning less than one's male partner, and experiencing more severe forms of violence.

Social Learning, Marital Status, and Violence

As already discussed, social learning theory predicts that children who witness or experience violence are more likely to be in a violent relationship when they mature. Given the high rate of violence among cohabitors, from a social learning perspective it is arguable that cohabitors were more likely to have been exposed to violence as children. Though Jackson (1996) tests this theory and finds that differential learning does not account for higher levels of violence among cohabitors, descriptive comparisons by marital status are not provided.

The results presented in table 6.4 show that, in the present study, women in a common-law union are significantly more likely than married women to report that their partner's father was violent toward their partner's mother. While a higher percentage of PC than non-PC marrieds report that their partner's father was violent, the differences are not significant.

Cohabiting women are also significantly more likely than married women to report that their father was violent toward their mother. Almost one in four cohabiting women indicated having come from a violent home compared to 16.1 percent of married women. The marital status group with the highest percentage reporting having come from a violent home, however, is PC married women. These women are almost twice as likely as non-PC married women to have come from a violent home.

It seems that there is a tendency for currently cohabiting women to be partnered with men who came from violent homes. There is a much greater tendency, however, for currently and previously cohabiting women themselves to have come from a violent home. It appears that men who witness violence at home are slightly more likely to choose to cohabit, but women who witnessed violence in their home are much more likely to choose to cohabit. Having seen their mothers victimized by their father, it is not surprising that many of these women would choose to cohabit either as an alternative or a precursor to marriage.

The results in table 6.5 suggest that women who report that their partner's father was violent toward his mother are significantly more likely to report both lifetime and one-year violence than are women whose partner's father was not violent. These women are more than twice as likely to report violence at some point in their marital/common-law relationship and three times as likely to report violence in the past year. Furthermore, each component of violence in table 6.1 is significantly more likely to be reported by women whose partner's father was violent. These differences are particularly high on the severe physical assault variables with women whose partner's father was violent being an average of seven times more likely to report severe physical assault by their partner.

There are also significant differences in the lifetime and one-year prevalence of violence in table 6.5 between women who did and did not report that their father was violent toward their mother. Again, there are significant differences on each component of violence in table 6.1. Overall, it appears that women whose father was violent toward their mother are just under twice as likely as those who did not come from a violent home to report violence by their current partner. They are, however, twice as likely to report psychological aggression, being slapped, both moderate and severe physical assault, and sexual coercion.

In general, social learning appears to be a powerful and consistent correlate of violence. Men witnessing their father's violent behavior toward their mother seems to be more strongly related to violence than women witnessing their father being violent toward their mother. Nevertheless, both variables are significant. Witnessing parental violence, then, is related to a greater propensity for men to use violence and for women to have violence used against them. It appears that some men may learn to become victimizers and some women may learn to become victims.

Based on the descriptive analyses, it seems that there may be a connection between witnessing violence as a child, choosing to cohabit, and perpetrating/experiencing violence. While Jackson (1996) found that differential learning does not account for higher levels of violence among cohabitors, this theory needs to be put to a more accurate test. Jackson's (1996) analysis is missing two key control variables, age and duration of relationship. As has already been discussed, cohabitors tend to be young, and, as will be discussed, their unions tend to be short-lived. Without controlling for these variables, especially the latter, any test of one or more theories that attempt to understand marital status differences in violence should be interpreted with caution.

Dating Violence, Marital Status, and Violence

To date, there has not been a study that investigates a possible connection between violence that occurs while dating and violence that occurs while living married or common-law. Of interest in this regard is whether those who are in a violent dating relationship are more likely to choose to cohabit as an alternative or precursor to getting married. Perhaps because of their partner's violence, these individuals are selected into cohabitation, which, in turn, accounts for the higher rate of violence among cohabitors.

While the percentages are relatively small, table 6.4 shows that almost twice as many women in a common-law than a marital union reported having experienced violence while dating their partner. However, among marrieds, nearly three times as many PC married women reported having experienced dating violence with their current partner compared to non-PC married women. Clearly, currently cohabiting women and, even more so, women who cohabited with someone other than their partner before marriage are significantly more likely to be with a partner who begins to be violent toward them while they are dating. It may be that women who cohabit are more likely to be selected into that type of relationship because they are experiencing violence with their partner, which predisposes cohabiting relationships to have higher rates of violence than marital unions. However, the results of the PC marrieds indicate that this is not just a phenomenon of selection into cohabitation. Recall that these are married women who did not necessarily cohabit with their current husband. One can nevertheless conclude that there is a possibility of a link between women who cohabit and a greater likelihood of continuing a violent dating relationship into a more committed common-law or marital union. It is important to reiterate, however, that far more cohabiting and married women who did not experience dating violence report experiencing violence during the lifetime of their current relationship. In a cross-tabulation of lifetime prevalence of violence by dating violence, it is found that 15.4 percent of women who did not report dating violence reported violence while living married or common-law with their partner. Just because one does not experience dating violence clearly does not mean that one will not experience violence while married/common-law.

The results in table 6.5 indicate that there is a significant relationship between experiencing violence while dating a partner and experiencing violence while living married/common-law to that same partner. Women who report dating violence also report significantly higher rates of violence in the lifetime of their marital/common-law relationship and in the year prior to the study. This is not surprising, as one would expect men who are violent while dating to be likely to continue their violence into a marital/common-law relationship. Women who experienced violence while dating their current partner are three times more likely to report that violence has occurred since becoming married or common-law and more than four times more likely to report having been victimized in the year prior to the survey. Like the social learning variables, respondents who experienced dating violence with their current partner are significantly more likely to report each individual component of violence than are women who did not report dating violence. Most notable are the differences in table 6.1 with respect to the prevalence of physical assault, particularly as it increases in severity. Women who reported dating violence are six times more likely to report being slapped, nine times more likely to be choked or hit with something that could hurt, and thirteen times more likely to be threatened with or have a knife or gun used on them by their partner.

Overall, there is a relationship between experiencing violence while dating a man and experiencing violence while living married/common-law to that same man. Cohabiting and PC married women are more likely to report experiencing dating violence than are non-PC married women. For cohabitors it appears possible that there is a connection between experiencing violence while dating a partner, choosing to cohabit, and experiencing violence while cohabiting. Despite experiencing dating violence, PC married individuals chose to get married. There also appears to be a connection, then, between living with someone other than one's marital partner, a willingness to translate a violent dating relationship into a marriage, and the experience of marital violence.

Previous Marriage, Marital Status, and Violence

Spanier (1983) has shown that half of cohabiting couples in the United States are previously married. More than one-third of Canadian cohabitors have previously been married (38 percent of men and 33 percent of women) (Stout, 1991). Ellis (1989) reports that between 30 to 52 percent of separated or divorced women indicate violence as a reason for the dissolution of their marriage. Ellis (1989) therefore deduces that a significant proportion of cohabiting males bring a history of violence to their relationships which, in turn, increases the probability that they will be violent toward their cohabiting partners.[13]

The results in table 6.4 indicate that women currently living common-law are more than three times as likely as married women to report having been previously married. Similarly, PC married women are three times as likely as non-PC married women to report having been previously married. Overall, non-PC married women are by far the least likely to have been previously married followed by PC marrieds and cohabitors.

Table 6.5 shows that an almost identical percentage of women who had and had not been married prior to their current relationship report violence at some time during their current relationship. However, women who have been married previously are significantly more likely to report violence in the year prior to the study than women not previously married. This difference between the lifetime and one-year prevalence rates, like other such differences in the present study, may be due to the time dependence of the independent variable. In this case, it may be that women who are previously married are more likely to be in the early stages of their current relationship because they have had to go through the process of being married, divorced, and finding a new partner.[14] It is expected that when asked about violence in the past year women who have been with their partner for a shorter period of time are more likely to report violence. But, when asked about violence in the lifetime of the relationship there is no difference because nonpreviously married women who experienced violence in the early part of their relationships are also included.

An inspection of the individual variables comprising violence in table 6.1 shows that eight of the eleven variables that are combined to produce the overall lifetime prevalence variable do have significant differences between respondents who report having or not having been previously married. Most of these differences are on the edge of significance. However, the differences in severe physical assault are significant at a higher level of confidence with previously married women being more likely to have been beaten up or kicked, bit, or hit with a fist at some point during their current relationship. Hence, while differences between the lifetime and one-year prevalence variables may to some extent be an artifact of their construction, there are nevertheless important and significant differences between previously and nonpreviously married women on individual measures of lifetime prevalence of violence.

Overall, there does appear to be some relationship between being previously married and experiencing violence, particularly severe physical assault. There is also a relationship between being divorced and being one who is willing to cohabit. Based on the descriptive analysis, it appears possible that there is a connection between being divorced, being a cohabitor, and experiencing violence by one's current partner. While it is not possible to determine whether PC remarried women cohabited after their divorce or prior to their first marriage, there nevertheless appears to be something about PC remarried women that leads them to be more likely to experience violence than women who are not previously married. However, it is important to reiterate that these results are based on descriptive analyses and are thus tentative.

Previous Partner Violence, Marital Status, and Violence

No study to date has explored the role of having experienced violence by a previous partner in understanding marital status differences in violence. It seems reasonable to posit that women who have experienced violence by a past partner may have a mistrust of men in general and therefore may be inclined to cohabit rather than commit to marriage. These same women may also be more likely to experience violence either because they tend to be in violent relationships and/or because of factors linked to cohabitation relationships.

The results in table 6.4 indicate that, while large percentages of common-law and married women who had a previous partner report that he was violent, women in common-law unions are significantly more likely to report that this was the case. Interestingly, PC and non-PC married women are not significantly different with almost equal percentages reporting having had a previous partner who was violent.

Women who indicate that they have been threatened and/or physically or sexually attacked by a previous husband/common-law partner are significantly more likely to also report experiencing violence by their current partner. Significant differences are found on both the lifetime and one-year prevalence measures as shown in table 6.5. For both overall violence measures women who report having experienced violence by a previous partner are almost twice as likely to also report violence by their current partner. With respect to the individual components of violence in table 6.1, all but one are significant and all are in the direction of women with previously violent spouses being more likely to report violence in their current relationship. The differences increase slightly with severity such that women having had a violent previous partner are more than twice as likely to report both moderate and severe physical assault.

There is a relationship, then, between having experienced violence by a previous marital or common-law partner and reporting violence by a current partner. There is also a relationship between having experienced violence by a previous partner and choosing to cohabit. Based on the descriptive results it seems possible that there may be some connection between experiencing violence by a previous partner, choosing to cohabit, and experiencing violence.

Region, Marital Status, and Violence

Wu and Balakrishnan (1995) have noted that ideological differences between French Quebec and English Canada may affect cohabitation behavior between these regions. Persons in Quebec are far more likely than persons in the rest of Canada to choose to live in a common-law union (Statistics Canada, 1997). It is interesting, then, to explore differences between regions in Canada in terms of cohabitation behavior and violence. For instance, given the higher rate of cohabitation in Quebec and the higher rate of violence among cohabitors, it seems possible that Quebec will have a higher rate of violence than other regions of Canada.

Table 6.4 shows that there are significant differences both in the percentages of marrieds and cohabitors as well as in the percentages of PC and non-PC marrieds coming from the different regions of Canada. Cohabitors are most likely to come from Quebec followed by Ontario, the Prairies, British Columbia, and Atlantic Canada. Marrieds are most likely to come from Ontario followed by Quebec, the Prairies, British Columbia, and Atlantic Canada. Among marrieds, non-PC marrieds are most likely to come from Ontario followed by Quebec, the Prairies, British Columbia, and Atlantic Canada. PC marrieds are most likely to come from Ontario followed by Quebec, British Columbia, the Prairies, and Atlantic Canada.

The first point of interest here is how the high prevalence of cohabitation in Quebec is reflected in the large percentage of cohabitors in the sample coming from Quebec. Second, the comparison among marrieds in British Columbia indicates that women in this region may be more likely than those in other regions to live with someone other than their current husbands prior to getting married. Indeed, an examination of the row percentages on these comparisons shows that British Columbia is the region with the highest percentage of its respondents reporting being PC married followed by the Prairies, Ontario, Quebec, and Atlantic Canada. It appears, then, that while Quebec is the region most likely to have respondents who cohabit, many of these women are either living common-law as an alternative to marriage or are marrying the man with whom they are cohabiting.

Table 6.5 demonstrates that significant differences were reported across categories of region for both the lifetime and one-year prevalence rates. In both time frames, the highest rates are in British Columbia. The next highest rates are in the Prairies and Ontario and these alternate from one time frame to the other. In both time frames the second lowest rate is in the Atlantic region and the lowest rate is in Quebec. An inspection of each component of violence in table 6.1 shows that the differences between regions tend to be most significant on the verbal abuse, psychological aggression, and minor physical assault variables. There are no differences in moderate physical assault, though the choking component does have significant differences. Ontario has the lowest rate of reporting being choked followed by Quebec. There are also significant differences in severe physical assault. These differences seem to be due to differences in reports of being kicked, bit, or hit with a fist and they follow the same pattern as the overall violence variables. However, it is noteworthy that there are not significant differences in terms of being threatened with or having a knife or gun used nor are there significant differences in terms of being beaten. As well, there are no significant differences in reports of sexual coercion.

Overall, region is related to violence and marital status is related to region. It is possible, then, that there is some connection between region, marital status, and violence. The fact that Quebec has the lowest overall prevalence of violence is interesting in the context of marital status differences in violence against women since Quebec has by far the highest rate of cohabitation. Interestingly, a cross-tabulation of violence in the past year by marital status controlling for region shows differences between cohabitors and marrieds as a whole in the predicted direction within every region. That is, in every region cohabitors have higher one-year prevalence rates of violence. However, the difference between co-habitors and marrieds as a whole reaches statistical significance in only two of the regions, Quebec and the Prairies.[15] It is on the less physically consequential components of violence where the differences across regions tend to be highly significant and on which Quebec women report the lowest rates. These are also the variables on which cohabitors and non-PC marrieds are more alike than PC marrieds in terms of rates of violence. This indicates, then, that it may not be that cohabitors in Quebec are less likely to be violent than cohabitors in the other regions of Canada. Rather, it may be that marrieds who cohabited with someone else prior to marriage are less likely to experience violence in Quebec. Given that there are greater numbers of common-law unions in Quebec, it is reasonable to suggest that living together is more acceptable there than in other regions of Canada. Indeed, Hobart and Grigel (1992) found attitudes toward cohabitation to be more favorable among francophone than anglophone students in Canada. Having lived with someone else prior to marriage, then, may be less likely to be a bone of contention among these couples in Quebec.

To investigate this possibility, a series of cross-tabulations were performed between violence and region while controlling for marital status. The lifetime prevalence of violence among non-PC married women in Quebec is significantly lower than in any other region in Canada (p < 0.01). In other words, even among women in Canada who have never cohabited with anyone other than their current partner, Quebec women are the least likely to report having experienced violence during their relationship. This indicates that there may be something operating in Quebec culture that leads to lower rates of violence against women generally. Quebec women may be less likely to report violence or there may actually be less violence against women taking place in Quebec.[16] While the differences between regions for non-PC marrieds are significant (p < 0.01), they are not particularly large. The lifetime prevalence for Quebec non-PC marrieds is 12.9 percent, and for British Columbia non-PC marrieds, the region with the highest lifetime prevalence, the rate is 19.7 percent. PC marrieds in Quebec, on the other hand, are far less likely to report violence than are PC marrieds in any other region in Canada (p < 0.05). PC marrieds in Quebec are half as likely to report violence during their relationship than their counterparts in Ontario, British Columbia, and the Prairie Provinces, and they are one-third as likely as PC married women in Atlantic Canada to report violence.[17] This supports the notion that the greater acceptability of cohabitation in Quebec makes it easier for PC married couples in Quebec to establish a nomos that is less prone to violence. Cohabiting women in Quebec are, in fact, significantly less likely to report violence over the lifetime of their relationship than are women in any other region in Canada. Of cohabitors in Quebec, 14.2 percent reported violence. This is compared to 17.3 percent in Ontario, 20.5 percent in British Columbia, 20.6 percent in Atlantic Canada,[18] and 24.2 percent in the Prairies. The magnitude of these differences are similar to those among non-PC marrieds and, like non-PC marrieds, indicate that there may be something about Quebec society that leads to lower overall rates of violence against women there.

With respect to one-year rates of violence, non-PC married women in Quebec are again significantly less likely than non-PC married women in the rest of the country to report violence ($p < 0.05$). The differences between PC marrieds across regions are not significant with the one-year rates. Nevertheless, a similar pattern emerges with PC marrieds in Quebec being at least half as likely as PC marrieds in other regions to report violence in the past year.[19] Interestingly, cohabitors in Quebec are not significantly more likely than cohabitors in any other region of the country to report having experienced violence in the year prior to the study.

In terms of verbal abuse, there are significant differences across regions with cohabitors in Quebec reporting the lowest rates ($p < 0.05$).[20] There are also significant differences across regions in reports of psychological aggression with cohabitors in Ontario reporting the lowest rates followed by cohabitors in Quebec ($p < 0.05$). Quebec cohabitors are the least likely to report minor physical assault ($p < 0.10$). However, there are no significant differences across regions in rates of moderate physical assault, severe physical assault, and sexual coercion for cohabitors. Thus, it appears that where there are differences in violence between cohabitors in Quebec and those elsewhere, they tend to be on the less physically consequential components of violence. The forms of violence for which cohabitors outscore other marital status categories, then, are also those which appear to occur at similar levels among cohabitors across the nation.

Relationship Factors, Marital Status, and Violence

There are a number of variables in the present study that are identified as relationship factors. Relationship factors are defined here as those characteristics of the respondent and/or her partner that tend to occur within the context of their relationship together.

Marital Status, Duration of Relationship, and Violence

For the most part, studies of violence against women have found duration of relationship to be negatively related to marital violence. When discussing differences between marital and common-law unions the duration variable acquires special significance because common-law unions tend to have much shorter average durations (Burch and Madan, 1986; Halli and Zimmer, 1991). For instance, Boba's (1996) investigation of the National Survey of Families and Households in the United States shows the average length of relationship for marrieds in the sample to be 20.35 years compared to only 2.67 years for cohabitors.

Johnson's (1996) descriptive analysis of the VAWS indicates a strong negative relationship between duration and violence, particularly for cohabitors. Common-law couples together for less than three years reported three times the prevalence of violence in comparison to marrieds of the same duration.

While both cohabiting and married couples must form rules for ending conflicts, Ellis (1989) has argued that the shorter duration of cohabitation relationships means that they have less time to develop rules for conflict resolution. According to Ellis (1989) ambiguity in norms of conflict resolution may lead to the use of violence to establish such norms. Similar to norms of conflict resolution, ambiguity or absence of norms for regulating sexual relations may also lead to higher rates of violence among cohabitors. Ellis (1989:247) argues that cohabitors, more than marrieds, have violent conflicts about sex because, as a function of the recency of their relationships, "they are more likely to experience the strain associated with the presence of relatively ambiguous norms governing sexual relations."

An examination of duration of relationship by marital status in table 6.6 shows significant differences on all comparisons. In the present study there is a strong negative relationship between duration of relationship and living common-law. The majority of cohabitors have been together for less than 4 years. While cohabitation relationships tend to be of short duration, marital unions tend to be of long duration. More than three-quarters of married respondents have been with their partner for ten or more years. Among marrieds, women who did not live with anyone else prior to getting married are most likely to have been with their current partner for ten or more years. On the other hand, the distribution of PC marrieds across categories of duration of relationship is far more even than any other marital status category. The higher percentage of PC mar-

Table 6.6. *Relationship Variables by Marital Status (in Percent).*

Marital Status

Selection Var.	C-Law	Married	Non-PC	PC
Duration				
< 4 years	57.0	8.0	6.8	23.5
4-9 years	29.0	15.5	13.9	37.3
10+ years	13.9	76.5‡	79.2	39.3‡
Jealous				
Yes	9.7	5.3	5.1	8.1
No	90.3	94.7‡	94.9	91.9‡
Know Whereabouts				
Yes	13.2	10.0	9.8	13.9
No	86.8	90.0‡	90.2	86.1‡
Freq. of Drinking				
Never	7.2	15.8	16.0	12.4
Never pst. mth.	10.7	15.5	15.8	12.2
1-2 times mth.	34.0	26.3	26.3	27.0
Once per week	20.1	15.9	15.8	17.4
2-3 times/week	17.5	14.1	13.9	17.4
4-6 times/week	5.5	5.5	5.4	6.0
Every day	5.0	6.8‡	6.7	7.6†
Freq. Heavy Drink.				
Didn't 5+	60.5	78.5	79.5	65.0
1 past month	15.8	9.2	9.0	12.0
2-4 past month	16.7	9.3	8.6	18.0
≥ 5 past month	6.9	3.0‡	2.8	5.0‡
Limit Contact				
Yes	5.9	3.9	3.8	5.8
No	94.1	96.1‡	96.2	94.2†
Prevents Inc. Access				
Yes	2.8	2.0	2.0	—
No	97.2	98.0	98.0	97.6
Live w/ Child. < 25				
Yes	36.7	56.0	55.4	63.2
No	63.3	44.0‡	44.6	36.8‡
Depression				
Yes	3.2	2.9	2.7	5.1
No	96.8	97.1	97.3	94.9‡

‡ p < 0.01; † p < 0.05; — not statistically reliable

Table 6.7. *Lifetime and One-Year Prevalence Rates by Relationship Variables (in Percent).*

Prevalence

Selection Variable	Lifetime	One-Year
Duration		
< 4 years	12.5	10.2
4-9 years	17.3	9.9
10+ years	16.8‡	7.6‡
Jealous		
Yes	54.7	39.7
No	13.9‡	6.4‡
Know Whereabouts		
Yes	44.5	31.0
No	13.0‡	5.7‡
Freq. of Drinking		
Never	15.9	8.0
Never pst. mth.	14.9	7.6
1-2 times mth.	14.8	6.8
Once per week	13.3	6.9
2-3 times/week	17.4	8.1
4-6 times/week	21.3	12.5
Every day	25.6‡	16.5‡
Freq. Heavy Drink.		
Didn't 5+	14.0	7.0
1 past month	15.7	6.8
2-4 past month	24.5	12.2
≥ 5 past month	40.2‡	24.6‡
Limit Contact		
Yes	68.1	55.9
No	14.1‡	6.3‡
Prevents Inc. Access		
Yes	68.4	57.9
No	15.1‡	7.3‡
Live w/ Child. < 25		
Yes	17.3	8.2
No	15.1†	8.5
Depression		
Yes	36.8	27.1
No	15.7‡	7.8‡

‡ p < 0.01; † p < 0.05

rieds than non-PC marrieds in the "less than 4 years" category may be because PC marrieds were married later because they were previously living with another person(s). But, once formed, PC marrieds' relationships appear to endure longer than cohabiting unions. In terms of duration of relationship, then, cohabitors, non-PC marrieds, and PC marrieds are three distinct groups.

Table 6.7 demonstrates that there are significant differences across categories of duration of relationship with both the lifetime and one-year prevalence rates of violence. As expected, lifetime prevalence rates tend to increase with increasing duration of relationship. There is a slight decrease in lifetime prevalence among those reporting having been together for ten or more years. This could be due to a cohort effect such that women who became married/common-law with their partner some time ago may have been less likely to experience violence. However, a more probable explanation is that women who have been together with their partner for a long time, and therefore include women who are older, may forget occurrences of violence that happened long ago. They may also be less likely to report violence that happened long ago perhaps because they feel that it is "water under the bridge" and is not worth reporting. Having also been subject to different social attitudes surrounding violence against women, older women may also be less willing to report violence by their partner. However, the results for age in table 6.5 show little difference in the one-year prevalence of violence for women aged 35 and above. This suggests that age is not a factor in differential reporting. It must also be added that violent relationships are more likely to end than nonviolent unions. Thus, the decrease in the longest duration category may also be due to a greater tendency for violent unions to terminate before reaching this duration category.

Also as expected, unlike the lifetime prevalence rates the one-year rates decrease with increasing duration. This may be connected to the greater violence among young people. However, not all people beginning a marital or common-law relationship are young. The higher rates among short duration relationships, then, may also be due to the ending of violent relationships in the older duration categories and/or, as Ellis (1989) has argued, to a greater likelihood of a conflictual environment when trying to establish norms of interaction.

The results of the cross-tabulations for each component of violence are presented in table 6.8. It is evident from an examination of table 6.8 that the only significant differences in lifetime prevalence with respect to the duration variable occur on psychological aggression, minor physical

Table 6.8. *Lifetime Prevalence of Each Component of Violence by Relationship Variables (in Percent).*

	Verbal Abuse	Psych. Aggression	Minor Physical Assault			Moderate Physical Assault				Severe Physical Assault				Sexual Coercion
	Name Calling	Threat	Push	Slap	Total	Choke	Throw	Hit	Total	T.Gun	Kick	Beat	Total	Forced Sex
Duration														
<4 years	5.7	4.8	7.9	2.1	8.5	—	3.2	1.4	3.7	—	2.2	—	2.3	—
4-9 years	7.0	6.9	12.5	3.5	12.8	1.2	4.0	1.6	4.4	—	2.5	1.5	2.8	—
10+ years	6.9	6.4*	11.0‡	4.5‡	11.5‡	1.2	3.1	1.0	3.9	0.7	2.1	1.4	2.8	2.0‡
Jealous														
Yes	33.1	27.4	35.8	18.7	37.9	5.3	17.1	8.4	20.5	6.0	10.9	9.2	15.0	12.5
No	5.2‡	4.9‡	9.3‡	3.1‡	9.7‡	0.8‡	2.4‡	0.7‡	3.0‡	0.3‡	1.7‡	0.9‡	1.9‡	0.9‡
Know Where														
Yes	26.3	20.7	30.0	14.6	31.7	4.0	12.3	6.0	14.6	4.0	7.2	5.3	9.6	6.5
No	4.5‡	4.6‡	8.6‡	2.8‡	8.9‡	0.7‡	2.2‡	0.6‡	2.8‡	0.3‡	1.6‡	0.9‡	1.9‡	1.0‡
Freq. of Drinking														
Never	6.9	6.2	10.3	3.9	10.8	1.9	3.0	—	4.4	—	2.3	1.6	2.7	2.4
Never pst. mth.	6.3	5.0	10.0	4.0	10.5	—	3.3	1.2	3.5	—	2.8	1.9	3.3	1.5
1-2 times mth.	5.6	5.0	9.7	3.2	10.2	—	2.4	1.1	3.0	—	1.5	1.0	1.9	1.4
Once per week	5.2	5.2	8.7	2.3	8.8	—	3.5	1.1	3.7	—	1.4	1.3	1.6	—
2-3 times/week	6.1	6.3	12.1	4.1	12.4	—	2.7	—	3.5	—	1.6	—	2.1	—
4-6 times/week	9.9	11.0	16.3	7.0	17.1	—	4.6	—	6.2	—	3.7	—	4.8	—
Every day	14.3‡	12.1‡	15.6‡	8.8‡	17.1‡	—‡	7.0‡	—	8.3‡	—‡	5.7‡	—	7.0‡	4.6‡
Freq. Hvy. Drink.														
Didn't 5+	5.7	4.7	9.0	3.2	9.4	0.8	2.5	0.8	3.0	0.5	1.8	1.1	2.1	1.3
1 past month	5.2	7.4	11.1	4.2	11.9	—	3.6	1.8	5.0	—	2.5	—	3.1	—
2-4 past month	10.1	8.9	16.5	5.6	17.0	—	5.1	2.2	5.5	—	2.8	1.8	3.4	—
≥5 past month	21.1‡	23.6‡	31.1‡	14.3‡	31.4‡	6.4‡	12.1‡	—‡	15.7‡	—‡	6.4‡	5.3‡	9.3‡	6.8‡
Limit Contact														
Yes	51.3	38.7	47.5	28.7	51.2	11.6	21.7	11.3	28.4	9.3	19.7	13.0	24.9	13.0
No	4.9‡	4.8‡	9.2‡	3.0‡	9.6‡	0.6‡	2.5‡	0.7‡	3.0‡	0.3‡	1.5‡	0.8‡	1.7‡	1.0‡

‡ p < 0.01; † p < 0.05; * p ≤ 0.10; — not statistically reliable

Table 6.8 continued.

	Verbal Abuse	Psych. Aggression	Minor Physical Assault			Moderate Physical Assault				Severe Physical Assault				Sexual Coercion
	Name Calling	Threat	Push	Slap	Total	Choke	Throw	Hit	Total	T.Gun	Kick	Beat	Total	Forced Sex
Prev. Inc. Access														
Yes	53.9	35.4	40.1	20.3	41.6	9.6	20.3	10.7	24.9	—	16.3	10.2	18.6	13.6
No	5.8‡	5.6‡	10.2‡	3.7‡	10.6‡	0.9‡	2.9‡	1.0‡	3.5‡	0.5‡	1.9‡	1.1‡	2.3‡	1.3‡
Live w/ Ch. <25														
Yes	6.7	6.6	12.2	4.1	12.6	1.1	3.2	1.2	4.0	0.8	2.1	1.5	2.7	1.4
No	6.9	5.9	9.3‡	4.0	9.8‡	1.1	3.4	1.2	4.0	0.5*	2.3	1.2	2.7	1.6
Depression														
Yes	23.8	20.2	23.1	13.0	25.1	—	8.9	—	10.1	—	7.3	6.9	9.7	6.9
No	6.3‡	5.8‡	10.5‡	3.7‡	10.9‡	1.0‡	3.1‡	1.1‡	3.8‡	0.5‡	2.1‡	1.2‡	2.5‡	1.4‡

assault, and sexual coercion. With the exception of sexual coercion, for which there are too few cases to provide reliable comparisons, it appears that the forms of violence that are most prevalent in the population are also those that women are significantly more likely to report the longer they stay with their partner.

Overall, cohabitors and, to a lesser extent, PC marrieds are more likely than non-PC marrieds to be in shorter duration relationships than non-PC marrieds and it appears that violence is negatively related to duration of relationship. Yllö and Straus's (1981) data show the relationship between violence and duration in common-law unions to be more curvilinear in comparison to marrieds. For respondents cohabiting less than two years, the rate of male to female violence is 12.5 percent. Among cohabitors together for three to ten years, the rate jumps to 30 percent. Those cohabiting more than ten years report no violence.[21] It is possible that the difference between these findings and those of the present study may be due to the small subsample of cohabitors ($n = 37$) in Yllö and Straus's (1981) study. These researchers do not provide sample sizes by duration, but given the small subsample of cohabitors and the fact that cohabitation relationships tend to be of short duration, it is reasonable to argue that these factors may be responsible for the zero rate of violence among cohabitors in the "over 10 years" category. Based on the descriptive analysis in the present study, however, it appears that there may be a connection between living together or having lived with someone before getting married, having not been together for very long, and experiencing violence.

Marital Status, Sexual Proprietariness, and Violence

Dobash and Dobash (1995) note that there is little evidence supporting differences between marrieds and cohabitors in terms of sexual jealousy. However, Wilson et al. (1995:343) argue that, given lesser commitment, youth, and greater autonomy, "There is reason to suppose that husbands may be less secure in their proprietary claims over wives in common-law unions than in registered unions." It seems possible, then, that the lack of a marriage license renders men in cohabitation relationships more likely to be jealous and also more likely to keep tabs on their partner.

There are significant differences between all marital status groups in terms of sexual proprietariness. Table 6.6 shows that cohabiting women are more likely than married women to report that their partner is jealous and does not want them talking to other men. PC marrieds are also significantly more likely to report that their partner is jealous compared to non-PC marrieds, though the magnitude of the difference is small (3 percent).

Like jealousy, women in a common-law union are significantly more likely than married women to report that their partner insists on knowing who she is with and where she is at all times. PC married women report a slightly higher rate of their partner wanting to know their whereabouts than do cohabiting women.

There is a pattern for women who are cohabiting or who have cohabited with someone other than their husband to be in a relationship where their partner is jealous and wants to know their whereabouts. This finding leads to two possibilities. The fact that this occurs at similar levels in cohabiting and PC married unions may indicate that higher rates of jealousy in common-law than marital unions are not because of the lower commitment in the former relationships. However, it is also possible that these men are jealous because of a lack of commitment. Cohabitors do not have a formal commitment and PC marrieds, while having a formal commitment, may feel that their partner is less committed to them than do non-PC marrieds.

Table 6.7 indicates that both variables comprising the concept of sexual proprietariness are significantly related to lifetime and one-year prevalence of violence. Women whose partner is jealous are more than three times as likely to report that violence has occurred during the lifetime of their marital/common-law relationship and more than six times as likely to report that violence has occurred in the year prior to the study. Similarly, women whose partner insists on knowing her whereabouts at all times are more than three times as likely to report that violence has occurred during their relationship and more than five times as likely to report that violence occurred in the year prior to the study. The results in table 6.8 demonstrate that both jealousy and knowing whereabouts are significantly related to every component of violence and in the predicted direction. The largest differences for both jealousy and knowing whereabouts are found on the moderate physical assault, severe physical assault, and sexual coercion variables. Women who have a jealous partner are twelve times more likely to report being hit with something that could hurt and women with a partner who insists on knowing her whereabouts are ten times more likely to report this act of violence. The biggest difference on both sexual proprietariness variables is for being threatened with or having a knife or gun used on a woman. Respondents whose partner is jealous are twenty times more likely to report this act of violence, and those with a partner who insists on knowing her whereabouts are thirteen times more likely to report this act of violence. The biggest difference between the two indicators of sexual proprietariness is on being beaten and being forced into sexual activity. Women with a jealous partner are ten times more likely than women without a jealous partner to report being beaten. While still very high, women with a partner who insists on knowing her whereabouts are five times as likely to report being beaten. The same pattern is also present on forced sexual activity. There is something about jealousy that, even more so than keeping tabs, puts women at risk of being beaten up and forced to engage in sexual activities against their will.

Overall, women who are cohabiting or have cohabited at some point are more likely than other women to have a partner who is jealous and wants to know her whereabouts at all times. Sexual proprietariness appears to be strongly positively related to violence. The descriptive analysis appears to hint at the evidence Dobash and Dobash (1995) report is lacking in the family violence field. That is, it appears possible that there is a connection between cohabiting or having cohabited, having a partner who is sexually proprietary, and experiencing violence. However, it must be cautioned that the magnitudes of the marital status differences in the sexual proprietariness variables are small.

Marital Status, Partner's Alcohol Consumption, and Violence

The role of alcohol consumption in violence is an issue of contention among researchers. Reviewing several studies of the link between alcohol intoxication and/or abuse and violence, Tolman and Bennett (1990:91,92) conclude that "chronic alcohol abuse by the male rather than acute intoxication is a better predictor of battering" and that "evidence for the mechanisms by which alcohol abuse affects battering is at best tentative." Indeed, while it has been reported that "substance abuse is the variable that best differentiates violent from non-violent men" (Bennett, 1995:761), it is generally agreed that the link between alcohol and violence is not one of direct cause-and-effect (Bushman and Cooper, 1990; DeKeseredy and MacLeod, 1997; Johnson, 1996).

Horwitz and White (1998) found that of cohabiting, married, and single men, cohabiting men have significantly more alcohol problems. The only study of marital status differences in violence that includes alcohol as a variable was conducted by Stets (1991). Stets reports that cohabitors are more likely than marrieds to exhibit drunkenness. Based on past research then, it seems possible that cohabiting unions are more likely to involve alcohol problems and that this may be indirectly linked to their higher rate of violence.

Table 6.6 indicates that there are significant differences between cohabitors and marrieds in terms of frequency of drinking in the present study. Married men are more likely to never drink and to have not consumed alcohol in the month prior to the survey. Men in a common-law union are more likely to have consumed alcohol one to two times in the month prior to the study, once per week, or two to three times per week. Equal proportions are reported to have consumed alcohol four to six times per week. However, married men are more likely than cohabiting men to drink every day. There are also significant differences between the two marital groups. Non-PC marrieds are more likely to never drink and to have not consumed alcohol in the month prior to the study. PC marrieds, however, are more likely to report drinking from one to two times per month through to drinking every day. The highest rate of drinking every day is among PC marrieds followed by non-PC marrieds and cohabitors.

There are also significant differences in the frequency of heavy drinking across all marital status comparisons. While the majority of men fall into the category of not having had five or more drinks on one occasion in the month prior to the survey, married men are more likely than cohabitors to fall into this category. Cohabiting men, on the other hand, are more likely than married men to have consumed alcohol heavily on one occasion once in the past month or two to four times in the past month. Moreover, cohabiting men are more than twice as likely to have consumed alcohol heavily on five or more occasions in the month prior to the study. With respect to the two married groups, the pattern is the same as for common-law versus marrieds. That is, non-PC married men are more likely than PC married men to have not consumed alcohol heavily in the month prior to the study. PC married men, on the other hand, are more likely than non-PC married men to have consumed alcohol heavily on one occasion once in the past month, two to four times in the past month, or five or more times in the past month.

Among the two indicators of partner's alcohol consumption, heavy drinking is the most clearly related to marital status. But in both cases there appears to be a greater tendency of cohabitors and PC marrieds to drink compared to non-PC marrieds.

Table 6.7 demonstrates that both measures of spousal alcohol consumption are significantly related to lifetime and one-year rates of violence. With respect to the frequency of drinking, men who never drink actually have slightly higher perpetration rates of lifetime and one-year violence than do men who had an average of one drink or less per week in the month prior to the study. One possible explanation for this is that men who never drink hold very traditional patriarchal attitudes that do not condone "the drink" but do condone violence toward one's "wife." However, once one looks at men who drink on average more than once per week the relationship between frequency of drinking and violence, both lifetime and one-year, becomes positive. Among men who drink on average at least two to three times per week, the more frequently they drink the more likely their partner is to report experiencing violence. With respect to the individual components of violence in table 6.8, all but two variables, being hit with something that could hurt and being beaten up, have significant differences. The only noteworthy pattern of deviation from the overall violence variables is that in the combined moderate and severe physical assault variables women whose partners drink on average two to three times per week reported lower lifetime prevalence rates than women whose partners never drink. In general, there appears to be something about men who never drink and something about men who drink frequently that seems to be related to their perpetration of violence.

A similar relationship is present between the frequency of heavy drinking and violence. The results in table 6.7 show that frequency of heavy drinking by a respondent's partner is clearly positively related to the lifetime prevalence rate of violence. The more frequently that a woman's partner drinks heavily the more likely she is to report experiencing violence to have occurred at some point during the relationship. While the one-year rate of violence is slightly higher among women whose partner did not drink heavily than among those whose partner consumed alcohol heavily once in the month prior to the survey, in general there is also a positive relationship between frequency of partner's heavy drinking and one-year violence. In terms of the individual components of violence in table 6.8, all of the differences across categories of heavy drinking are significant. The direction of the relationship is clearly positive for psychological aggression, minor physical assault, moderate physical assault, and severe physical assault. While half of the estimates could not be reported due to insufficient cases, there is also some indication of a negative relationship between partner's heavy drinking and sexual coercion. It is only with verbal abuse that women with partners who did not drink heavily in the month prior to the study report slightly higher rates of violence than women with partners who consumed alcohol heavily on one occasion. Even so, the difference is very small.

In general, there is a relationship between violence and partner's alcohol consumption. Men who drink occasionally appear to be the least likely to be violent followed by men who never drink and then men who drink frequently. The more frequently men drink heavily the more likely they are to be violent.

Overall, there is a tendency for cohabiting men and PC married men to drink compared to non-PC marrieds. The relationship between alcohol consumption and violence is somewhat complex. It seems that men who never drink, who are most likely to be non-PC married, are more likely than men who drink relatively rarely to be violent. Similarly, men who drink every day, who are most likely to be PC married, also have a high rate of violence. However, with respect to heavy drinking it is cohabiting and PC married men who are most likely to drink heavily. Heavy drinking is positively related to violence. It appears possible, then, that there is a linkage among marital status, alcohol consumption, and violence. Non-PC married men may be more traditional, which makes them less likely to drink but more likely to hold more traditional patriarchal attitudes condoning violence against women. On the other hand, cohabiting and PC married men may be less traditional but more likely to drink frequently and heavily which is, in turn related to the use of violence.

Marital Status, Social Isolation, and Violence

As discussed in chapter 3, previous researchers have hypothesized that cohabitors are more likely than marrieds to be socially isolated and that this lack of support by family and friends is, in turn, linked to their higher likelihood of reporting violence.

Table 6.6 demonstrates that women in common-law relationships are significantly more likely than married women to report that their partner socially isolates them by trying to limit their contact with family or friends. PC married women are also significantly more likely than non-PC married women to report that their husband socially isolates them. Barring some intervening variable that prevents cohabiting and/or PC married women from actually being socially isolated, cohabiting and PC married women appear more likely than non-PC married women to be isolated from family and friends.

The results of the cross-tabulations in table 6.7 show that the relationship between having a partner who tries to limit their contact with family or friends and violence is significant and in the expected direction for both the lifetime and one-year time frames. Over the lifetime of the relationship, women whose partner limits their contact are more than four times more likely to report that violence has occurred. Women whose partner limits their contact with family or friends are more than eight times more likely to report having experienced violence in the year prior to the survey. Since becoming married/common-law, 68.1 percent of respondents whose partner socially isolates them report having experienced violence. In the past year, 55.9 percent of women whose partner socially isolates them report violence. With respect to each component of violence in table 6.8, large differences are found on every variable. The differences for each violence variable range from five times for being pushed, grabbed, or shoved to thirty-one times for being threatened with or having a knife or gun used. Other particularly high differences include women with a partner who socially isolates them being ten times more likely to report verbal abuse, nineteen times more likely to report being choked, sixteen times more likely to report being hit with something that could hurt, thirteen times more likely to report being kicked, bit, or hit with a fist, sixteen times more likely to report being beaten, and thirteen times more likely to report being forced into sexual activity. The differences between women with and without a partner who socially isolates them are the largest of any other variable in the present study. Clearly, men who try to socially isolate their partner are far more likely to be violent toward their partner than men who do not try to isolate their partner.

Based on the descriptive analyses, cohabiting and PC married women are more likely than non-PC married women to have a partner who tries to socially isolate them. There is a very strong relationship between having such a partner and experiencing violence. It appears, then, that there may be a connection between living together or having lived with someone else prior to marriage, having a partner who tries to limit a woman's contact with family or friends, and experiencing violence.

Marital Status, Dominance, and Violence

The review of explanatory frameworks for understanding marital status differences in violence indicates that patriarchy may be applicable in this regard. That is, cohabiting men may be more likely than married men to hold a patriarchal ideology and therefore behave in a patriarchal, domineering manner.

While slightly more cohabitors and PC marrieds than non-PC marrieds report that their partner prevents them from knowing about or having access to family income, the results of the cross-tabulations in table

6.6 show that there does not appear to be a significant relationship between this measure of dominance and marital status. One possible explanation for this is that most women in the sample worked in the year prior to the study. Despite the fact that married women are more likely than cohabiting women to earn less than their partner, because the majority of sampled women are themselves income earners there may be less need for them to have access to "family income."

With respect to violence, similar differences to those found with social isolation are also found with respect to having a partner who prevents his partner from knowing about or having access to family income, even if she asks. Table 6.7 indicates that women whose partner dominates them in this way are four times more likely than those whose partner does not dominate them to report experiencing violence since becoming married/common-law. In the lifetime of their relationship, 68.4 percent of women with a partner who dominates them by preventing income access report experiencing violence. These women are seven times more likely to report having experienced violence in the year prior to the survey with a prevalence rate of 57.9 percent. With respect to the individual components of violence in table 6.8, while the differences are not as dramatic as those for social isolation, they are large and significant. The differences range from three times for being pushed, grabbed, or shoved, to ten times for being choked, hit with something that could hurt, and sexually coerced. Women with a partner who dominates them by preventing income access are also eight times more likely to be kicked, bit, or hit with a fist, and nine times more likely to be verbally abused and beaten.

Overall, women with a partner who dominates them by preventing income access are more likely to experience violence than women without such a partner. However, based on the descriptive analyses there does not appear to be a connection between marital status and dominance.

Marital Status, Presence of Children, and Violence

Ellis (1989) has reported that the presence of children among married couples tends to inhibit violence. Common-law couples are more often childless than married couples (Wilson, Johnson, and Daly, 1995) and hence one might expect this to be a contributing factor to higher rates of violence among cohabitors. Boba's (1996) data show that cohabitors are less likely than marrieds to have children in the home. The results of Boba's (1996) multivariate analysis are unclear since with controls for structural variables childlessness is linked to lower odds of violence but with additional controls for relationship quality, relationship dependence, and gender ideology this relationship is reversed. Since Boba (1996) does not separate cohabitors from marrieds in this comparison it is not possible to determine exactly how this variable operates by marital status.

Table 6.6 shows that there is a significant relationship between marital status and having children under the age of 25 living at home. More than half of married women (56.0 percent) compared to 36.7 percent of cohabiting women report that they have at least one child at home. Interestingly, more PC married women (63.2 percent) than non-PC married women (55.4 percent) report having a child at home. Since PC married women are more likely to have been with their partner for less time than non-PC married women, it is possible that this difference is largely due to non-PC marrieds' children being more likely to be older and to have already left home. In addition, PC married women or their partners may be more likely to have one or more children from an earlier relationship. Unfortunately, it is not possible to determine whether one or more of the children are from a current or a previous relationship.

The difference in the lifetime prevalence of violence between women who do and do not live with children less than 25 years of age, as is indicated in table 6.7, is small (2.2 percent). As well, there is not a significant difference in reports of violence in the year prior to the study for women who do and do not have children. The only component of violence for which there seems to be a significant difference is on the item involving being pushed, grabbed or shoved. As shown in table 6.8, of women who live with children under the age of 25, 12.2 percent report being pushed, grabbed, or shoved at some time during their relationship compared to 9.3 percent of women who do not have children under age 25 at home. The only other component of violence to reach significance involves being threatened with or having a knife or gun used on a respondent. Women with children living at home less than age 25 are slightly more likely (0.3 percent) to report having experienced this form of violence. Overall, at best there appears to be a very weak relationship between having children under age 25 at home and experiencing violence.

Overall, married women, particularly PC married women, are more likely than cohabiting women to have children under age 25 living at home. However, there appears to be a weak relationship between having children and experiencing violence. Based on the descriptive analyses, the relationship among marital status, presence of children, and violence appears to be complex and will require a multivariate approach for further clarification.

Marital Status, Depression, and Violence

Stets (1991) reasoned that depression is one result of a lack of social support. Hypothesizing that cohabitors have less social support, Stets (1991) argued that an association between cohabitors' depression and violence is indicative of a spurious relationship with social isolation. Stets (1991) did indeed find that cohabitors are more likely than marrieds to be depressed. However, an examination of Stets's results (1991:675 table 3) indicates that depression has a significant impact on violence even after controlling for a number of other social support/isolation variables. This indicates that there may be something more than social isolation that links depression to violence. Horwitz and White (1998), however, report finding no differences in depression between cohabitors and other marital status groups in their longitudinal study of a young adult cohort. It is important to add, though, that among the limitations of Horwitz and White's (1998) study is that it only includes 136 cohabitors. The results of these studies indicate that very little is known about differences between marrieds and cohabitors in terms of depression and what role it might play in understanding marital status differences in violence. Nevertheless, the results of past studies render the role of depression worthy of further investigation.

Table 6.6 shows that there are no significant differences between cohabiting and married respondents in terms of using drugs or medication for depression in the month prior to the survey. However, PC married women are significantly more likely than non-PC married women to report using drugs or medication for depression. Assuming that all three groups are equally likely to use medication for depression, it appears that PC married women are more likely than non-PC married and cohabiting women to be depressed.

As indicated in table 6.7, there is a significant relationship between being a woman who is depressed and experiencing violence both at some time during the relationship and in the year prior to the study. Women who are depressed are twice as likely to report having experienced violence at some time during their relationship and three times as likely to report that violence has occurred in the year prior to the study. Significant differences are also found on every component of violence in table 6.8. Most of these differences are in the neighborhood of two to three times for depressed women compared to nondepressed women. However, the magnitude of the difference on one variable, sexual coercion, stands out. Women who are depressed are nearly five times as likely to report being forced into any sexual activity against their will by being threatened, held down, or hurt in some way. Of course, the causal ordering of the relationship between depression and violence is unclear. It is possible that higher depression among victimized groups is a consequence of their victimization. Causal ordering aside for the moment, there is clearly a relationship between being depressed and experiencing violence.

Overall, based on the descriptive analyses, PC married women appear to be more likely than non-PC married and cohabiting women to be depressed. There is a relationship between being depressed and experiencing violence. There may be a connection, then, between being PC married, being depressed, and experiencing violence.

Summary

Violence within current marital and common-law relationships is quite prevalent in Canada. In 1993, 16.3 percent of Canadian women living married or common-law reported experiencing violence during their relationship. The most common form of violence involves being pushed, grabbed, or shoved. However, the population estimates demonstrate that even the least common form of violence, being threatened with or having a knife or gun used, is experienced by many women.

The results of the descriptive analyses support the first hypothesis of the study. There is a relationship between marital status and violence such that cohabitors and PC marrieds do report higher rates of violence than do non-PC marrieds. However, an examination of each component of violence separately shows that this relationship varies depending on what component of violence is being investigated. The descriptive analysis shows that cohabitors and non-PC marrieds do not significantly differ on the less physically consequential variables of verbal abuse, psychological aggression, and minor physical assault. PC marrieds, on the other hand, are significantly more likely than both non-PC marrieds and cohabitors to report these behaviors. The separate analyses of each component of violence show that the second hypothesis of the study is also supported. That is, cohabitors and PC marrieds are significantly more likely than non-PC marrieds to report severe violence. More specifically, cohabitors and PC marrieds are significantly more likely than non-PC marrieds to report moderate and severe physical assault.

The findings of the descriptive analyses also provide an application of Nock's (1995) method for understanding marital status differences. The differences between PC and non-PC marrieds indicate that simply being married does not result in similar levels of these forms of violence. Rather, there appears to be something about having lived with someone other than one's current marital partner that leads women to be particularly likely to report experiencing verbal abuse, psychological aggression, and minor physical assault. As well, the findings that both cohabitors and PC marrieds are significantly more likely to report moderate and severe physical assault suggest that the status of the relationship does not matter.

The results also show that all of the selection and relationship characteristics are related to violence. From the descriptive analyses, then, it appears that while marital status differences are not due to the status of the relationship it is quite possible that some combination of both selection and relationship characteristics are responsible for the marital status-violence relationship.

In line with the third hypothesis of the study, the descriptive results indicate that cohabitors and PC marrieds differ significantly from non-PC marrieds on characteristics that select them into less committed relationships. Based on this analysis, it appears possible that cohabitors and PC marrieds are a select group of people. They tend to be younger than non-PC marrieds, to be age heterogamous, to be education and income inconsistent, to have witnessed interparental violence, to have experienced violence while dating their partner, and they are more likely to have been previously married. Current cohabitors are also more likely to have come from the Quebec region and to have a previous partner who was violent. Neither cohabitors nor PC marrieds, however, seem to be a select group in terms of socioeconomic status. That is to say, they do not seem to be selected into their respective marital status based on socioeconomic characteristics.

Consistent with the fourth hypothesis of the study, the descriptive results suggest that cohabitors and PC marrieds differ significantly from non-PC marrieds on relationship characteristics. It seems, based on this analysis, that cohabitors' and PC marrieds' relationships differ from those of non-PC marrieds. Cohabitors and PC marrieds tend to have shorter duration unions, to have sexually proprietary partners, to drink alcohol, and to have a socially isolating male partner. However, based on the descriptive analyses, there are no significant marital status differences in terms of dominance, PC and non-PC marrieds are more alike than cohabitors with respect to having children, and only PC marrieds stand out as being significantly more likely to be depressed.

There also appears to be some preliminary support for the hypothesis that cohabitors' and PC marrieds' differential selection and relationship characteristics are linked to their greater likelihood of violence. For both cohabitors and PC marrieds there does appear to be a possible connection among violence and age, age heterogamy, income consistency, social learning, dating violence, previous marriage, duration of relationship, sexual proprietariness, and alcohol consumption. However, a number of findings from the descriptive analyses suggest that the underlying reality of marital status differences in violence is more complex than these tentative connections. For instance, based on the descriptive analyses, education consistency, previous partner violence, and coming from Quebec appear only to be linked to violence for cohabitors. Similarly, based on the descriptive analyses, depression may only be significantly linked to violence for PC marrieds.

While these findings are consistent with previous research showing that cohabitors are more likely than non-PC marrieds to experience violence, the higher rates of violence among PC marrieds are somewhat surprising, particularly on those components for which they even exceed cohabitors. Further, the importance of some, but not all, of both selection and relationship variables suggests that the etiology of violence against women in different types of unions is complex. It must be reiterated at this point that the connections among marital status, selection variables, relationship variables, and violence as described in this chapter are only tentative. They are based on the kind of conjecture that, unfortunately, characterizes so much of the literature on marital status differences in violence. Until the effects of all of these variables are considered simultaneously through multivariate analyses, one cannot begin to know how the pieces of this puzzle fit together.

Notes

1. The only difference between the operational definitions of violence used by the authors of the VAWS and that presented here is the addition of the verbal abuse variable in the present study. Using the original variable (ALLVCSP), the marital status differences are larger. The lifetime prevalence rates are 15.1 percent for marrieds and 18.1 percent for cohabitors. In terms of the one-year

prevalence rates, cohabitors report four times the rate of marrieds (8.7 and 2.2 percent, respectively). The addition of the verbal abuse variable, then, reduces marital status differences.

2. When examining the subsample of marrieds alone, the weights were re-scaled in the appropriate manner.

3. In terms of all three marital status groups, using the original VAWS vari-able with a lifetime time frame there is a similar pattern to the new variable with non-PC marrieds having the lowest rate (14.6 percent), followed by cohabitors (18.1 percent), and PC marrieds (21.7 percent). However, the pattern is different with the one-year time frame. Non-PC marrieds have the lowest rate (1.9 per-cent), followed by PC marrieds (6.2 percent), and cohabitors (8.7 percent).

4. Since one-year time frames have some built in control for duration of re-lationship, it is possible that the differences between the rates with one-year and lifetime time frames in the present study allude to the importance of controlling for duration of relationship in understanding marital status differences in vio-lence.

5. The exact estimates for each of the cross-tabulations on the prevalence of each component of violence by each independent variable are presented in table 6.1 and table 6.8.

6. According to Statistics Canada's guidelines, estimates based on data with the PERWGHT weighting factor should be based on fifteen or more records. "When the number of contributors to the weighted estimate is less than this, the weighted estimate should not be released regardless of the value of the Ap-proximate Coefficient of Variation" (Statistics Canada, 1994:22).

7. The incidence measure in the VAWS excludes verbal abuse.

8. One-year incidence rates are based on respondents whose first incident (DVJ21) and most recent incident (DVJ22) happened in the twelve months prior to the survey. If only the most recent incident were used, this would give the number of incidents that had *ever* occurred in the relationship among those who experienced at least one incident in the twelve months prior to the survey. To restrict the estimate to only those incidents that occurred in the past twelve months, it is necessary to include only those respondents whose first incident occurred in the past twelve months.

9. The differences between the lifetime and one-year prevalence rates may raise concern about the potential for differences in the operation of violence with risk markers. However, trivariate analyses for both time frames between age and violence while controlling for duration of relationship show that prevalence rates with both time frames operate in the same manner provided that duration of rela-tionship has been controlled. The detailed results of this analysis are presented in appendix B.

10. It is possible that these results are confounded by age. An analysis was performed between respondent's education and marital status controlling for

respondent's age. The results show that for all women except those aged 45-54, cohabitors are more likely than marrieds to have less than high school education. However, cohabiting women under age 30 are also more likely than their married counterparts to have a university degree. On the other hand, married women aged 30 and over are more likely to have a university degree. These results may suggest a tendency for highly educated women age 30 and over to marry. As well, if highly educated women under age 30 are cohabiting as an alternative to marriage, then as these women become older the numbers of older cohabiting women will increase. It is evident that respondent's age is an important variable to control in the multivariate analyses.

11. It is possible that these relationships are due to the partner's age. Since partner's age is not reported, a rough approximation is calculated by taking the mid-point of each age difference category and adding or subtracting from the respondent's age depending on whether the partner is older or younger. Cross-tabulations of verbal abuse, psychological aggression, and the minor physical assault item of being pushed, grabbed, or shoved by the partner's education controlling for partner's age show that in virtually all of the age categories men with some post-secondary education have higher rates than those with a high school diploma. Thus, it would appear that these results are not due to a confounding effect of age.

12. Caution must be exercised in the interpretation of these results because respondent's age is being used. As the cross-tabulation of age difference by marital status has shown, the majority of respondents' partners are older than they. Caution must also be exercised because on some of the trivariate comparisons there were too few cases to provide reliable estimates. Also, reliable comparisons with PC marrieds cannot be made because there were too few cases of unemployed PC marrieds in every age category.

13. Previous marriage has also been found to be a risk marker of divorce (Richardson, 1996).

14. An examination of duration of relationship by previous marriage appears to provide support for this contention. A larger proportion of previously than nonpreviously married women are in the early stages of their current relationship. Of women together with their current partner for less than four years, 29.2 percent were previously married while 11.2 percent were not previously married. Of women together with their partner for four to nine years, 28.4 percent were previously married while 15.5 percent were not previously married. Finally, 42.4 percent of previously married women had been with their current partner for ten or more years compared to 72.8 percent of nonpreviously married women.

15. Caution must be used when interpreting the result for the Atlantic region because there were too few common-law women reporting violence to produce a reliable estimate.

16. An examination of uxoricide data lends some support to this hypothesis. Based on uxoricide data from 1978 to 1997 (Fitzgerald, 1999), Quebec's uxoricide rate per million couples (10.0) is lower than the national average (11.5). The only provinces that have a lower uxoricide rate are Newfoundland (3.4) and Prince Edward Island (6.2). However, the other two provinces comprising the Atlantic region, Nova Scotia (10.5) and New Brunswick (11.6), have higher uxoricide rates than Quebec.

17. Caution must be exercised when interpreting the results for the Atlantic and Quebec regions on this cross-tabulation because the small number of cases reporting violence.

18. Only fourteen cases contributed to this estimate. It is therefore not reliable and should be interpreted cautiously.

19. Caution must be exercised when interpreting this result because three of the five estimates are based on too few cases to be reliable.

20. All cross-tabulations of cohabitors by region must be interpreted with caution due to the small number of cases having experienced a given form of violence within most of the regions.

21. The same pattern surfaced with respect to couple violence (31.2 percent; 50 percent; 0 percent respectively).

Chapter 7

Logistic Regression Results

Based on the review of past research and the descriptive analyses, it is evident that combining cohabitors and marrieds into one group when studying violence is both a theoretical and methodological mistake. Cohabitors and marrieds are very different. The descriptive analyses also support the notion that PC marrieds are a unique group. These findings beg the question of what it is about each of these groups that makes them unique with respect to experiences of violence. Within the theoretical synthesis of the present study, it is therefore necessary to identify the importance of selection and relationship variables for understanding marital status differences in violence. To this end, a number of logistic multiple regressions are performed.[1] What follows begins with the results and implications of these analyses on the overall lifetime prevalence of violence.[2] Following this, the results for each component of violence are examined and the implications of these analyses in relation to the overall analysis are articulated.

The Role of Selection and Relationship Variables in Determining Marital Status Differences in Lifetime Prevalence of Violence

As shown in table 7.1, without controls for selection and relationship variables PC marrieds have 45 percent greater odds of lifetime prevalence of violence compared to non-PC marrieds. While the difference is

Table 7.1. *Results of Logistic Regressions on Lifetime Prevalence of Violence for Selection and Relationship Variables.*

	Marital Status $n = 8365$	Selection $n = 7282$	Relationship $n = 7984$	Full Model $n = 7023$
Covariates	Odds Ratio	Odds Ratio	Odds Ratio	Odds Ratio
Marital Status				
PC Married	1.446‡	1.105	1.444†	1.149
Cohabitor	1.114	1.007	1.068	1.020
Non-PC married	1.000	1.000	1.000	1.000
Age		1.001		0.982†
Age Difference				
Partner 6+ older		0.903		0.958
Partner 1-5 older		0.883		0.942
Partner 1-5 younger		0.829		1.035
Partner 6+ younger		1.263		1.597*
Same age		1.000		1.000
Woman's Education		0.958‡		1.005
Woman's Employment				
Worked past year		1.051		1.044
Did not work past year		1.000		1.000
Partner's Employment				
Did not work		0.928		0.849
Worked past year		1.000		1.000
Woman's Income		1.000		1.000
Income Consistency		1.000		1.000
Income Consistency Square		1.000		1.000
Education Consistency		0.821		0.490
Education Consistency Square		1.213		1.396†
Partner's Father Violent				
Yes/Think so		2.683‡		2.294‡
No/Do not think so		1.000		1.000
Woman's Father Violent				
Yes/Think so		1.538‡		1.466‡
No/Do not think so		1.000		1.000
Dating Violence				
Yes		3.602‡		2.681‡
No		1.000		1.000
Previous Marriage				
Yes		0.735*		0.801
No		1.000		1.000
Previous Partner Violence				
Yes, violent		1.524†		1.333*
No, not violent		1.000		1.000

‡ $p < 0.01$; † $p < 0.05$; * $p \leq 0.10$

Table 7.1 continued.

	Marital Status	Selection	Relationship	Full Model
	n = 8365	*n* = 7282	*n* = 7984	*n* = 7023
Covariates	Odds Ratio	Odds Ratio	Odds Ratio	Odds Ratio
Region				
Atlantic		0.824		0.816
Quebec		0.643‡		0.666‡
Prairies		0.993		0.995
British Columbia		1.130		1.167
Ontario		1.000		1.000
Duration			1.008†	1.030‡
Jealousy				
Yes			2.842‡	2.624‡
No			1.000	1.000
Know Whereabouts				
Yes			2.406‡	2.361‡
No			1.000	1.000
Heavy Drinking			1.073‡	1.052‡
Frequency of Drinking			1.008‡	1.005
Limit Contact				
Yes			4.901‡	4.942‡
No			1.000	1.000
Prevent Income Access				
Yes			5.955‡	5.716‡
No			1.000	1.000
Children < 25				
Yes			1.447‡	1.303‡
No			1.000	1.000
Depression				
Yes			2.268‡	2.134‡
No			1.000	1.000

not as large, cohabitors have 11 percent greater odds of violence compared to non-PC marrieds. It is remarkable that PC marrieds are so much more likely to experience violence. Is this result due to their cohabitation per se? Is it due to characteristics that they are more likely to possess than cohabitors? While PC marrieds are more likely than cohabitors to experience some forms of violence, many of the descriptive analyses imply a similarity between cohabitors and PC marrieds. Do risk markers of violence operate in the same fashion for both PC marrieds and cohabitors? These unanticipated questions must be answered. Needless to say, to meet the demands of zero tolerance, we must understand why it is that women who are currently cohabiting or who have cohabited in the past are any more likely to report experiencing violence during their current relationship.

The second model in table 7.1, containing the logistic regression controlling for selection factors, shows that with these controls the odds for cohabitors are reduced to being virtually identical to non-PC marrieds. Based on this model, it appears that the greater odds of cohabiting women to experience violence over the course of their relationship can be accounted for by factors that select them into cohabitation. As well, controlling for selection factors reduces the odds of lifetime prevalence of violence for PC marrieds compared to non-PC marrieds by 34 percent. Selection factors, then, play an important role in the greater odds of lifetime prevalence of violence for both cohabitors and PC marrieds relative to non-PC marrieds.

The selection factor that has the greatest impact on the odds of lifetime prevalence of violence is dating violence. Women who reported having experienced violence while dating their current partner have 260 percent greater odds of reporting violence while living married or common-law with their partner. Another selection variable that significantly impacts lifetime prevalence of violence is education consistency. The logistic regression analysis for selection factors shows that for each unit of increase in respondent's to partner's education there is a 21 percent increase in the odds of lifetime prevalence of violence. In other words, the more educational resources a woman has relative to her partner the greater her odds of experiencing violence at some time during her relationship. A third variable that seems to be particularly important involves partner's social learning. Women whose partner's father was violent have 168 percent greater odds of reporting having experienced violence during their relationship. Additional selection factors that also seem to play some role are women's social learning (54 percent increased odds), women having experienced violence by a previous partner (52 percent increased odds), living in Quebec (36 percent reduced odds), women who have partners six or more years younger than they (26 percent increased odds), and having been previously married (26 percent reduced odds). It appears, then, that selection factors, particularly dating violence, education consistency, and partner's social learning, have a large impact on the higher odds of violence reported by cohabitors and PC marrieds relative to non-PC marrieds.

In the third model in table 7.1 only the relationship variables and marital status are entered. Controlling for relationship factors, the odds of lifetime prevalence of violence for PC marrieds compared to non-PC marrieds remain virtually unchanged. Therefore, relationship factors appear to have no effect on differences between PC marrieds and non-PC marrieds. Relationship factors have a limited effect on the odds of lifetime prevalence of violence for cohabitors compared to non-PC marrieds, with only a 4 percent reduction in odds. An inspection of the impact and significance of the relationship variables in table 7.1 shows that relationship factors are nevertheless very important determinants of lifetime prevalence of violence. This analysis demonstrates that these relationship factors do not account for the observed marital status differences.

To acquire the most accurate odds ratio for a given variable, it is important to control for the effects of all other covariates. When both selection and relationship factors are entered into the full model, the odds of lifetime prevalence of violence for cohabitors and PC marrieds relative to non-PC marrieds are not reduced as much as when selection factors alone are controlled. This appears to reaffirm that it is primarily selection factors that lead those who cohabit or who have cohabited to have a greater propensity than those who have never cohabited to experience at least one form of violence over the course of their relationship.

While the logistic regressions already discussed provide insights into the impact of selection and relationship variables on marital status differences in violence, these regressions cannot identify which variables are important for each marital status group and in what manner. Also, they do not allow one to compare cohabitors to PC marrieds. To get an idea of the relative impact of the predictor variables for each marital status group what follows analyzes separate logistic regression models for each group on lifetime prevalence of violence.[3] Table 7.2 provides the results of these logistic regressions. A quick inspection of the direction and magnitude of the effects of variables across marital status groups shows several differences. This is even further evidence of the importance of analyzing the marital status groups separately.

Age, Marital Status, and Violence

Recall from the previous logistic regressions that it is the block of selection factors that contributed to the greatest marital status reductions in lifetime prevalence of violence. This analysis did not indicate how each variable operates for each marital status group. Previous research has found that age does not account for marital status differences in violence (Boba 1996; Stets 1991; Stets and Straus 1989; Yllö and Straus 1981). In

Table 7.2. *Results of Logistic Regressions on Lifetime Prevalence of Violence for Marital Status Subgroups.*

Covariates	Cohabitor $n = 863$ Odds Ratio	PC Married $n = 478$ Odds Ratio	Non-PC Married $n = 5682$ Odds Ratio
Age	0.948†	0.965	0.995
Age Difference			
Partner 6+ older	0.736	2.308	0.938
Partner 1-5 older	0.991	1.859	0.925
Partner 1-5 younger	0.975	2.163	1.015
Partner 6+ younger	1.890	2.815	1.429
Same age	1.000	1.000	1.000
Woman's Education	1.044	1.051	0.997
Woman's Employment			
Worked past year	0.798	1.141	1.053
Did not work	1.000	1.000	1.000
Partner's Employment			
Did not work	0.989	0.335*	0.805
Worked past year	1.000	1.000	1.000
Woman's Income	1.000	1.000	1.000
Income Consistency	1.000*	1.000†	1.000
Income Consistency Square	1.000*	1.000*	1.000
Education Consistency	1.806	0.031†	0.563
Education Consistency Square	0.820	3.470†	1.350*
Partner's Father Violent			
Yes/Think so	1.781*	3.277‡	2.449‡
No/Do not think so	1.000	1.000	1.000
Woman's Father Violent			
Yes/Think so	1.437	1.133	1.587‡
No/Do not think so	1.000	1.000	1.000
Dating Violence			
Yes	2.389†	4.129‡	2.641‡
No	1.000	1.000	1.000
Previous Marriage			
Yes	0.712	1.389	0.062
No	1.000	1.000	1.000
Previous Partner Violence			
Yes, violent	2.215†	1.124	1.083
No, not violent	1.000	1.000	1.000

‡ p < 0.01; † p < 0.05; * p ≤ 0.10

Table 7.2 continued.

Covariates	Cohabitor $n = 863$ Odds Ratio	PC Married $n = 478$ Odds Ratio	Non-PC Married $n = 5682$ Odds Ratio
Region			
Atlantic	1.155	0.936	0.777
Quebec	0.696	0.264‡	0.718‡
Prairies	1.056	1.008	0.988
British Columbia	0.968	0.600	1.318†
Ontario	1.000	1.000	1.000
Duration	1.100‡	1.074†	1.020†
Jealousy			
Yes	1.177	4.466‡	3.112‡
No	1.000	1.000	1.000
Know Whereabouts			
Yes	3.498‡	1.404	2.371‡
No	1.000	1.000	1.000
Heavy Drinking	1.046	1.050	1.059‡
Frequency of Drinking	1.004	1.014	1.004
Limit Contact			
Yes	5.915‡	7.933‡	5.047‡
No	1.000	1.000	1.000
Prevent Income Access			
Yes	3.169*	1.143	7.207‡
No	1.000	1.000	1.000
Children < 25			
Yes	0.795	1.628	1.438‡
No	1.000	1.000	1.000
Depression			
Yes	3.702†	2.043	1.984‡
No	1.000	1.000	1.000

their study of violence across marital status categories, Yllö and Straus (1981) investigate the existence of a spurious association due to age. Using analysis of variance, the differences between marrieds and cohabitors remain after controlling for the effect of age (F = 6.72, p < 0.01). Stets and Straus (1989) also test for spuriousness with age. Employing log-linear analysis, these researchers found that age and marital status have independent effects on violence. Moreover, they found that there is no significant interaction between these variables. Stets (1991) controlled for the effect of age in a logit regression and also found that the marital status differences in violence persist. Boba's (1996) data also show that controlling for the effect of age the difference between cohabitors and marrieds remains significant. Thus, the available data suggest that age alone does not account for the different rates of violence between marrieds and cohabitors.

The findings of the regressions on lifetime prevalence of violence do support past studies that indicate that age is nevertheless a stronger predictor of violence for cohabitors than marrieds. Indeed, consistent with the findings of the descriptive analysis, age has no effect on the odds of violence over the lifetime of the relationship for non-PC marrieds. However, controlling for all other variables in the model, for each one year increase in the age of a woman who lived with someone else before getting married there is a 3 percent decrease in odds of violence having occurred during their relationship. For cohabitors a one year increase in age leads to a 5 percent decrease in odds of lifetime prevalence of violence. On the other hand, married women who have never cohabited are essentially no less likely to report some form of violence having occurred during the relationship as they age. Thus, while the impact of age is only moderate, young women who have cohabited before marriage, and particularly young cohabitors, are at greater risk of violence in their relationships than are older women in these unions.

Age Heterogamy, Marital Status, and Violence

The research on age heterogamy generally indicates that the more age heterogamous the couple the greater the likelihood of problems in the relationship. The descriptive analysis in the present study shows that this is also the case with respect to violence, especially when the male partner is six or more years younger than his female partner. Furthermore, cohabitors and PC marrieds are overrepresented in this group. Controlling for all other variables in the model, the results of the logistic regressions in table 7.2 demonstrate that relatively large increases in odds of lifetime prevalence of violence are restricted to the "partner 6 or more years younger" category for cohabitors and non-PC marrieds. Cohabiting women who have a partner who is six or more years younger than they have 89 percent higher odds of reporting violence at some time during their relationship than do their cohabiting counterparts who are of the same age as their partner. For non-PC marrieds the odds are not as large, but non-PC marrieds in this category nevertheless have 43 percent higher odds of violence than do non-PC married women who are of the same age as their partner. These findings contradict the assertion of Wu and Balakrishnan (1995) who argue that any age difference will lead to conflict. Rather, for all three marital status groups the highest likelihood of violence is when the male partner is six or more years younger than the female. Nevertheless, PC marrieds have surprisingly higher odds of lifetime prevalence of violence regardless of the age heterogamy category one examines. The fact that every category of age heterogamy is associated with higher odds of lifetime prevalence of violence for only PC marrieds is indicative that there is something about PC marrieds that renders them particularly prone to the effects of age heterogamy. It appears that PC marrieds are sensitive to any age differences between the couple, and, given that this is not the case in the other two marital status groups, this is either a direct or indirect result of the female partner having cohabited with someone else.

SES, Marital Status, and Violence

As with the descriptive results, education, employment, and income are discussed here in turn.

Education. Researchers using multivariate techniques of analysis have found that education differences do not account for higher violence among cohabitors. Stets and Straus (1989) control for the effect of education in their study and find that it does not account for marital status differences in violence.[4] These researchers did not find a significant interaction between education and marital status. Stets (1989) also controls for education and finds that, when included in the full model, it does not have a significant effect on the role of marital status. In Boba's logistic regression model, education does significantly affect men's violence but controlling for education does not account for marital status differences.

The descriptive analysis in the present study indicates that differential selection by education is not a distinguishing factor in understanding marital status differences in violence. While the results of the logistic regressions do support this case in general, they also provide some interesting nuances of the effect of education for cohabitors and PC marrieds. Controlling for all other variables in the model, the effect of respondent's education on lifetime prevalence of violence is not large for any of the marital status groups. Interestingly, however, while woman's education has no effect for non-PC married women, a one unit increase in the education variable is linked to a 4 percent increase in odds of lifetime prevalence of violence for cohabitors and a 5 percent increase for PC marrieds. While the descriptive analysis surprisingly indicated that cohabitors and

PC marrieds tended to be more highly educated, this higher education is also surprisingly linked to increased odds of violence for these groups, though the effects are relatively small. It may be that cohabiting and PC married women with partners who are less educated than they are experience violence due to status inconsistency. An examination of the results of the education consistency will indicate whether this is due to educational status differences between couples in these groups.

Employment. In a multivariate analysis Boba (1996) finds that neither men's nor women's employment has a significant effect on men's violence, and employment does not account for marital status differences in violence. Consistent with the descriptive analysis and with previous research (Boba, 1996), there does not appear to be much effect of woman's employment on odds of lifetime prevalence of violence. The direction of the effect of employment, however, is interesting. For both groups of marrieds, having a relationship in which the woman works is linked to an increase in odds of lifetime prevalence of violence. This is contrary to the descriptive results that indicated that it may be only PC married women whose employment is linked to violence. One possible explanation for this is that, when other variables are taken into account, married men in general are more likely to feel proprietary about their wives and thus feel insecure about their wives working. It is clear, however, that the situation is not the same for women who cohabit. Cohabiting women who are employed report 20 percent lower odds of violence compared to cohabiting women who are unemployed. In other words, it is cohabiting women who do not work that face higher odds of violence. This is also contradictory to what one would expect based on the descriptive analyses. It seems possible that cohabiting men are less proprietary than married men. But why, then, do cohabiting men have a higher likelihood of violence when their partner does not work? It may be that cohabiting men feel that because they are not married they should not be supporting a partner, and, when faced with this reality, are thus more likely to become violent. It is also possible that having a dependent partner allows men more freedom to become violent with less fear of their partner leaving. The discussion of education and income consistency may shed more light on tenability of this hypothesis.

Despite the findings of the descriptive analyses, which hinted at a limited link among violence, cohabitation and male unemployment, the logistic regressions indicate that living with a man who is unemployed does not increase the likelihood of violence over the course of the relationship, regardless of marital status. If anything, men who work are more likely to be violent, particularly for PC married men. PC married men that did not work in the year prior to the study actually had 66 percent lower odds of violence compared to their employed counterparts. Clearly, when all other control variables are taken into account, male violence against women is not a syndrome of the frustrated unemployed. *Income and Income Consistency.* As found in the descriptive analysis, the amount of income a woman earns does not affect the odds of lifetime prevalence of violence. This is consistent with Boba's (1996) multivariate analysis in which income does not have a significant effect on violence and does not account for marital status differences in violence. As well, consistent with the findings of previous research (Anderson, 1997), when controlling for all other variables in the model, the ratio of female to male income does not have an impact on the odds of lifetime prevalence of violence. Despite the fact that the descriptive analysis showed that the effects of income consistency varied by marital status group, controlling for other variables in the model eliminates the impact of income consistency on the odds of lifetime prevalence of violence. This lack of effect for both woman's income and income consistency exists in all the remaining logistic regression analyses in the present study. Suffice it to state that both the amount of money a woman earns and her income relative to that of her partner have no impact on her odds of experiencing violence. Links to violence between education and employment thus appear not to be due to actual income differences, but rather to status differences.

Education Consistency, Marital Status, and Violence

Unlike previous research that shows education consistency not to affect violence (Anderson, 1997), the present study does find education consistency to have a large impact on lifetime prevalence of violence. While the descriptive analysis indicated the possibility of a link between being a cohabiting woman, having more education than one's partner and experiencing violence, the logistic regression analysis on lifetime prevalence of violence indicates the opposite. For each unit increase in a cohabiting woman's education relative to her partner's education, there is an 18 percent decrease in her odds of lifetime prevalence of violence. Contrary to the relationship hypothesized by Ellis and DeKeseredy (1989), education inconsistency in favor of women does not lead to higher odds of violence for cohabitors. Rather, the present analysis shows this to be the case for marrieds, particularly PC marrieds. While for each unit increase in female to male education levels there is a 35 percent increase in odds for non-PC marrieds, for PC marrieds there is a 247 percent increase in odds of lifetime prevalence of violence. These findings are consistent with those for women's employment. It would appear that married men are more affected by their wives being more educated than they. This could be indicative of a patriarchal belief by these men that the man in the relationship should have greater resources.

Social Learning, Marital Status, and Violence

Consistent with previous research (Jackson, 1996), a partner's social learning has a significant impact on lifetime prevalence of violence regardless of marital status. The descriptive analysis in the present study indicates that men whose father was violent may be selected into common-law unions and that this may explain higher rates of violence in these union types. Partner's social learning has an impact on the odds of lifetime prevalence of violence the most for marrieds, according to the logistic regression results controlling for all other variables. While cohabiting women living with a partner whose father was violent toward his wife have 78 percent higher odds of lifetime prevalence of violence, PC married women and non-PC married women in the same category have 228 percent and 145 percent increased odds, respectively. The fact that the odds are higher in marital relationships despite men in all groups having the same social learning experiences may indicate that some married men still view "the marriage license as a hitting license."

Woman's social learning also has an impact on the odds of lifetime prevalence of violence, though the effects are not as large in any of the marital status groups as they are on the partner's social learning variable. This variable has the least impact on odds for PC married respondents. PC married women whose father was violent have 13 percent higher odds of reporting violence having occurred at some time during their relationship. For cohabitors the effect is larger with a 44 percent increase in odds of lifetime prevalence of violence. Interestingly, non-PC married women with a violent father have a 59 percent increase in odds. Again, while the descriptive analysis indicated that woman's social learning may select these women into violent cohabiting unions, it is clear from the logistic regressions that woman's social learning has the largest impact on non-PC married women. Despite having similar social learning experiences in all three groups, it appears that this subset of non-PC married women are most likely to experience violence. It may be that cohabiting as well as PC married women who witnessed their father being violent toward their mother are more likely to be sensitive to violence and were thus selected into cohabitation out of fear of having such a union. Nevertheless, the differences between cohabitors and non-PC married women on this variable are relatively small. It must be reiterated that the descriptive analyses and the logistic regressions show men's social learning to be more strongly related to violence than women's social learning.

Dating Violence, Marital Status, and Violence

The descriptive analyses of dating violence indicate that there may be something about common-law couples and PC marrieds that makes them more likely than non-PC marrieds to translate a violent dating relationship into a violent union. The logistic regressions, however, show dating violence to have a significant impact across all marital status groups. While dating violence increases the odds of lifetime prevalence of violence by 139 percent for cohabitors and 164 percent for non-PC marrieds, this variable has by far the largest impact on PC marrieds with a 313 percent increase in odds for those having experienced violence while dating one's current partner. While it is possible that some cohabitors are selected into cohabitation because of the violence they experience with their partner while dating, dating violence cannot account for the higher rates of violence among cohabitors. It appears instead to have a particularly large impact on the lifetime prevalence of violence experienced by women who have lived with someone other than their current husband. Consistent with the descriptive analyses, it seems that PC married women's willingness to translate a violent dating relationship into a marriage is linked to their experience of violence in marriage. This suggests that PC married women are a unique group who have fewer options, or perceive themselves as having fewer options, in terms of potential mates.

Previous Marriage, Marital Status, and Violence

Interestingly, the odds of violence are reduced for both cohabitors and non-PC marrieds who reported having been married prior to their current relationship. Previously married cohabitors have 29 percent lower odds of violence than nonpreviously married cohabitors. The impact of having been married previously is larger for non-PC marrieds.

Marrieds who have not previously cohabited but have been previously married have 94 percent lower odds of violence than do non-PC marrieds who have not been previously married. It would appear that non-PC marrieds who have been divorced and, to a lesser extent, divorced cohabitors have found themselves in relationships that are less likely to be violent than their counterparts who have not experienced a failed marriage. The finding that previous marriage for cohabitors is negatively related to violence is consistent with those of previous research (Yllö and Straus, 1981). On the other hand, Yllö and Straus (1981) found previous marriage to be positively related to marital violence. However, these researchers did not make the PC/non-PC distinction. While the findings of the present study for non-PC marrieds are not consistent with Yllö and Straus (1981), the findings for PC marrieds are consistent with past research. PC married women who have also had a failed marriage have 39 percent higher odds of reporting violence having occurred during their current marriage compared to their counterparts who have not had a failed marriage. It would appear that these women, who have had a failed marriage, a failed common-law relationship, and are now remarried, are particularly prone to report experiencing violence at some time during their current marriage. It appears that these are women who, for some reason, are caught in a cycle of problematic relationships. Perhaps these women come from social environments where better choices are not available.

Previous Partner Violence, Marital Status, and Violence

The analyses of bivariate relationships indicate that there may be a connection between a woman having experienced violence in a previous marriage or common-law relationship, choosing to cohabit, and experiencing violence by her current partner. The results of the logistic regression on lifetime prevalence of violence support the findings of the descriptive analyses. While previous partner violence increases the odds of lifetime prevalence of violence for all marital status groups, the effects are relatively small for marrieds compared to cohabitors. Previous partner violence is linked to an 8 percent increase in odds for non-PC marrieds and a 12 percent increase in odds of violence for PC marrieds. For cohabitors, on the other hand, previous partner violence is linked to a 122 percent increase in odds of violence. While these women may have chosen to cohabit rather than marry or remarry because of their violent experiences with their previous partner, they nevertheless still have higher odds of experiencing some for violence during their current relationship compared to their PC and non-PC married counterparts.

Region, Marital Status, and Violence

The region of Canada where a woman lives was found in the descriptive analysis to affect reporting of violence. Consistent with the descriptive analysis, the logistic regression analyses show that the region associated with the lowest odds of lifetime prevalence of violence is Quebec. This is true of all three marital status categories. Thus, it is not that cohabitation is more socially accepted in Quebec, but, instead, there is either something about Quebec society that renders men there less likely to be violent or violence is less likely to be reported by Quebec respondents. One possible explanation for these findings involves the cultural shift in Quebec away from a traditional, patriarchal society. Wu and Baer (1996), using a nationally representative sample of 5,045 women aged 18-49, compare francophones to anglophones in terms of attitudes toward family life and gender roles. Among the findings of these researchers is that francophones tend to be less committed to traditional values about marriage and relationships, and they are more supportive than anglophones of egalitarian gender roles. Similarly, it has been found that Quebecers are less traditional than those living in the rest of Canada concerning the rights and roles of women in society (Baer, Grabb, and Johnston, 1990). These findings do indeed point to a shift in Quebec away from a traditionalism and patriarchalism. This is surprising given that a large portion of Quebecers are Catholic and that Catholics are typically more conservative than Protestants (Wu and Balakrishnan, 1992). To understand this one might look to what is known as the Quiet Revolution.

The Quiet Revolution essentially refers to the social, political, and cultural changes that occurred in Quebec in the 1960s. Prior to the 1960s, the Catholic Church had been a major agent of social control in Quebec. According to Satzewich (1998), the Catholic Church helped to ensure the survival of the French-Canadian culture by preventing French-Canadian workers and farmers from becoming more educated, having small families, joining unions, and becoming professionals and entrepreneurs. Without these interventions, the decline in population and loss of way of life, including the French language, would mean the loss of French Canadian culture. Despite the control of the Church, in the 1940s and 1950s a new francophone middle class arose. Partially because of their initiatives the Quiet Revolution occurred (Satzewich, 1998). The changes during the Quiet Revolution included a questioning of the Catholic Church's authority in all areas of life (Satzewich, 1998). As Pollard and Wu (1998:8) summarize, "With the Quiet Revolution came a change in ideology, from traditionalism and patriarchy to individualism, secularism, and gender equality."

It seems probable that the higher rate of cohabitation in Quebec is linked to an ideological shift away from the Church's authority through marriage. It also seems possible that the cultural shift in Quebec society from patriarchy to egalitarianism is linked to lower rates of violence against women in Quebec. At the societal level, then, there does seem to be a connection between patriarchy and violence against women. This is consistent with Yllö and Straus (1990) who find that patriarchal norms, measured via an index that taps the extent to which residents of various American states feel that husbands should dominate decision-making within the family, are positively related to violence against women. The more patriarchal the norms concerning marital power in a given state, the higher is the rate of violence against women. To be sure, the Quebec situation poses an important hypothesis that deserves further development and research in the future.

Duration of Relationship, Marital Status, and Violence

Despite the fact that the logistic regressions on selection and relationship characteristics showed selection factors to have the largest overall impact on lifetime prevalence of violence, a quick inspection of the effects of relationship factors on the odds in table 7.2 shows that some of these variables also operate differently across marital status groups. To get a complete picture of marital status differences it is important to also investigate the relationship variables.

Consistent with the descriptive analysis, the logistic regressions on the duration variable show it to be positively related to lifetime prevalence of violence for all three marital status groups. The impact of the duration variable differs depending on marital status. A one-year increase in duration of relationship is linked to a 2 percent increase in odds of lifetime prevalence of violence for non-PC marrieds, a 7 percent increase in odds for PC marrieds, and a 10 percent increase in odds for cohabitors. It must be reiterated, however, that on average the duration of common-law relationships is short. The majority of cohabitors in the present study have been together for less than four years.

In their analysis Yllö and Straus (1981) control for the effect of duration and find that it does not account for the different rates of violence between marrieds and cohabitors (F = 7.24, p < .01). Similarly, in a multivariate analysis Boba (1996) found that duration was not a significant predictor of men's violence and it did not account for marital status differences. It is not surprising, then, that duration of relationship itself does not appear to account for marital status differences in violence. Rather, the real importance of including duration of relationship in the model is as a control variable to account for the effects of the shorter durations of cohabitors' and PC marrieds' unions.

Sexual Proprietariness, Marital Status, and Violence

The logistic regressions suggest partial support for the greater impact of sexual proprietariness among cohabitors and those who have cohabited before marriage. However, the results are not as straightforward as those of the descriptive analyses, which indicate sexual proprietariness having the largest impact on cohabitors followed by PC marrieds and non-PC marrieds. Having a partner who is jealous increases the odds of violence over the course of the relationship by 347 percent for PC married women and 211 percent for non-PC married women. Surprisingly, having a jealous cohabiting partner increases the odds of lifetime prevalence of violence by only 18 percent. It seems that having a partner who is jealous has by far the biggest impact on those who have the commitment of marriage. Perhaps men who are jealous but who feel that their partner can leave them more easily are less apt to be violent. Clearly, jealousy alone does not account for higher rates of violence among cohabitors. While having a jealous partner does not have much impact on the odds of violence for cohabitors, having a partner who "keeps tabs" does. The odds of violence occurring during the relationship for cohabiting women are 250 percent higher if their partner is one who insists on knowing whom she is with and where she is at all times. Having such a partner also increases the odds for non-PC marrieds by 137 percent and by only 40 percent for PC marrieds. It would seem possible that the lack of formal commitment in cohabiting unions combined with being a man who takes the initiative to actively watch over or "keep tabs" on "his woman" make these men particularly likely to be violent.

Partner's Alcohol Consumption, Marital Status, and Violence

Previous research has shown cohabitors to have more problems with alcohol (Horwitz and White, 1998; Stets, 1991). In a logistic regression, Stets (1991) finds that a respondent having a drinking problem makes a significant contribution to marital status differences in violence. The results of the logistic regressions in the present study, however, indicate that alcohol consumption does not differentiate the marital status groups in terms of odds of violence. The frequency with which a respondent's partner consumed alcohol in the month prior to the study has virtually no effect on the odds of lifetime prevalence of violence for any group. The frequency of heavy drinking does, however, impact the odds of lifetime prevalence of violence. For each additional time in the month prior to the study that a respondent's partner consumed more than five drinks, there is a 5 percent increase in odds for cohabitors and PC marrieds and a 6 percent increase in odds for non-PC marrieds. The common conjecture that the alcohol consumption of cohabitors leads to their higher rates of violence is not supported on the basis of the present analysis. Contrary to the descriptive results, which indicated that not drinking among non-PC married men would be linked to violence, the multivariate analysis shows that heavy drinking even among non-PC married men is linked to violence. The finding that a partner's alcohol consumption does not differentiate the marital status groups in terms of violence is also in contradiction to the only other study that has investigated the effect of alcohol on marital status differences in violence (Stets, 1991). One possible explanation for this disparity is that Stets's (1991) sample consists of both female and male respondents and the measure of alcohol consumption asked the respondent whether she or he had a problem with drinking too much alcohol. Stets's (1991) measures, then, are faced with two problems in terms of comparisons to the results in the present study. First, Stets (1991) is investigating violence by either male or female cohabiting partners, depending on whether or not the respondent is male or female, and it may well be that the causes of violence perpetrated by females are different than those perpetrated by males. Thus, combining the role of alcohol consumption for both females and males may confound the linkages of this variable to violence. Second, the measure of alcohol abuse itself may pose problems. It seems possible that some respondents would not report having "a problem of drinking too much alcohol." As well, this measure is open to interpretation. What some see as too much may not be perceived as such by others. Rather, one needs a more quantifiable measure of alcohol consumption, such as the one employed in the present study, to more objectively measure alcohol use and abuse.

Social Isolation, Marital Status, and Violence

The possibility of a relationship between being a cohabitor or a PC married woman, having a partner who is socially isolating, and experiencing violence is alluded to by the analyses of bivariate relationships. The results of the logistic regressions show that non-PC married women with a socially isolating partner have 405 percent increased odds, cohabiting women with such a partner have 492 percent increased odds, and PC married women in the same category have 693 percent increased odds of violence during their relationship. While having a socially isolating partner has the largest impact for PC marrieds and cohabitors, the results indicate more generally that having a socially isolating partner has a large impact on the odds of violence over the lifetime of the relationship regardless of marital status. This finding may be linked to the measure of social isolation employed in the present study. While the measure does indicate isolation or attempted isolation from family and friends, the source of this isolation is different from isolation imposed by ideologies based in societal disdain of cohabitation. However, with the increasing prevalence, and therefore acceptance, of unmarried cohabitation, it is likely that social isolation due to ideology has diminished. Despite this ideological shift, cohabitors nevertheless have higher rates of all forms of violence than non-PC marrieds, with the exception of verbal abuse. It would seem that social isolation is not a salient explanation for marital status differences in violence against women.

Dominance, Marital Status, and Violence

The descriptive analysis indicates that dominance is related to violence but that domineering behavior through limiting access to family income is not related to marital status. However, the logistic regression models in table 7.2 show that domineering behavior does affect the odds of violence differently across marital status groups. Having a domineering partner does not affect the odds of violence much for PC married women with an increase of only 14 percent over their counterparts without a domineering partner. Having a domineering partner does significantly impact the odds of violence for cohabitors with a 217 percent increase compared to cohabitors with a domineering partner. However, by far the largest impact of the dominance variable is for non-PC marrieds. Non-PC married women with a domineering partner have 621 percent greater odds of reporting violence having occurred during the course of their relationship compared to non-PC married women without a domineering partner. It would appear that married women who have never lived common-law are particularly susceptible to violence by a domineering partner. It may be that the institution of marriage combined with the traditionalism of these women allows domineering patriarchal men greater latitude to translate their domination into violence.

Presence of Children, Marital Status, and Violence

According to the results of the descriptive analysis there may be a weak connection between being married, having children, and experiencing violence. The results of the logistic regression support this finding. PC married women with children have 63 percent higher odds and non-PC married women with children have 44 percent higher odds of lifetime prevalence of violence compared to their childless counterparts. Contrary to Ellis (1989), the presence of children among married couples does not inhibit violence but instead increases its odds.[5] It may be that for marrieds the presence of children is an additional strain that leads men to vent their frustrations through violence against their wives. Interestingly, having children reduces the odds of lifetime prevalence of violence for cohabitors by 20 percent. It may be that common-law relationships that include children indicate greater commitment to a permanent loving relationship, given the fact that most cohabitors prefer to marry before having children (Cunningham and Antill, 1995). Alternatively, it may be that, because of the children, men in these relationships do not want to risk venting their frustration through violence since the absence of a formal commitment renders it easier for their partners to leave.

Depression, Marital Status, and Violence

Finally, according to the results of the bivariate analyses, there may be a connection between being PC married, being depressed, and experiencing violence. However, the logistic regression analyses show this not to be the case, or at least not the whole story. Women who had taken drugs or medication for depression in the month prior to the study in the two married groups have very similar odds of reporting that violence had occurred during the relationship. Non-PC married women who are depressed have 98 percent higher odds and depressed PC married women have 104 percent higher odds of violence than their non-depressed counterparts. Depressed cohabiting women, on the other hand, have 270 percent higher odds of reporting violence during their relationship. This finding is consistent with that of Stets (1991) such that depression has a larger impact on violence experienced by cohabitors than marrieds. However, while Stets (1991) attributes this to cohabitors' social isolation, as has already been discussed, both Stets's (1991) own analysis as well as that of the present study indicate that the role of depression is not linked to social isolation. So what then is the link among depression, cohabitation, and violence? It is not that cohabitors are more likely to be depressed because the descriptive analysis found PC married women most likely to report being depressed. The question then becomes, Why is it that depressed cohabiting women have a higher likelihood of reporting violence than do depressed PC married and non-PC married women? Due to their greater likelihood of experiencing moderate and severe physical violence, one possibility is that cohabitors are more likely to be depressed as a consequence of violence. Perhaps depression is not as much a cause of violence, but it may be a consequence of violence. An examination of the post-violence variables in the next chapter may shed light on this hypothesis.

Three Distinct Types of Violent Experiences

One can conclude based on the analysis thus far that the three marital status groups are quite distinct. The above analysis can, indeed, provide an overall profile of the characteristics in each union type that are particularly likely to lead to some form of violence during the relationship.

Violence among Cohabitors

First, with respect to cohabiting relationships, those that seem particularly likely to be violent include women who are young and who are childless. The results on the age heterogamy variable for this group indicate that the only category that has higher odds than partners of the same age is where the partner is six or more years younger. Given these findings it follows that it is particularly young men in these relationships who are being violent. Second, cohabiting women who have low levels of education relative to their partner and who do not work are particularly likely to report violence. The men in these cohabiting relationships therefore are with women who are dependent on them. It may be that frustration over providing for a cohabiting partner and/or the power afforded by a woman's dependence contribute to violence by these men. Third, cohabiting women who have experienced violence by a previous partner are particularly likely to report violence by their current partner. This combined with their lack of relative resources may be connected to the finding that depressed cohabitors are particularly likely to report violence. Finally, cohabiting women with a partner who "keeps tabs" are more likely to report violence. For cohabitors, then, the occurrence of violence may have more to do with youth, relative powerlessness/dependence of women, and being limited to a pool of violent and proprietary men.

Violence among PC Marrieds

For PC marrieds differential educational resources seem to be particularly related to violence. The more educational resources a PC married woman has relative to her partner the greater her likelihood of reporting violence. As well, any age heterogamy is linked to increased odds of violence for these women. PC married women who have been married previously and those who reported violence while dating their current partner are also more likely to report violence in their current marriage. In addition to the fact of the respondent having lived with someone prior to marriage other than her current husband, the aforementioned characteristics all seem to point to greater social marginality. Moreover, PC married men who learned violence from their father, who are jealous and socially isolating are particularly likely to be violent. It seems possible that PC married couples' greater social marginality is linked to their relationship choices and their experience of violence.

Violence among Non-PC Marrieds

The only variable that stands out for non-PC marrieds compared to the other marital status groups is dominance. While several other variables have an important effect on the odds of violence for non-PC marrieds, having a dominating partner who prevents access to family income is particularly likely to lead to reports of violence. This seems to reflect an underlying dimension of patriarchy, which underlies the notion of a man controlling familial income. Apparently, men married to more traditional women and who behave in a patriarchal manner through controlling family income are particularly likely to be violent toward their wives. This may be because these men feel that by virtue of their marriage license they have the right to be violent or because they believe their more traditional wives will allow it or are unable to prevent it.

Theoretical Implications of Logistic Regressions on Lifetime Prevalence of Violence

The results thus far have clearly demonstrated that marital status is an important variable for understanding the causes of male partner violence against women. The next step in this research is to verify the relevance of the various theories for understanding marital status differences. With respect to these explanatory frameworks, a number of conclusions can be drawn from the logistic regressions.

Feminist and Resource Theories

Contrary to the findings of previous research (Lenton, 1995b), the results of the descriptive analyses in the present study show that men in all marital status groups roughly equally exhibit domineering behavior rooted in patriarchal beliefs. It is possible that the difference in results between Lenton's (1995b) study and the present work are due to the different measures employed. Using the VAWS data, Lenton (1995b) created a patriarchy index from five variables: jealousy, limiting contact, knowing whereabouts, name calling, and preventing income access. Lenton (1995b:314) asserts that these items "seem to tap similar sentiments" to Smith's definition of patriarchal ideology. Smith defines patriarchal ideology as "(a) a set of beliefs that legitimizes male power and authority over women in marriage, or in a marriage-like arrangement, and (b) a set of attitudes or norms supportive of violence against wives who violate, or who are perceived as violating, the ideals of familial patriarchy" (cited in Lenton, 1995b:314). Preventing income access does appear to tap dominance indicating legitimized male power and authority over women and this is why it is selected to represent patriarchy in the present study. However, while Lenton (1995b) argues that all of these measures have some face validity, the present work has argued that they more suitably measure other concepts. Lenton (1995b) also argues that the similarity in findings between her study and that of Smith (1990a) contributes to the construct validity of her measure. However, Lenton (1995b) does not detail the precise convergence between the results of the two studies. Needless to say, finding that the measures employed by Lenton (1995b) relate to violence in the same way as Smith's (1990a) measures does not necessarily mean that the two sets of variables are measuring the same concept. This is not to say that the measure of patriarchy employed in the present study is wholly adequate. To more adequately test feminist theory a more elaborate measure than patriarchal dominance is required. Such a measure would look at both the ideological and structural components of patriarchy as well as at the relationships between both levels (Dobash and Dobash, 1979).

While men in the present study exhibit domineering behavior at similar levels regardless of marital status, the results of the logistic regressions have shown that men are most likely to be violent when they are married to women who have never cohabited. The fact that cohabiting men who prevent their partner from having access to family income are not as likely to be violent as their married counterparts indicates that patriarchy does not account for the higher rates of violence for cohabitors. Furthermore, drawing on resource theory, feminist theory argues that status inconsistency has an underlying dimension of patriarchy. The results of the present study suggest that this does not account for violence against cohabiting women since income consistency makes no difference to odds of violence, and higher female to male education levels actually reduce the odds of violence among cohabitors. Based on the present study, it would appear that neither feminist theory nor resource theory are able to account for violence among cohabitors.

Routine Activities Theory

The results thus far do indicate some support for routine activities theory. As routine activities theory would predict, the youth and child-lessness of cohabiting couples is linked to increased odds of violence. Routine activities theory would also argue that cohabitors are more likely to engage in potentially conflict producing activities such as going to the bar. The fact that the cohabiting couple is not married may mean that they tend to engage in these activities separately, that is the "boys/girls night out." The importance of cohabiting men being sexually proprietary through wanting to know with whom their partner is and where she is at all times may be indicative of concern over such activities. While alcohol consumption does not differentiate marital status groups, it nevertheless appears possible that young cohabiting men's concern about their part-ners arising from their more separate lifestyle combined with sharing a residence contribute to violence in these unions. Overall, the majority of the predictions of routine activities theory do seem to be supported by the data.

Social Learning Theory

As already discussed, social learning does have an impact on the odds of violence in the present study. However, given that neither social learning variable in the present study has a larger impact on violence for cohabitors than marrieds, it appears that social learning cannot account for higher violence among cohabitors. Instead, the results of the logistic regressions show social learning to have by far the greatest impact on odds of violence for marrieds. Even with the methodological improve-ment over past research (Jackson, 1996) via controls for age and duration of relationship, the results of the present study suggest that social learn-ing theory cannot account for the higher prevalence of violence among cohabitors.

Sex-Role Theory

With respect to sex-role theory, previous research (Boba 1996) found that cohabitors are more likely than marrieds to be egalitarian regarding attitudes toward working when asked about the man being the sole breadwinner. This egalitarianism is positively linked to violence in Boba's (1996) study. However, the results of the logistic regressions in the present study suggest that egalitarianism is associated with reduced odds of violence for cohabitors. Common-law unions in which a woman worked are linked to reduced odds of violence. One possible explanation for the disparity in findings between Boba (1996) and the present study is that the former is measuring attitudes while the latter measures behavior. Attitudes are, of course, very different from behavior. It may be that there is a *perception* of egalitarianism among cohabitors in Boba's (1996) sample, but in reality these cohabitors are less egalitarian as shown by their higher likelihood of violence. On the other hand, cohabitors in the present study who *behave* in an egalitarian way, in the sense that the female partner works, are less likely to experience violence. For marrieds, egalitarianism in terms of female employment does not reduce the likelihood of violence to the same degree. Marrieds may present a case, then, in which what appears to be egalitarian behavior does not necessarily reflect egalitarian attitudes. That is, it seems possible that married men are more traditional and when confronted with a wife who works they are slightly more likely than cohabitors to be violent.

Social Isolation

As already discussed at some length, social isolation as measured by a man's attempts to limit his partner's contact with family and friends is found in the present study to be linked to violence, but it does not lead to appreciably higher odds of violence for cohabitors compared to the other marital status groups. In conjunction with the fact that cohabitation is increasingly accepted in society, this suggests that the persistence of higher rates of violence among cohabitors is not due to social isolation.

The DAD Model

With respect to the DAD model, it has already been discussed that neither income nor education dependency of cohabiting men on women is linked to increased odds of violence. Contrary to Ellis and DeKeseredy's (1989) hypothesis cohabiting males do not appear to be resorting to violence to achieve their status of dominance. As Ellis and DeKeseredy (1989) had hypothesized, neither does alcohol dependency appear to be disproportionately linked to violence among cohabitors. Even considering differential availability for violence via controlling for duration of relationship, jealousy has the least effect on odds of violence for cohabitors compared to other marital status groups. Moreover, some factors Ellis and DeKeseredy (1989) posit to reduce deterrence, namely, social isolation and low income, do not appear to be important in this regard. The youthfulness of cohabitors may be a factor leading to lower deterrence.

The testing of Ellis and DeKeseredy's (1989) theory fills a major gap in our knowledge of marital status differences in violence. DeKeseredy and Ellis (1989) base their theoretical framework on a synthesis of research findings from other selected studies. While this is an appropriate approach, it is only as good as the evidence on which it is based. The present study identifies weaknesses in several of these studies that may account for the contradictory findings presented here. These results show that the most commonly cited explanatory synthesis for understanding marital status differences in violence is inadequate. At the very least the results identify a need for further theorizing and empirical testing in this area.

The Selection versus Relationship Dichotomy

The results of the first set of logistic regressions points to the prime importance of selection variables in understanding marital status differences in lifetime prevalence of violence. The second set of logistic regressions, on the other hand, shows that most of the relationship variables operate differently for different groups. Based on these analyses it appears that while marital status differences in violence have the strongest link to the type of people who are selected into cohabitation, these selection variables may also operate through characteristics of the relationship in the production of violence. It may be that the selection versus relationship method creates a false dichotomy. There may be a complex causal web of both selection and relationship variables operating in the production of marital status differences in violence.

The Role of Selection and Relationship Variables in Determining Marital Status Differences in Verbal Abuse

The descriptive analyses have shown that the marital status/violence relationship varies depending on the type of violence one investigates. Since the lifetime prevalence variable combines all forms of violence, it is important to analyze each type of violence separately to identify important deviations from the patterns already identified in the lifetime prevalence variable.

Table 7.3 provides the results of the logistic regressions on verbal abuse controlling for selection and relationship variables. Consistent with the descriptive analysis, without controls PC marrieds have higher odds of verbal abuse compared to non-PC marrieds while cohabitors and non-PC marrieds have virtually identical odds. Controlling for selection factors dramatically reduces the odds of verbal abuse for PC marrieds relative to non-PC marrieds such that the former only have 5 percent greater odds of verbal abuse than the latter. Interestingly, while the cohabitors and non- PC marrieds are almost identical without controls, with controls for selection factors the odds of verbal abuse for cohabitors compared to non-PC marrieds are reduced by 15 percent. This suggests that selection factors are particularly pertinent to the verbal abuse experienced by women who are currently cohabiting or who have cohabited prior to marriage. The selection variables that have by far the largest impact on verbal abuse are having experienced violence while dating (352 percent increased odds) and a partner's social learning (187 percent increased odds).

The third model in table 7.3 shows that controlling for relationship variables reduces the odds of verbal abuse for PC marrieds compared to non-PC marrieds by 20 percent. Relationship factors alone do not account for as much of the difference between PC marrieds and non-PC marrieds as do selection factors. With relationship controls the odds for cohabitors compared to non-PC marrieds, on the other hand, are reduced by 24 percent. Relationship factors, then, appear to have a greater effect on verbal abuse for cohabitors than PC marrieds relative to non-PC marrieds. An inspection of the odds for relationship factors in the model indicates that several are important determinants of verbal abuse. The variable that has the greatest impact on odds of verbal abuse is dominance through preventing access to income (898 percent increased odds). Social isolation (584 percent increased odds), depression (325 percent increased

Table 7.3. *Results of Logistic Regressions on Verbal Abuse for Selection and Relationship Variables.*

Covariates	Marital Status n = 8372 Odds Ratio	Selection n = 7282 Odds Ratio	Relationship n = 7989 Odds Ratio	Full Model n = 7023 Odds Ratio
Marital Status				
PC Married	1.489†	1.047	1.287	1.027
Cohabitor	0.988	0.842	0.757	0.662*
Non-PC married	1.000	1.000	1.000	1.000
Age		1.004		0.998
Age Difference				
Partner 6+ older		0.830		0.755
Partner 1-5 older		0.741†		0.768
Partner 1-5 younger		0.640†		0.709
Partner 6+ younger		1.098		1.132
Same age		1.000		1.000
Woman's Education		0.910‡		0.956†
Woman's Employment				
Worked past year		1.127		1.230
Did not work past year		1.000		1.000
Partner's Employment				
Did not work		0.924		0.815
Worked past year		1.000		1.000
Woman's Income		1.000†		1.000*
Income Consistency		1.000		1.000
Income Consistency Square		1.000		1.000
Education Consistency		1.832		0.945
Education Consistency Square		0.969		1.174
Partner's Father Violent				
Yes/Think so		2.873‡		2.244‡
No/Do not think so		1.000		1.000
Woman's Father Violent				
Yes/Think so		1.137		1.052
No/Do not think so		1.000		1.000
Dating Violence				
Yes		4.519‡		2.995‡
No		1.000		1.000
Previous Marriage				
Yes		0.919		0.962
No		1.000		1.000

‡ $p < 0.01$; † $p < 0.05$; * $p \leq 0.10$

Table 7.3 continued.

	Marital Status	Selection	Relationship	Full Model
	$n = 8372$	$n = 7282$	$n = 7989$	$n = 7023$
Covariates	Odds Ratio	Odds Ratio	Odds Ratio	Odds Ratio
Previous Partner Violence				
Yes, violent		1.199		0.915
No, not violent		1.000		1.000
Region				
Atlantic		0.804		0.808
Quebec		0.537‡		0.556‡
Prairies		0.938		0.826
British Columbia		0.973		0.860
Ontario		1.000		1.000
Duration			1.004	1.020
Jealousy				
Yes			2.418‡	2.549‡
No			1.000	1.000
Know Whereabouts				
Yes			2.700‡	2.436‡
No			1.000	1.000
Heavy Drinking			1.047‡	1.029*
Frequency of Drinking			1.017†	1.012*
Limit Contact				
Yes			6.838‡	6.974‡
No			1.000	1.000
Prevent Income Access				
Yes			9.984‡	9.190‡
No			1.000	1.000
Children < 25				
Yes			1.061	0.919
No			1.000	1.000
Depression				
Yes			3.247‡	3.359‡
No			1.000	1.000

odds), and the sexual proprietariness variables of knowing the whereabouts (170 percent increased odds) and jealousy (142 percent increased odds) also have a large impact on verbal abuse.

In the full model, the greatest reductions occur in odds of verbal abuse for both PC marrieds and cohabitors. For PC marrieds the odds are reduced to just 3 percent in comparison to non-PC marrieds. For cohabitors, the odds are reduced a further 10 percent from the relationship model such that cohabitors have 33 percent lower odds of verbal abuse in comparison to non-PC marrieds. It appears that both selection and relationship factors work in combination in the reduction in odds of verbal abuse for cohabitors compared to non-PC marrieds. An inspection of both the selection and relationship variables in the full model indicates relatively little change in most of the odds. However, the direction of two of the variables, education consistency and presence of children, is changed indicating the need to further investigate specific links between selection and relationship variables.

The results of the logistic regressions in table 7.4 provide some interesting insights in terms of understanding the marital status differences in verbal abuse uncovered in the descriptive analysis and the logistic regressions in table 7.3. Recall that without controls PC marrieds have significantly higher odds of verbal abuse than do cohabitors and non-PC marrieds. The logistic regressions on selection and relationship variables also suggest that it is primarily selection variables that account for this difference, though relationship variables still appear to play some role. An inspection of the regressions on verbal abuse for marital status subgroups further specifies the relative role of the predictive variables. The selection variables that seem to be particularly important determinants for PC marrieds are education consistency, partner's social learning, and previous marriage. Women who have lived with someone other than their current marital partner and who have more education than their current partner have much higher odds of being called names than do educationally inconsistent cohabitors and non-PC marrieds. For each unit increase in female to male level of education there is a 252 percent increase in the odds of verbal abuse for PC marrieds. This is compared to a 16 percent increase for non-PC marrieds and an 80 percent decrease for cohabitors. While partner's social learning increases the odds of verbal abuse for all marital status groups it has by far the largest impact on PC marrieds. Cohabiting women whose partner's father was violent have 115 percent higher odds of verbal abuse and their non-PC married counterparts have 135 percent higher odds. PC married women whose partner was subject to social learning, on the other hand, have 449 percent higher odds of verbal abuse.

The effect of previous marriage is also interesting for PC marrieds. Cohabitors and non-PC marrieds who were previously married have decreased odds of verbal abuse compared to their non-previously married counterparts. On the other hand, PC marrieds who were also previously married have 208 percent increased odds of verbal abuse. There appears to be something about PC marrieds, then, that makes verbal abuse par-

Table 7.4. *Results of Logistic Regressions on Verbal Abuse for Marital Status Subgroups.*

Covariates	Cohabitor $n = 863$ Odds Ratio	PC Married $n = 478$ Odds Ratio	Non-PC Married $n = 5682$ Odds Ratio
Age	0.948†	0.965	0.995
Age Difference			
Partner 6+ older	0.736	2.308	0.938
Age 1.027	0.972	0.992	
Age Difference			
Partner 6+ older	0.415	0.582	0.803
Partner 1-5 older	1.431	0.972	0.712*
Partner 1-5 younger	0.988	0.648	0.696
Partner 6+ younger	0.234	1.205	1.689
Same age	1.000	1.000	1.000
Woman's Education	0.866*	0.902	0.966
Woman's Employment			
Worked past year	2.268	1.448	1.208
Did not work	1.000	1.000	1.000
Partner's Employment			
Did not work	0.704	0.072†	0.873
Worked past year	1.000	1.000	1.000
Woman's Income	1.000†	1.000	1.000
Income Consistency	1.000	1.000†	1.000
Income Consistency Square	1.000	1.000*	1.000
Education Consistency	123.367*	0.024	1.027
Education Consistency Square	0.197*	3.516	1.163
Partner's Father Violent			
Yes/Think so	2.146	5.494‡	2.350‡
No/Do not think so	1.000	1.000	1.000
Woman's Father Violent			
Yes/Think so	1.199	0.627	1.012
No/Do not think so	1.000	1.000	1.000
Dating Violence			
Yes	4.277‡	2.386	2.510‡
No	1.000	1.000	1.000
Previous Marriage			
Yes	0.287*	3.081*	0.080
No	1.000	1.000	1.000
Previous Partner Violence			
Yes, violent	2.027	0.700	0.700
No, not violent	1.000	1.000	1.000

‡ $p < 0.01$; † $p < 0.05$; * $p \le 0.10$

Table 7.4 continued.

Covariates	Cohabitor n = 863	PC Married n = 478	Non-PC Married n = 5682
	Odds Ratio	Odds Ratio	Odds Ratio
Region			
Atlantic	0.473	0.097*	0.915
Quebec	0.188‡	0.563	0.678†
Prairies	0.706	0.733	0.791
British Columbia	0.924	0.329	0.919
Ontario	1.000	1.000	1.000
Duration	1.064	1.018	1.015
Jealousy			
Yes	0.639	3.380*	3.126‡
No	1.000	1.000	1.000
Know Whereabouts			
Yes	3.071†	5.313‡	2.469‡
No	1.000	1.000	1.000
Heavy Drinking	0.954	1.088	1.045†
Frequency of Drinking	1.085‡	0.946	1.010
Limit Contact			
Yes	8.726‡	3.200	8.407‡
No	1.000	1.000	1.000
Prevent Income Access			
Yes	29.023‡	12.617†	9.581‡
No	1.000	1.000	1.000
Children < 25			
Yes	0.972	1.026	0.904
No	1.000	1.000	1.000
Depression			
Yes	7.640‡	4.021*	3.342‡
No	1.000	1.000	1.000

ticularly likely to occur when the woman has more education than the man, when she has been previously married, and when he had been exposed to parental violence as a child. All of these findings are consistent with the overall analysis of lifetime prevalence of violence and thus point to the greater proprietariness and insecurity of men married to these women, the view of some of these men that the marriage license is a license to be abusive, and some limitation placed on the relationship choices made by women in these unions.

The addition of relationship variables to the selection variables only reduces the marital status difference for PC marrieds compared to non-PC marrieds by 2 percent. This is also reflected in the logistic regressions for marital status subgroups. The most noteworthy difference for PC marrieds on the relationship variables involves the sexual proprietariness variable of insisting on knowing the woman's whereabouts. Non-PC married and cohabiting women with a partner who keeps tabs on them have 147 percent and 207 percent higher odds of verbal abuse, respectively, compared to their counterparts without such a partner. By contrast, PC married women with a partner who keeps tabs on them have 431 percent higher odds of verbal abuse. It would seem possible that the selection variables already discussed directly, and, through the sexual proprietariness variables, indirectly influence PC married women's experiences of verbal abuse.

The logistic regression on selection and relationship variables for cohabitors also shows that both selection and relationship controls have an important impact and that the combination of both sets of variables provided the greatest reduction in odds of verbal abuse. There are some interesting differences on the selection variables. Unlike for the other marital status groups and for the overall lifetime prevalence variable, the odds of verbal abuse actually increase with age for cohabitors. For each unit of increase in age for cohabiting women there is a 3 percent increase in odds of reporting verbal abuse. It would appear that older cohabiting women are more likely to be verbally abused than younger cohabiting women. It must be reiterated that cohabitors tend to be young and therefore it may still be primarily young men in this group who are perpetrating verbal abuse. While with the overall violence variable cohabiting women who work have reduced odds, with respect to verbal abuse working cohabiting women have increased odds. Non-PC married women who work have 21 percent higher odds, employed PC married women have 45 percent higher odds, and cohabiting women who are employed have 127 percent higher odds of verbal abuse. Thus, while the analysis of lifetime prevalence of violence indicates that, overall, female employment does not lead cohabiting men to be violent, this analysis shows that female employment is an issue for these men. Instead of venting their feelings through other means of violence, cohabiting men with an employed partner rely on verbal attacks. This may be because these women are not dependent on them and the lack of a marriage license means that it is easier for the woman to dissolve the union. While dating violence is a particularly important variable for PC marrieds in terms of overall violence, this importance is transferred to cohabitors with respect to verbal abuse. Having experienced some form of violence while dating one's current partner is linked to 328 percent increased odds of verbal abuse for cohabitors compared to an increase of 139 percent for PC marrieds and 151 percent for non-PC marrieds. Cohabitors, then, appear more likely than other marital status groups to translate violent dating experiences into verbal abuse. While married women who have experienced violence in a previous marriage or common-law union are equally less likely to report verbal abuse in their current marriage, cohabiting women who reported previous partner violence have 103 percent higher odds of verbal abuse. Consistent with the overall analysis of violence, while these women may have chosen to cohabit because of their previous violent experiences, they nevertheless have higher odds of verbal abuse than their PC and non-PC married counterparts.

Recalling that relationship factors have a larger effect than selection factors on the difference in verbal abuse between cohabitors and non-PC marrieds, it is apparent that this may largely be due to the effect of dominance. While dominance has a large impact on verbal abuse in all marital status groups, it has a particularly large impact on the verbal abuse reported by cohabitors. Cohabiting women with a partner who exhibits domineering behavior through limiting access to family income have far higher odds of verbal abuse than do cohabiting women without such a partner. While married women with a domineering partner also have higher odds than those without such a partner, the difference is not as great for marrieds as it is for cohabitors. Though the overall analysis of violence indicates that domineering men are most likely to be violent when married to nonpreviously cohabiting women, the present analysis shows that dominance, and therefore patriarchy, does have an impact on the verbal abuse reported by cohabiting women. The only other relationship variable that seems to be particularly important relative to other marital status groups is depression. Consistent with the overall analysis of violence, taking drugs or medication for depression is linked to more than double the odds of verbal abuse for cohabitors compared to PC marrieds and non-PC marrieds.

The Role of Selection and Relationship Variables in Determining Marital Status Differences in Psychological Aggression

As shown in table 7.5, consistent with the descriptive analysis, in the absence of controls PC marrieds have 77 percent higher odds of psychological aggression and cohabitors have 11 percent higher odds of psychological aggression compared to non-PC marrieds.

Table 7.5. *Results of Logistic Regressions on Psychological Aggression for Selection and Relationship Variables.*

Covariates	Marital Status $n = 8369$ Odds Ratio	Selection $n = 7281$ Odds Ratio	Relationship $n = 7986$ Odds Ratio	Full Model $n = 7022$ Odds Ratio
Marital Status				
PC Married	1.769‡	0.761	1.387*	0.661
Cohabitor	1.114	0.679†	0.848	0.953†
Non-PC married	1.000	1.000	1.000	1.000
Age		0.995		0.962‡
Age Difference				
Partner 6+ older		1.112		1.136
Partner 1-5 older		1.112		1.098
Partner 1-5 younger		1.066		1.268
Partner 6+ younger		1.419		1.835*
Same age		1.000		1.000
Woman's Education		0.919‡		0.960*
Woman's Employment				
Worked past year		1.103		1.124
Did not work past year		1.000		1.000
Partner's Employment				
Did not work		0.965		0.929
Worked past year		1.000		1.000
Woman's Income		1.000		1.000
Income Consistency		1.000*		1.000
Income Consistency Square		1.000		1.000
Education Consistency		4.802†		3.920*
Education Consistency Square		0.676*		0.710
Partner's Father Violent				
Yes/Think so		3.749‡		3.080‡
No/Do not think so		1.000		1.000
Woman's Father Violent				
Yes/Think so		1.602‡		1.585‡
No/Do not think so		1.000		1.000
Dating Violence				
Yes		3.686‡		2.682‡
No		1.000		1.000
Previous Marriage				
Yes		0.654		0.750
No		1.000		1.000

‡ $p < 0.01$; † $p < 0.05$; * $p \leq 0.10$

Table 7.5 continued.

Covariates	Marital Status n = 8369 Odds Ratio	Selection n = 7281 Odds Ratio	Relationship n = 7986 Odds Ratio	Full Model n = 7022 Odds Ratio
Previous Partner Violence				
Yes, violent		1.401		1.148
No, not violent		1.000		1.000
Region				
Atlantic		1.128		1.221
Quebec		0.686†		0.729*
Prairies		1.374†		1.440†
British Columbia		1.333*		1.310
Ontario		1.000		1.000
Duration			0.996	1.037‡
Jealousy				
Yes			2.552‡	2.005‡
No			1.000	1.000
Know Whereabouts				
Yes			1.954‡	1.839‡
No			1.000	1.000
Heavy Drinking			1.071‡	1.063‡
Frequency of Drinking			1.012*	1.010
Limit Contact				
Yes			4.517‡	4.309‡
No			1.000	1.000
Prevent Income Access				
Yes			2.745‡	3.059‡
No			1.000	1.000
Children < 25				
Yes			1.053	0.925
No			1.000	1.000
Depression				
Yes			2.301‡	2.051
No			1.000	1.000

When controls for selection variables are introduced the odds of psychological aggression for both PC marrieds and cohabitors in comparison to non-PC marrieds are reduced dramatically. The odds of psychological aggression are reduced by 91 percent for PC marrieds while cohabitors' odds are reduced by 43 percent. In both groups, with controls for selection it is observed that the odds of psychological aggression become lower than for non-PC marrieds. The selection variables that have the largest impact on psychological aggression are partner's social learning

(275 percent increased odds), dating violence (269 percent increased odds), and education consistency (32 percent decreased odds per unit increase in female to male years of education).

Controlling for relationship factors also reduces the odds of psychological aggression for both groups. However, the reduction is much less than with selection variables. With controls for relationship variables, PC marrieds still have 39 percent higher odds of psychological aggression compared to non-PC marrieds. Cohabitors have 15 percent lower odds compared to non-PC marrieds with controls for relationship factors but it must be reiterated that this reduction is not as great as when only selection factors are controlled. While the relationship variables are not as important as selection variables in determining marital status differences, several are nevertheless important determinants of psychological aggression. Social isolation through a respondent having her contact with family and friends limited is linked to 352 percent increased odds of psychological aggression. As well, women who are dominated through having access to income limited by their partner have 175 percent increased odds of psychological aggression. Sexual proprietariness, particularly through jealousy (155 percent increased odds), and depression (130 percent increased odds) are also linked to this form of violence.

Interestingly, controlling for both selection and relationship factors provides the greatest reduction in odds for both groups. In the full model, PC marrieds have 34 percent lower odds and cohabitors have 41 percent lower odds of psychological aggression compared to non-PC marrieds. For both groups, selection factors appear to be more powerful than relationship variables in accounting for the higher odds compared to non-PC marrieds. However, relationship factors, in combination with selection factors, also clearly play a role in terms of understanding why those who cohabit have higher rates of psychological aggression. An inspection of both selection and relationship variables in the full model shows that the majority of variables tend to decline somewhat in importance in comparison to when they are entered as separate models. However, in the full model women having a partner who is six or more years younger now have 84 percent higher odds of psychological aggression in comparison to those with a partner who is of the same age. The duration variable also becomes significant in the full model such that for every year that a couple is together there is a 4 percent increase in the odds of psychological aggression. Finally, the odds of psychological aggression for women with a dominating partner are also increased such that women with a partner who prevents her access to family income now have 206 percent higher odds of this form of violence than do women without such a partner. Clearly, links between selection and relationship variables and psychological aggression need to be more clearly specified.

A quick overview of the results of the logistic regressions in table 7.6 shows that the majority of the variables that have a particularly large impact on psychological aggression belong to the PC married category. Consistent with the overall analysis of violence, men whose father had been violent and who are the husbands of PC married women have far higher odds of psychological aggression than cohabitors and non-PC marrieds. Social learning by PC married men is linked to increases in odds of psychological aggression that are more than double those for non-PC marrieds and eighteen times those for cohabitors. While the overall analysis of violence indicates that woman's social learning has the smallest impact on PC marrieds it, in fact, has the largest impact on PC marrieds with respect to psychological aggression. PC married women whose father had been violent have higher odds of psychological aggression than their counterparts whose father had not been violent and this is at a level more than three times that of non-PC marrieds and more than ten times that of cohabitors. This is compared to an increase in odds of 64 percent for non-PC married women and only 23 percent for cohabitors. As well, the results on psychological aggression for previous partner violence are in contradiction to the overall analysis of violence. PC married women who experienced violence by a previous partner have 113 percent higher odds of psychological aggression while cohabitors in the same category have only 22 percent increased odds.

Given that the largest reductions in odds occur when the full model is entered in the logistic regressions for selection and relationship factors, it is not surprising that there are a few relationship variables that have a large impact on odds of psychological aggression for PC marrieds. PC married women with a partner who is jealous have 173 percent higher odds of psychological aggression than their counterparts without a jealous partner. Non-PC married women with a jealous husband have 107 percent increased odds and cohabitors with such a partner have 45 percent increased odds of psychological aggression. It seems that jealousy plays an important role in the psychological aggression experienced by PC marrieds. Interestingly, while heavy drinking did not have a large impact on the overall violence variable, it does have an important impact on the odds of psychological aggression for PC marrieds. For each additional occasion in the month prior to the study that a PC married woman's partner consumed five or more drinks, there is a 13 percent increase in the odds of psychological aggression. It appears that frequent

Table 7.6. *Results of Logistic Regressions on Psychological Aggression for Marital Status Subgroups.*

Covariates	Cohabitor $n = 862$ Odds Ratio	PC Married $n = 468$ Odds Ratio	Non-PC Married $n = 5682$ Odds Ratio
Age	0.880‡	0.958	0.980
Age Difference			
Partner 6+ older	1.683	1.124	1.056
Partner 1-5 older	1.818	1.472	1.031
Partner 1-5 younger	1.706	1.291	1.278
Partner 6+ younger	4.479	0.453	1.839
Same age	1.000	1.000	1.000
Woman's Education	1.087	0.867*	0.955*
Woman's Employment			
Worked past year	0.577	0.926	1.338*
Did not work	1.000	1.000	1.000
Partner's Employment			
Did not work	0.411	0.725	0.968
Worked past year	1.000	1.000	1.000
Woman's Income	1.000	1.000	1.000
Income Consistency	1.000	1.000	1.000‡
Income Consistency Square	1.000	1.000	1.000‡
Education Consistency	1.878	0.930	8.736†
Education Consistency Square	0.721	1.258	0.560*
Partner's Father Violent			
Yes/Think so	1.317	6.771‡	3.367‡
No/Do not think so	1.000	1.000	1.000
Woman's Father Violent			
Yes/Think so	1.233	3.317‡	1.637‡
No/Do not think so	1.000	1.000	1.000
Dating Violence			
Yes	2.283*	2.557	2.891‡
No	1.000	1.000	1.000
Previous Marriage			
Yes	1.127	0.538	0.122
No	1.000	1.000	1.000
Previous Partner Violence			
Yes, violent	1.222	2.128*	0.770
No, not violent	1.000	1.000	1.000

‡ p < 0.01; † p < 0.05; * p ≤ 0.10

Table 7.6 continued.

Covariates	Cohabitor n = 862	PC Married n = 468	Non-PC Married n = 5682
	Odds Ratio	Odds Ratio	Odds Ratio
Region			
Atlantic	2.338	2.333	1.107
Quebec	0.767	1.430	0.725*
Prairies	2.401*	2.367	1.282
British Columbia	2.118	0.733	1.286
Ontario	1.000	1.000	1.000
Duration	1.206‡	1.054	1.021
Jealousy			
Yes	1.453	2.731*	2.069‡
No	1.000	1.000	1.000
Know Whereabouts			
Yes	1.874	0.558	2.182‡
No	1.000	1.000	1.000
Heavy Drinking	1.067	1.130†	1.070‡
Frequency of Drinking	1.037	1.010	1.006
Limit Contact			
Yes	3.320†	2.661	4.979‡
No	1.000	1.000	1.000
Prevent Income Access			
Yes	3.944*	7.167*	2.815‡
No	1.000	1.000	1.000
Children < 25			
Yes	0.925	1.141	0.956
No	1.000	1.000	1.000
Depression			
Yes	4.084†	0.719	2.116‡
No	1.000	1.000	1.000

heavy drinking is particularly linked to PC married men's threats to hit their partner with a fist or something else that could hurt them. Finally, while dominance is again positively related to the dependent variable for all marital status groups, with respect to psychological aggression it is most strongly linked to odds reported by PC married women. PC married women with a domineering partner have 617 percent higher odds of psychological aggression compared to a 294 percent increase for cohabitors and a 182 percent increase for non-PC marrieds.

The logistic regressions on selection and relationship factors show that for cohabitors it is the combination of both sets of controls that have the greatest impact, with selection variables having a larger impact on the odds of psychological aggression relative to relationship variables. The only selection variable that stands out as having a particularly large impact for cohabitors relative to other marital status groups is a woman's age. For each one year increase in woman's age, there is a 12 percent decrease in odds of psychological aggression for cohabitors, compared to a 4 percent decrease for PC marrieds and a 2 percent decrease for non-PC marrieds. For cohabitors, psychological aggression seems particularly likely to occur among those who are young. As with the selection variables, there is only one relationship variable that stands out as being particularly linked to the odds of psychological aggression for cohabitors. Depressed cohabiting women have 308 percent higher odds of reporting having experienced psychological aggression during their relationship, compared to a 117 percent increase for depressed non-PC marrieds and a 38 percent decrease for depressed PC marrieds. Consistent with the analyses of the lifetime prevalence of violence and verbal abuse variables, there is something about being a depressed cohabiting woman that is particularly linked to the odds of reporting psychological aggression.

The Role of Selection and Relationship Variables in Determining Marital Status Differences in Minor Physical Assault

The results of the logistic regressions in table 7.7 show that without controls both PC marrieds and cohabitors have significantly higher odds than non-PC marrieds of the most common form of violence reported by Canadian women. As well, consistent with the nonphysical forms of violence already discussed, PC marrieds have higher odds (43 percent) of minor physical assault relative to non-PC marrieds than do cohabitors (25 percent).

With controls for selection variables, the odds of minor physical assault are reduced to virtually identical levels for the two groups in comparison to non-PC marrieds. PC marrieds have 7 percent higher odds and cohabitors have 8 percent higher odds of minor physical assault than do non-PC marrieds. Selection factors, however, account for a greater portion of the odds for PC marrieds than cohabitors. It appears that the strongest selection variables in predicting the odds of minor physical assault are partner's social learning (187 percent increased odds), dating violence (151 percent increased odds), and education consistency (31

Table 7.7. *Results of Logistic Regressions on Minor Physical Assault for Selection and Relationship Variables.*

	Marital Status	Selection	Relationship	Full Model
	$n = 8368$	$n = 7282$	$n = 7985$	$n = 7023$
Covariates	Odds Ratio	Odds Ratio	Odds Ratio	Odds Ratio
Marital Status				
PC Married	1.433†	1.073	1.364†	1.094
Cohabitor	1.246†	1.077	1.221	1.171
Non-PC married	1.000	1.000	1.000	1.000
Age		0.996		0.965‡
Age Difference				
Partner 6+ older		0.990		1.011
Partner 1-5 older		0.980		0.956
Partner 1-5 younger		0.914		1.062
Partner 6+ younger		1.374		1.778†
Same age		1.000		1.000
Woman's Education		0.949‡		0.994
Woman's Employment				
Worked past year		0.934		0.873
Did not work past year		1.000		1.000
Partner's Employment				
Did not work		0.915		0.847
Worked past year		1.000		1.000
Woman's Income		1.000		1.000†
Income Consistency		1.000		1.000
Income Consistency Square		1.000		1.000
Education Consistency		0.637		0.372*
Education Consistency Square		1.305*		1.525†
Partner's Father Violent				
Yes/Think so		2.873‡		2.390‡
No/Do not think so		1.000		1.000
Woman's Father Violent				
Yes/Think so		1.586‡		1.538‡
No/Do not think so		1.000		1.000
Dating Violence				
Yes		2.508‡		1.787‡
No		1.000		1.000
Previous Marriage				
Yes		0.718		0.774
No		1.000		1.000

‡ $p < 0.01$; † $p < 0.05$; * $p \leq 0.10$

Table 7.7 continued.

	Marital Status	Selection	Relationship	Full Model
	$n = 8368$	$n = 7282$	$n = 7985$	$n = 7023$
Covariates	Odds Ratio	Odds Ratio	Odds Ratio	Odds Ratio
Previous Partner Violence				
Yes, violent		1.589†		1.376*
No, not violent		1.000		1.000
Region				
Atlantic		0.922		0.921
Quebec		0.638‡		0.643‡
Prairies		1.102		1.091
British Columbia		1.328†		1.363†
Ontario		1.000		1.000
Duration			1.006*	1.044‡
Jealousy				
Yes			1.940‡	1.623‡
No			1.000	1.000
Know Whereabouts				
Yes			2.323‡	2.317‡
No			1.000	1.000
Heavy Drinking			1.067‡	1.048‡
Frequency of Drinking			1.007	1.004
Limit Contact				
Yes			3.962‡	3.798‡
No			1.000	1.000
Prevent Income Access				
Yes			2.156‡	2.384‡
No			1.000	1.000
Children < 25				
Yes			1.531‡	1.420‡
No			1.000	1.000
Depression				
Yes			1.851‡	1.735†
No			1.000	1.000

percent increased odds per unit increase in female to male years of education).

The relationship variables also reduce the odds for both groups, though not nearly as much as do the selection variables. Controlling for relationship variables leads to a 9 percent decrease in odds of minor physical assault for PC marrieds and a 3 percent decrease for cohabitors compared to non-PC marrieds. Despite their lack of effect in terms of differentiating martial status groups, most of the relationship factors do significantly affect the odds of minor physical assault with social isolation (296 percent increased odds), sexual proprietariness as measured by partner insisting on knowing whereabouts (132 percent increased odds), and dominance (116 percent increased odds) being particularly powerful variables.

In the full model the odds of minor physical assault are reduced for both marital status groups. However, in neither group do the odds reach the level found when controlling for selection factors alone. Clearly, in determining marital status differences in minor physical assault, it is selection factors that are key. With respect to the odds for the selection and relationship variables in the full model, there are only two significant changes. First, the odds of minor physical assault for women with a partner who is six or more years younger than they are more than doubled such that they now have 78 percent higher odds in comparison to women whose partners are the same age as they. Second, the odds for dating violence are nearly halved such that women who experienced violence while dating their partner now have 79 percent higher odds of minor physical assault than women who did not report experiencing dating violence. The fact that there are few such changes in the full model may be further indicative of the central importance of the selection variables in determining marital status differences in minor physical assault.

Since it is selection factors that are key to understanding marital status differences in minor physical assault, it is especially interesting to see how the odds of this component of violence differ across selection variables for the marital status groups. The results of the logistic regressions in table 7.8 show that while, similar to the overall analysis, woman's age is negatively related to minor physical assault, the relationship between this variable and minor physical assault appears to be even stronger for cohabitors in comparison to PC marrieds. For each year increase in age, the odds of minor physical assault decrease 1 percent for non-PC marrieds, 5 percent for PC marrieds, and 9 percent for cohabitors. Particularly among cohabitors, then, it is the young who are experiencing minor physical assault. Age heterogamy is also related to minor physical assault for all groups. Consistent with the overall analysis, a woman having a partner who is six or more years younger than she is most strongly linked to increased odds of minor physical assault. Cohabiting women with a much younger partner have 308 percent higher odds of minor physical assault than their cohabiting counterparts with partners of the same age. This is compared to PC married women in the same category who have 214 percent higher odds and non-PC married women

Table 7.8. *Results of Logistic Regressions on Minor Physical Assault for Marital Status Subgroups.*

	Cohabitor $n = 863$	PC Married $n = 478$	Non-PC Married $n = 5682$
Covariates	Odds Ratio	Odds Ratio	Odds Ratio
Age	0.907‡	0.953	0.987
Age Difference			
Partner 6+ older	1.035	2.695	0.953
Partner 1-5 older	1.252	2.013	0.913
Partner 1-5 younger	1.497	2.120	0.986
Partner 6+ younger	4.078†	3.142	1.327
Same age	1.000	1.000	1.000
Woman's Education	1.034	1.063	0.980
Woman's Employment			
Worked past year	0.677	0.699	0.914
Did not work	1.000	1.000	1.000
Partner's Employment			
Did not work	0.936	0.236*	0.810
Worked past year	1.000	1.000	1.000
Woman's Income	1.000	1.000	1.000†
Income Consistency	1.000	1.000*	1.000
Income Consistency Square	1.000	1.000*	1.000
Education Consistency	1.051	0.015*	0.437
Education Consistency Square	0.995	4.754†	1.462†
Partner's Father Violent			
Yes/Think so	1.446	4.093‡	2.597‡
No/Do not think so	1.000	1.000	1.000
Woman's Father Violent			
Yes/Think so	1.634*	2.200†	1.587‡
No/Do not think so	1.000	1.000	1.000
Dating Violence			
Yes	0.903	2.483	2.065‡
No	1.000	1.000	1.000
Previous Marriage			
Yes	1.083	0.932	0.030
No	1.000	1.000	1.000
Previous Partner Violence			
Yes, violent	1.608	1.615	1.037
No, not violent	1.000	1.000	1.000

‡ p < 0.01; † p < 0.05; * p ≤ 0.10

Table 7.8 continued.

Covariates	Cohabitor $n = 863$ Odds Ratio	PC Married $n = 478$ Odds Ratio	Non-PC Married $n = 5682$ Odds Ratio
Region			
Atlantic	1.380	2.185	0.819
Quebec	0.665	0.261†	0.672‡
Prairies	1.167	1.020	1.084
British Columbia	0.961	0.810	1.532‡
Ontario	1.000	1.000	1.000
Duration	1.134‡	1.111†	1.025†
Jealousy			
Yes	1.113	4.252†	1.604†
No	1.000	1.000	1.000
Know Whereabouts			
Yes	3.857‡	0.543	2.440‡
No	1.000	1.000	1.000
Heavy Drinking	1.048	1.036	1.056‡
Frequency of Drinking	1.013	1.044†	1.000
Limit Contact			
Yes	5.088‡	6.265†	3.786‡
No	1.000	1.000	1.000
Prevent Income Access			
Yes	0.987	0.808	3.088‡
No	1.000	1.000	1.000
Children < 25			
Yes	0.887	2.188*	1.585‡
No	1.000	1.000	1.000
Depression			
Yes	2.512*	0.608	1.933†
No	1.000	1.000	1.000

who have 33 percent higher odds. Thus, cohabiting women with a much younger partner are particularly vulnerable to minor physical assault at some time during their relationship. Interestingly, while the overall analysis of violence indicates that the other categories of age heterogamy are not positively related to violence for cohabitors, with respect to minor physical assault there is a positive link to any category of age heterogamy. However, the odds for cohabitors still do not meet those of PC marrieds. For PC marrieds any age heterogamy is linked to at least a 101 percent increase in odds of minor physical assault. Clearly, there is something about age heterogamy generally that increases the odds of minor physical assault for cohabitors and particularly for PC marrieds.

While women's age and having a much younger partner are particularly important determinants of the odds of minor physical assault for cohabitors, education consistency, social learning, and dating violence seem to be important selection variables in determining the odds for PC marrieds. Education consistency has no effect on the odds of minor physical assault for cohabitors. For non-PC marrieds, for each unit increase in female to male years of education there is a 46 percent increase in the odds of minor physical assault. For PC marrieds, on the other hand, each unit increase in female to male years of education is linked to a 375 percent increase in odds of minor physical assault. With respect to partner's and respondent's social learning, PC marrieds exposed to the effects of social learning have nearly twice the odds of minor physical assault compared to the next highest marital status group. PC married men whose father had been violent have 309 percent higher odds of perpetrating minor physical assault and PC married women whose father had been violent have 120 percent higher odds of experiencing minor physical assault. Similar to the analysis of lifetime prevalence of violence, dating violence has the largest impact on the odds for PC marrieds. PC marrieds who experienced violence while dating their partner have 148 percent higher odds of minor physical assault and non-PC marrieds have 107 percent higher odds. Interestingly, cohabiting women who experienced violence while dating their partner actually have 10 percent reduced odds of minor physical assault. As will be shown in table 7.12, this is also the case with respect to severe physical assault. Cohabiting women who experience dating violence have 25 percent reduced odds of severe physical assault. One possible explanation for these findings is that cohabiting women who did not report violence while dating their partner dated for a shorter period of time prior to moving in with their partner. For instance, there may have been more pressure from these men to start cohabiting, and there would be less opportunity for acts of violence to occur while dating. In this case it is not surprising that these are also women who are reporting physical assaults. However, since the duration of dating is not recorded in the VAWS, this hypothesis cannot be verified.

The results of the separate logistic regressions for relationship variables tend to be consistent with the results of the regressions on lifetime prevalence of violence. PC married men who are jealous have far higher odds compared to jealous cohabiting and non-PC married men. Indeed, jealous PC married men have 325 percent increased odds of perpetrating minor physical assault. Cohabiting men who keep tabs on their partner, on the other hand, have the highest odds of minor physical assault. These men have 286 percent higher odds of perpetrating this form of violence compared to the group with the next highest odds, non-PC marrieds, who have 144 percent increased odds. Similar to the overall analysis of violence, social isolation has a large impact on the odds of violence for all three marital status groups, though the largest impact is on PC marrieds who have 527 percent increased odds of minor physical assault. As well, domineering behavior through limiting access to family income has the largest impact for non-PC marrieds with an increase in odds of 209 percent. Also consistent with the overall violence analysis, the presence of children is linked to the greatest increase in odds for PC marrieds who have 119 percent higher odds of minor physical assault while having children is again shown to reduce the odds of violence for cohabitors. Finally, depression is again linked to the greatest increase in odds of violence for cohabitors who have 151 percent higher odds of reporting minor physical assault.

The Role of Selection and Relationship Variables in Determining Marital Status Differences in Moderate Physical Assault

An inspection of the first model in table 7.9 shows that, in the absence of controls, both PC marrieds and cohabitors have significantly higher odds of moderate physical assault compared to non-PC marrieds. Consistent with the descriptive analysis, it is apparent that, with physical assaults that are beyond that which is minor in severity, cohabitors now have higher odds than do PC marrieds relative to non-PC marrieds. With controls for selection variables, the odds of moderate physical assault are reduced by 90 percent for PC marrieds such that they now have 33 percent lower odds of experiencing this form of violence than non-PC marrieds. Selection variables are clearly very important for understanding the higher odds of moderate physical assault of PC marrieds compared to non-PC marrieds. The odds of moderate physical assault are also reduced substantially, by 57 percent, for cohabitors compared to non-PC marrieds. However, cohabitors still have 10 percent greater odds of moderate physical assault compared to non-PC marrieds. In terms of the selection variables, it appears that dating violence (372 percent increased odds), partner's social learning (261 percent increased odds), and a woman hav-

Table 7.9. *Results of Logistic Regressions on Moderate Physical Assault for Selection and Relationship Variables.*

Covariates	Marital Status $n = 8368$ Odds Ratio	Selection $n = 7281$ Odds Ratio	Relationship $n = 7985$ Odds Ratio	Full Model $n = 7022$ Odds Ratio
Marital Status				
PC Married	1.574†	0.666	1.162	0.507*
Cohabitor	1.667‡	1.101	1.349	0.893
Non-PC married	1.000	1.000	1.000	1.000
Age		0.992		0.946‡
Age Difference				
Partner 6+ older		0.807		0.738
Partner 1-5 older		0.903		0.858
Partner 1-5 younger		0.644*		0.705
Partner 6+ younger		1.010		1.550
Same age		1.000		1.000
Woman's Education		0.895‡		0.947†
Woman's Employment				
Worked past year		0.876		0.712*
Did not work past year		1.000		1.000
Partner's Employment				
Did not work		0.993		0.865
Worked past year		1.000		1.000
Woman's Income		1.000		1.000
Income Consistency		1.000*		1.000‡
Income Consistency Square		1.000†		1.000‡
Education Consistency		1.381		0.564
Education Consistency Square		1.080		1.419
Partner's Father Violent				
Yes/Think so		3.611‡		2.887‡
No/Do not think so		1.000		1.000
Woman's Father Violent				
Yes/Think so		1.391†		1.363*
No/Do not think so		1.000		1.000
Dating Violence				
Yes		4.717‡		3.750‡
No		1.000		1.000
Previous Marriage				
Yes		0.553*		0.668
No		1.000		1.000

‡ p < 0.01; † p < 0.05; * p ≤ 0.10

Table 7.9 continued.

	Marital Status	Selection	Relationship	Full Model
	n = 8368	*n* = 7281	*n* = 7985	*n* = 7022
Covariates	Odds Ratio	Odds Ratio	Odds Ratio	Odds Ratio
Previous Partner Violence				
Yes, violent		1.983†		1.983†
No, not violent		1.000		1.000
Region				
Atlantic		0.857		0.886
Quebec		0.741*		0.753
Prairies		0.956		0.874
British Columbia		1.259		1.164
Ontario		1.000		1.000
Duration			1.001	1.053‡
Jealousy				
Yes			2.549‡	1.813‡
No			1.000	1.000
Know Whereabouts				
Yes			2.009‡	2.150‡
No			1.000	1.000
Heavy Drinking			1.069‡	1.057‡
Frequency of Drinking			1.005	0.999
Limit Contact				
Yes			4.274‡	3.724‡
No			1.000	1.000
Prevent Income Access				
Yes			2.654‡	2.538‡
No			1.000	1.000
Children < 25				
Yes			1.076	0.907
No			1.000	1.000
Depression				
Yes			0.971	0.697
No			1.000	1.000

ing experienced violence by a previous husband or common-law partner (98 percent increased odds) are particularly associated with increased odds of moderate physical assault.

Controlling for relationship factors also results in a reduction in odds for both groups. There is a 41 percent decrease in the odds for PC marrieds and a 32 percent decrease in odds for cohabitors compared to non-PC marrieds. While the effect of the relationship factors is not as dramatic as the selection factors, relationship factors do play a role in understanding marital status differences in moderate physical assault. With respect to the relationship variables, social isolation (327 percent increased odds), dominance (167 percent increased odds), and jealousy (155 percent increased odds) appear to be particularly important links to understanding moderate physical assault.

The full model is witness to the greatest reduction in the odds for both groups. PC marrieds now have nearly half the odds of non-PC marrieds in terms of experiencing moderate physical assault. With controls for selection and relationship factors cohabitors have 11 percent lower odds of moderate physical assault than do non-PC marrieds. Clearly, it is the combination of both selection and relationship variables that provides the greatest explanatory power for understanding marital status differences in moderate physical assault. Among the changes in odds of covariates from the selection and relationship models to the full model, the largest change appears to involve the education consistency variable. In the selection model, with a one-unit increase in the ratio of female to male years of education there is an 8 percent increase in odds of moderate physical assault. In the full model the odds ratio for this variable increases to 42 percent. Controlling for one or more relationship variables, then, leads to a larger impact of the education consistency variable. As in the analyses of other types of violence with similar overall results, the finding of the importance of both selection and relationship variables is indicative that the links between these two types of variables must be specified to enhance understanding of marital status differences in moderate physical assault.

The importance of the selection and relationship variables established in the previous logistic regressions is affirmed by the observation that a number of both selection and relationship variables in table 7.10 are linked to increased odds of violence for particular marital status groups. Again, young cohabitors have far higher odds of experiencing this form of violence. For each year increase in a cohabiting woman's age, her odds of experiencing moderate physical assault are reduced by 16 percent. For PC marrieds there is virtually no change in odds with age and for non-PC marrieds the odds are reduced by only 2 percent per year. Cohabiting women who are six or more years older than their partner also face high odds of moderate physical assault. These women have 376 percent increased odds of experiencing this form of violence. Cohabitors who experienced violence by a previous partner also have particularly high odds of violence. The difference in the odds of moderate physical

Table 7.10. *Results of Logistic Regressions on Moderate Physical Assault for Marital Status Subgroups.*

Covariates	Cohabitor n = 862 Odds Ratio	PC Married n = 478 Odds Ratio	Non-PC Married n = 5682 Odds Ratio
Region			
Atlantic	1.380	2.185	0.819
Age	0.839‡	1.007	0.977
Age Difference			
Partner 6+ older	0.847	1.297	0.661
Partner 1-5 older	1.673	1.946	0.775
Partner 1-5 younger	0.876	0.371	0.698
Partner 6+ younger	4.758	0.001	1.799
Same age	1.000	1.000	1.000
Woman's Education	1.041	1.137	0.916†
Woman's Employment			
Worked past year	0.338†	0.716	0.914
Did not work	1.000	1.000	1.000
Partner's Employment			
Did not work	1.080	0.116	0.863
Worked past year	1.000	1.000	1.000
Woman's Income	1.000	1.000	1.000
Income Consistency	1.000	1.000*	1.000†
Income Consistency Square	1.000	1.000*	1.000†
Education Consistency	0.403	0.001*	1.575
Education Consistency Square	1.340	9.404*	1.056
Partner's Father Violent			
Yes/Think so	3.053†	1.819	3.232‡
No/Do not think so	1.000	1.000	1.000
Woman's Father Violent			
Yes/Think so	0.389*	6.421†	1.516†
No/Do not think so	1.000	1.000	1.000
Dating Violence			
Yes	1.338	18.922†	6.091‡
No	1.000	1.000	1.000
Previous Marriage			
Yes	1.105	1.209	0.065
No	1.000	1.000	1.000
Previous Partner Violence			
Yes, violent	6.040†	3.329	0.927
No, not violent	1.000	1.000	1.000

‡ p < 0.01; † p < 0.05; * p ≤ 0.10

Table 7.10 continued.

Covariates	Cohabitor n = 862	PC Married n = 478	Non-PC Married n = 5682
	Odds Ratio	Odds Ratio	Odds Ratio
Region			
Atlantic	0.627	2.958	0.867
Quebec	0.476	1.145	0.839
Prairies	1.184	0.397	0.893
British Columbia	1.026	1.432	1.179
Ontario	1.000	1.000	1.000
Duration	1.188†	1.134*	1.021
Jealousy			
Yes	3.768†	1.613	1.542*
No	1.000	1.000	1.000
Know Whereabouts			
Yes	1.285	2.858	2.523‡
No	1.000	1.000	1.000
Heavy Drinking	1.166‡	1.139	1.041†
Frequency of Drinking	0.966	0.961	1.004
Limit Contact			
Yes	3.656†	12.673†	3.865‡
No	1.000	1.000	1.000
Prevent Income Access			
Yes	2.266	3.664	3.107‡
No	1.000	1.000	1.000
Children < 25			
Yes	0.838	2.037	0.938
No	1.000	1.000	1.000
Depression			
Yes	0.839	0.214	0.539
No	1.000	1.000	1.000

assault for cohabiting women with past experiences of partner violence are more than double those for PC marrieds and seventy-two times those for non-PC marrieds.

Some selection variables are also linked to particularly high odds for PC marrieds. As PC married women have more relative educational resources, they also face higher odds of this form of violence. For each unit increase in female to male education, a PC married woman's odds of moderate physical assault increase by 840 percent. As well, growing up with a violent father is particularly linked to moderate physical assault for PC married women. These women face 542 percent increased odds of moderate physical assault. Finally, in terms of selection variables, PC married women who reported experiencing violence while dating their partner face far higher odds of moderate physical assault during their relationship.

With respect to relationship variables, contrary to all of the other forms of violence it is cohabiting women with a jealous partner who have the highest odds of moderate physical assault. These women have more than four times higher odds of experiencing moderate physical assault compared to PC marrieds and non-PC marrieds. A cohabiting women whose partner consumed alcohol heavily in the month prior to the study also has high odds of this form of violence. For each additional occasion that a cohabiting woman's partner consumed alcohol heavily, there is a 17 percent increase in the odds of moderate physical assault.

A partner's heavy drinking also seems to have an important impact for PC marrieds with an increase of 14 percent per unit increase. Social isolation is also strongly linked to increased odds of this form of violence for PC marrieds. PC married women with a partner who tries to limit her contact with family or friends have far higher odds of moderate physical assault. Finally, while having children is linked to reduced odds of moderate physical assault for both cohabitors and non-PC marrieds, PC married women with children have 104 percent higher odds of experiencing this form of violence.

The Role of Selection and Relationship Variables in Determining Marital Status Differences in Severe Physical Assault

As with moderate physical assault, the results of the logistic regressions in table 7.11 show that without controls PC marrieds and cohabitors have higher odds of severe physical assault than do non-PC marrieds. Moreover, consistent with the descriptive analysis it is cohabitors who have the greatest odds of severe physical assault relative to non-PC marrieds.

With controls for selection variables, the odds of severe physical assault for PC marrieds are reduced by 79 percent and the odds for cohabitors are reduced by 69 percent compared to non-PC marrieds. In this model cohabitors have 30 percent lower odds and PC marrieds have 49 percent lower odds of severe physical assault compared to non-PC marrieds. It appears that partner's social learning (496 percent increased odds), dating violence (398 percent increased odds), experiencing vio-

Table 7.11. *Results of Logistic Regressions on Severe Physical Assault for Selection and Relationship Variables.*

Covariates	Marital Status $n = 8369$ Odds Ratio	Selection $n = 7282$ Odds Ratio	Relationship $n = 7986$ Odds Ratio	Full Model $n = 7023$ Odds Ratio
Marital Status				
PC Married	1.296	0.508	0.881	0.395*
Cohabitor	1.394*	0.699	0.958	0.541*
Non-PC married	1.000	1.000	1.000	1.000
Age		0.998		0.946‡
Age Difference				
Partner 6+ older		1.060		0.923
Partner 1-5 older		0.840		0.688
Partner 1-5 younger		0.690		0.618
Partner 6+ younger		2.145*		2.946†
Same age		1.000		1.000
Woman's Education		0.918‡		0.972
Woman's Employment				
Worked past year		0.868		0.673*
Did not work past year		1.000		1.000
Partner's Employment				
Did not work		0.991		0.842
Worked past year		1.000		1.000
Woman's Income		1.000		1.000
Income Consistency		1.000		1.000†
Income Consistency Square		1.000		1.000
Education Consistency		1.529		0.488
Education Consistency Square		0.984		1.427
Partner's Father Violent				
Yes/Think so		5.962‡		4.656‡
No/Do not think so		1.000		1.000
Woman's Father Violent				
Yes/Think so		1.254		1.285
No/Do not think so		1.000		1.000
Dating Violence				
Yes		4.980‡		3.318‡
No		1.000		1.000
Previous Marriage				
Yes		1.112		1.452
No		1.000		1.000

‡ $p < 0.01$; † $p < 0.05$; * $p \leq 0.10$

Table 7.11 continued.

	Marital Status	Selection	Relationship	Full Model
	n = 8369	*n* = 7282	*n* = 7986	*n* = 7023
Covariates	Odds Ratio	Odds Ratio	Odds Ratio	Odds Ratio
Previous Partner Violence				
Yes, violent		2.539†		1.853*
No, not violent		1.000		1.000
Region				
Atlantic		0.820		0.780
Quebec		0.660*		0.683
Prairies		0.959		0.868
British Columbia		1.284		1.157
Ontario		1.000		1.000
Duration			0.993	1.051†
Jealousy				
Yes			2.829‡	2.260‡
No			1.000	1.000
Know Whereabouts				
Yes			1.358	1.417
No			1.000	1.000
Heavy Drinking			1.043†	1.033*
Frequency of Drinking			1.021†	1.022†
Limit Contact				
Yes			7.148‡	5.668‡
No			1.000	1.000
Prevent Income Access				
Yes			2.127†	2.686‡
No			1.000	1.000
Children < 25				
Yes			0.990	0.802
No			1.000	1.000
Depression				
Yes			1.712*	1.182
No			1.000	1.000

lence by a previous partner (154 percent increased odds), and a respondent having a partner six or more years younger than she (115 percent increased odds) are particularly important selection variables for understanding severe physical assault.

Controlling for relationship factors also leads to a reduction in odds for both groups, though the reduction is not as great as that which occurred in the selection model. In the relationship model PC marrieds have 12 percent lower odds and cohabitors have 4 percent lower odds of severe physical assault compared to non-PC marrieds. Social isolation (615 percent increased odds), jealousy (183 percent increased odds), and dominance (113 percent increased odds) are the relationship variables that have the greatest impact on severe physical assault.

While both the selection and the relationship models account for marital status differences in odds of severe physical assault, it is in the full model where one can see the greatest reduction in odds for both groups. Controlling for both selection and relationship factors PC marrieds have 60 percent lower odds and cohabitors have 46 percent lower odds of severe physical assault compared to non-PC marrieds. While the selection model contributed to a greater reduction than the relationship model, it is evident that a combination of both selection and relationship variables play an important role in understanding marital status differences in severe physical assault. As with moderate physical assault, there is one particular point of interest regarding the changes in odds of covariates from the selection and relationship models to the full model. Again, the largest change appears to involve the education consistency variable. In the selection model, with a one unit increase in the ratio of female to male years of education there is a 2 percent decrease in odds of moderate physical assault. In the full model this changes such that there is a 42 percent increase in odds with a one unit increase in the ratio of female to male years of education. Controlling for one or more relationship variables leads to a larger impact of the education consistency variable and changes its direction. Again, the links between selection and relationship variables need to be investigated further.

As one would expect based on the previous logistic regressions on severe physical assault, there are several important marital status differences on both selection and relationship variables. Table 7.12 shows that respondent's age has an important impact for both cohabitors and PC marrieds. As with moderate physical assault, young cohabitors have high odds of violence. For each year increase in a cohabiting woman's age, her odds of experiencing severe physical assault are reduced by 18 percent. Surprisingly, the effect for PC marrieds is the same but in the opposite direction. Older PC married women have higher odds of experiencing severe physical assault than do younger PC married women. An inspection of the duration variable indicates that this, however, does not mean that as a PC married woman gets older she will face an increased likelihood of severe physical assault. Rather, the odds of this form of violence decrease slightly from the beginning of the relationship with the passage of time. There seems to be something about being an older PC

Table 7.12. *Results of Logistic Regressions on Severe Physical Assault for Marital Status Subgroups.*

Covariates	Cohabitor $n = 863$ Odds Ratio	PC Married $n = 478$ Odds Ratio	Non-PC Married $n = 5682$ Odds Ratio
Age	0.824†	1.181	0.959†
Age Difference			
Partner 6+ older	0.322	0.872	0.964
Partner 1-5 older	1.017	0.062	0.661
Partner 1-5 younger	1.597	0.045	0.513*
Partner 6+ younger	8.815*	0.951	3.428†
Same age	1.000	1.000	1.000
Woman's Education	0.991	0.610	0.978
Woman's Employment			
Worked past year	0.278*	2.966	0.854
Did not work	1.000	1.000	1.000
Partner's Employment			
Did not work	0.481	0.008†	1.047
Worked past year	1.000	1.000	1.000
Woman's Income	1.000	1.000*	1.000
Income Consistency	1.000	1.001*	1.000*
Income Consistency Square	1.000	1.000	1.000
Education Consistency	0.485	0.145	1.154
Education Consistency Square	1.719	3.691	1.011
Partner's Father Violent			
Yes/Think so	2.739	2.810	5.978‡
No/Do not think so	1.000	1.000	1.000
Woman's Father Violent			
Yes/Think so	0.759	5.689	1.385
No/Do not think so	1.000	1.000	1.000
Dating Violence			
Yes	0.747	17.057	4.860‡
No	1.000	1.000	1.000
Previous Marriage			
Yes	3.217	0.224	0.075
No	1.000	1.000	1.000
Previous Partner Violence			
Yes, violent	58.969*	4.978	1.400
No, not violent	1.000	1.000	1.000

‡ p < 0.01; † p < 0.05; * p ≤ 0.10

Table 7.12 continued.

Covariates	Cohabitor $n = 863$ Odds Ratio	PC Married $n = 478$ Odds Ratio	Non-PC Married $n = 5682$ Odds Ratio
Region			
Atlantic	0.301	191.890*	0.757
Quebec	0.261	118.898	0.829
Prairies	0.993	26.463	0.729
British Columbia	1.641	59.722*	0.935
Ontario	1.000	1.000	1.000
Duration	1.291‡	0.973	1.038*
Jealousy			
Yes	2.558	6.210	2.080†
No	1.000	1.000	1.000
Know Whereabouts			
Yes	3.438*	0.391	1.278
No	1.000	1.000	1.000
Heavy Drinking	1.141†	1.076	1.012
Frequency of Drinking	0.988	1.171*	1.023*
Limit Contact			
Yes	1.444	153.285†	8.089‡
No	1.000	1.000	1.000
Prevent Income Access			
Yes	4.808	1.369	2.753†
No	1.000	1.000	1.000
Children < 25			
Yes	0.964	0.121	0.811
No	1.000	1.000	1.000
Depression			
Yes	1.354	0.618	0.838
No	1.000	1.000	1.000

married woman that is linked to heightened odds of severe physical assault. Perhaps these are women who lived with someone for a long time and are therefore older when they get married. If women experience changes to the relationship through marriage to their cohabiting partner, or if they have cohabited with someone else for a long time, they may experience severe violence. Without more detailed information it is impossible to test these hypotheses.

With respect to age heterogamy, consistent with the majority of the regressions on other forms of violence, the largest impacts are in the "partner six or more years younger" category. Severe physical assault seems to be particularly linked to this category of age heterogamy for cohabitors. Cohabiting women with partners six or more years younger than they have 782 percent higher odds of severe physical assault. Previous marriage is also linked to appreciably higher odds of severe physical assault for cohabitors. Previously married cohabiting women have 222 percent higher odds of experiencing this form of violence. As well, cohabiting women who experienced violence by a previous marital or common-law partner report by far the highest increase in odds of severe physical assault.

With respect to PC married women, women's education seems to have a fairly large impact on odds of severe physical assault. On all other forms of violence women's education is not strongly linked to increased odds of violence for any group. This is also the case on severe physical assault for cohabitors and non-PC marrieds. However, a one unit change in the education variable leads to a 39 percent decrease in odds of severe physical assault for PC married women. It appears that PC married women with low educational levels are particularly likely to experience severe physical assault. Interestingly, it is also PC married women who work that have high odds of experiencing this form of violence. PC married women who worked in the year prior to the study have 197 percent higher odds of severe physical assault compared to PC married women who did not work. The logistic regressions also show that PC married women whose partners worked in the year prior to the study face 99 percent higher odds of experiencing violence. Education consistency is also linked to particularly high odds of this form of violence for PC married women. For each unit increase in female to male years of education for a PC married woman, the odds of experiencing severe physical assault are increased by 269 percent. As well, PC married women who grew up in a violent home are particularly likely to experience this form of violence. These women have 469 percent higher odds of severe physical assault compared to their counterparts who did not grow up in a violent home. Finally, PC married women who experienced violence while dating their partner are particularly likely to report severe physical assault.

With respect to relationship variables, as in the analysis of lifetime prevalence of violence cohabiting women with a partner who keeps tabs on her have particularly high odds of this form of violence. Cohabiting women whose partner insists on knowing with whom she is and where she is at all times have 244 percent higher odds of experiencing severe physical assault. Having a cohabiting partner who drinks heavily also appears important. For each additional occasion in the month prior to the study that a cohabiting woman's partner consumed five or more drinks, her odds of experiencing severe physical assault are increased by 14 percent. Contrary to the overall analysis of lifetime prevalence of violence, of women with a partner who is domineering it is those who are cohabiting who are particularly likely to report severe physical assault. Cohabiting women with a domineering partner have 481 percent higher odds of experiencing this form of violence. Along with the results on the minor physical assault component of violence, this suggests that patriarchy does play some role in certain forms of violence experienced by cohabiting women.

As with the overall analysis of lifetime prevalence of violence, of women with a jealous partner it is those who are PC married that have particularly high odds of violence. These PC married women have 521 percent higher odds of severe physical assault than their nonjealous counterparts. As well, it seems that PC married women with a partner who drinks frequently are prone to experience this form of violence. For each additional time in the month prior to the study that a PC married woman's partner consumed alcohol, there is a 17 percent increase in her odds of experiencing severe physical assault. The most dramatic impact on the odds for PC marrieds, however, is for those who have a partner that socially isolates them. PC married women with a partner who limits their contacts with family or friends have dramatically higher odds of severe physical assault than their counterparts without such a partner. Finally, while women in all three groups who have children face decreased odds of severe physical assault, having children seems to particularly insulate PC married women from severe physical assault. PC married women with children have 88 percent reduced odds of experiencing severe physical assault. It is interesting to note that having children is linked to increased odds of all other components of violence for PC married women. What is it about having children that insulates PC married women from severe violence but not from other forms of violence? This question cannot be answered with the information in the present study, but it is an interesting question for future research.

The Role of Selection and Relationship Variables in Determining Marital Status Differences in Sexual Coercion

Unlike any of the other regressions, table 7.13 shows that without controls both PC marrieds and cohabitors have lower odds of sexual coer-

Table 7.13. *Results of Logistic Regressions on Sexual Coercion for Selection and Relationship Variables.*

	Marital Status	Selection	Relationship	Full Model
	n = 8370	*n* = 7282	*n* = 7986	*n* = 7023
Covariates	Odds Ratio	Odds Ratio	Odds Ratio	Odds Ratio
Marital Status				
PC Married	0.858	1.426	0.451	0.679
Cohabitor	0.572*	0.767	0.566	0.608
Non-PC married	1.000	1.000	1.000	1.000
Age		1.022†		0.996
Age Difference				
Partner 6+ older		1.531		1.293
Partner 1-5 older		1.649		1.576
Partner 1-5 younger		0.847		0.912
Partner 6+ younger		1.548		1.517
Same age		1.000		1.000
Woman's Education		0.900†		0.981
Woman's Employment				
Worked past year		1.586*		1.701*
Did not work past year		1.000		1.000
Partner's Employment				
Did not work		1.052		0.871
Worked past year		1.000		1.000
Woman's Income		1.000		1.000
Income Consistency		1.000*		1.000
Income Consistency Square		1.000		1.000
Education Consistency		1.565		0.715
Education Consistency Square		1.151		2.271*
Partner's Father Violent				
Yes/Think so		3.513‡		2.128†
No/Do not think so		1.000		1.000
Woman's Father Violent				
Yes/Think so		1.777†		1.924†
No/Do not think so		1.000		1.000
Dating Violence				
Yes		2.109*		0.793
No		1.000		1.000
Previous Marriage				
Yes		1.498		3.752
No		1.000		1.000

‡ $p < 0.01$; † $p < 0.05$; * $p \leq 0.10$

Table 7.13 continued.

	Marital Status	Selection	Relationship	Full Model
	n = 8370	*n* = 7282	*n* = 7986	*n* = 7023
Covariates	Odds Ratio	Odds Ratio	Odds Ratio	Odds Ratio
Previous Partner Violence				
Yes, violent		1.627		2.312
No, not violent		1.000		1.000
Region				
Atlantic		0.886		0.992
Quebec		0.920		1.303
Prairies		1.036		1.011
British Columbia		1.214		1.332
Ontario		1.000		1.000
Duration			1.030‡	1.044*
Jealousy				
Yes			9.674‡	9.187‡
No			1.000	1.000
Know Whereabouts				
Yes			1.375	1.457
No			1.000	1.000
Heavy Drinking			1.076‡	1.070‡
Frequency of Drinking			1.000	1.016
Limit Contact				
Yes			2.479‡	2.928‡
No			1.000	1.000
Prevent Income Access				
Yes			2.638‡	1.476
No			1.000	1.000
Children < 25				
Yes			1.321	1.030
No			1.000	1.000
Depression				
Yes			1.380	1.297
No			1.000	1.000

cion than do non-PC marrieds. PC marrieds have 14 percent lower odds and cohabitors have 43 percent lower odds of sexual coercion compared to non-PC marrieds. In this regression one needs to understand why non-PC marrieds have higher odds of sexual coercion than PC marrieds and cohabitors.

With controls for selection variables, the odds of violence are increased for both groups. The odds of sexual coercion for PC marrieds are increased by 57 percent and the odds for cohabitors are increased by 20 percent. With these controls, PC marrieds have 43 percent greater odds of sexual coercion compared to non-PC marrieds. Cohabitors, on the other hand, still have 23 percent lower odds of sexual coercion than non-PC marrieds.

Interestingly, controlling for relationship factors has the opposite effect than controlling for selection factors on the odds of sexual coercion for PC marrieds. PC marrieds now have 55 percent lower odds of sexual coercion compared to non-PC marrieds. The odds for cohabitors, on the other hand, remain exactly the same as they were without controls.

In the full model the least change in odds takes place for PC marrieds compared to non-PC marrieds. As well, there is only a very small change in the odds for cohabitors compared to non-PC marrieds. Overall, it appears that selection variables provide the strongest link to understanding why non-PC marrieds have the highest odds of sexual coercion. As noted in the discussion of duration of relationship in chapter 6, Ellis (1989) has hypothesized that cohabitors are more likely to have violent conflicts about sex, due to the shorter duration of their relationships. However, cohabitors have low odds of sexual coercion compared to non-PC marrieds. In fact, it is not surprising that cohabitors have lower odds of sexual coercion since this group has been reported to have the most sexual activity (Boba, 1996; Call, Sprecher, and Schwartz, 1995). One would therefore expect less for forced sex in common-law unions. The difference between PC marrieds and non-PC marrieds, on the other hand, is more than accounted for by selection variables. Selection variables that seem to be particularly powerful are partner's social learning (251 percent increased odds), having experienced violence while dating (111 percent increased odds), and education consistency (15 percent increased odds per unit increase in female to male years of education). In other words, when controlling for selection variables such as differential social learning, dating violence, and educational differences between partners, the lower odds of sexual coercion for PC marrieds compared to non-PC marrieds is more than accounted for.[6]

Three Distinct Types of Violent Experiences Revisited

While the overall analysis of lifetime prevalence of violence pointed to three distinct types of experiences leading to violence for each of the marital status groups, it is important to identify the extent to which these different types remain when investigating each component of violence separately.

Violence among Cohabitors

With the exception of verbal abuse, youth is consistently a risk marker of violence for cohabitors. While cohabitors in general tend to be young, it appears that older cohabitors are more likely to resort to name calling than other more physically oriented forms of violence. Overall, however, it is apparent that youth is a particularly important risk marker for understanding the violent experiences of cohabitors.

For every subcomponent of violence, the childlessness of cohabitors is linked to higher odds of violence. The decreases in odds for each component of violence, however, are smaller than for the overall violence variable. It appears that the childlessness of cohabitors has the greatest effect on minor and moderate physical assault with an 11 percent and 16 percent increase in odds respectively.

While the overall analysis of violence shows that cohabiting women with low relative education levels have higher odds of experiencing violence, an examination of this variable for each component of violence separately suggests that the nature of this relationship is dependent on the severity of violence. On verbal abuse and psychological aggression the relationship is negative. A one unit increase in female to male years of education is linked to 80 percent reduced odds of verbal abuse and 28 percent reduced odds of psychological aggression for cohabitors. While the same change does not have any impact on odds of minor physical assault it is linked to 34 percent increased odds of moderate physical assault and 72 percent increased odds of severe physical assault. That the relationship of violence to precipitating factors changes with severity points to the importance of analyzing components of violence separately to arrive at a fuller understanding of the complete picture of violence. It appears that cohabiting women who have more education than their partner are less likely to experience less severe forms of violence but they are more likely to experience more severe forms of violence. With the exception of psychological aggression for non-PC marrieds, as both PC and non-PC married women have more relative education resources, they have consistently higher odds on each component of violence. In other words, any gender status inconsistency in education resources is linked to increased odds of all forms of violence for PC and non-PC marrieds. This begs the question of why it is that married men are more likely to use any form of violence when their partner has more education resources while cohabiting men tend to resort to severe violence when their partner has more education. It seems possible that when cohabiting men feel that their partner is dependent they do not resort to the more severe forms of violence. When cohabiting men themselves feel dependent only then do they choose more severe forms of violence. This finding further refines the hypothesis of Ellis and DeKeseredy (1989). Cohabiting men's dependency, as measured by relative education resources, has an impact on their violence in terms of moderate and severe physical assault.

The overall analysis of violence also indicated that cohabiting women who do not work face increased odds of violence. This holds true for all types of violence except verbal abuse. Cohabiting women who worked in the year prior to the study face 127 percent higher odds of verbal abuse than those who did not. In general, cohabiting women who do not work experience the greatest likelihood of physically oriented violence while, cohabiting women who do work, on the other hand, are more likely to be the recipients of verbal attacks. That cohabiting men with a partner who works tend to resort to verbal attacks suggests that the greater independence of the female partner may prevent these men from using more severe forms of violence.

Having been victimized by a previous partner was also shown to be a particularly important determinant of violence in the overall analysis. An inspection of the results for this variable on each component of violence shows that previous partner violence is also linked to increased odds of each component of violence. As already discussed, cohabiting women who experienced violence by a previous partner have particularly high odds of experiencing moderate and severe physical assault. It seems that cohabiting women who are subject to serial victimization face particularly high odds of moderate and severe forms of physical violence.

With respect to depression, on all but moderate physical assault this variable is linked to increased odds of violence. Moreover, where depression is positively linked to violence for marrieds, the effect does not approach the impact that this variable has for cohabitors. There is something about depression that is particularly linked to all forms of violence for cohabitors. As speculated earlier, this may be a consequence of experiencing more severe forms of violence or it may be linked to other factors that increase the likelihood of violence for cohabiting women such as a lack of relative resources or having experienced violence by a previous partner.

Finally, the overall analysis of violence shows that having a cohabiting partner who keeps tabs is strongly linked to violence. Interestingly, the importance of this variable for cohabitors relative to marrieds seems to be restricted to minor and severe physical assault. Indeed, on the other forms of violence keeping tabs has a larger relative impact on the odds for one or both of the married groups. It may be that cohabiting men who keep tabs are more likely to resort to physically assaultive behaviors due to some other characteristic such as youth.

Overall, for cohabitors the results of the analyses on each component of violence indicate that the importance of youth persists in terms of understanding the violent experiences of cohabiting women. The relative powerlessness of women in terms of education is linked to higher odds of verbal abuse and psychological aggression but to lower odds of moderate and severe physical assault. Nevertheless, women who do not work, and who therefore are dependent, face increased odds of all forms of violence except verbal abuse. The notion that these women may somehow be limited in their pool of potential mates is further supported by the finding that cohabiting women who had a violent partner in the past face higher odds of all forms of violence by their current partner. As well, the importance of keeping tabs for understanding minor and severe physical assault supports the notion that the insecurities of cohabiting men who are sexually proprietary in this way are translated into violence, particularly certain types of physical assault.

Violence among PC Marrieds

For a PC married woman, having more educational resources than her partner is a particularly strong predictor of lifetime prevalence in the overall analysis. An examination of the logistic regression results shows that this relationship persists for each component of violence. Women who have lived with someone other than their husbands before marriage and who have more educational resources than their husbands have higher odds of experiencing each form of violence. There is something about PC married women having more educational resources than their husbands that leads them to be particularly likely to experience violence. It appears possible that the importance of the female being more educated is just one component of PC marrieds' social marginality.

The overall analysis also pointed to the importance of PC married women being different in age from their partner, regardless of the magnitude or direction of the difference. An examination of each component of violence separately, however, indicates that the importance of any age heterogamy for PC marrieds is restricted to understanding minor physical assault. As table 7.8 shows, PC married women with a partner who is six or more years older have 170 percent increased odds, those with a partner one to five years older have 101 percent increased odds, those with a partner who is one to five years younger have 112 percent increased odds, and those with a partner six or more years younger have 214 percent increased odds of minor physical assault. Again, social marginality among PC marrieds, in this case in terms of age difference, leads to a greater likelihood of pushing, grabbing, shoving, and slapping.

Having been previously married was shown in the overall analysis to have distinguished PC married women as the only marital status group to have a positive relationship to this variable. An examination for each component of violence, however, shows that this relationship exists only on two components of violence. Table 7.4 shows that these women have 208 percent higher odds of experiencing verbal abuse and table 7.10 indicates that PC married women who are remarried have 21 percent higher odds of moderate physical assault. It seems that women who have lived common-law with someone other than their current husband and who were also previously married stand a particularly high chance of being abused verbally. These are women who have had serial relationships that were serious enough to be common-law or married, but at least two of which did not work. Consistent with social marginality, it may be that these are women who come from a social environment that places some limits on their relationship choices.

The analysis of lifetime prevalence of violence also indicated that PC married women who translated a violent dating relationship into a marriage also faced particularly high odds of violence. While the positive relationship persists for each component of violence, it is evident that the odds are appreciably higher in comparison to the other two groups only on the physical assault variables. This is particularly the case for moderate and severe physical assault where, as discussed earlier, PC married women have far higher odds. It appears that PC married women who translate a violent dating relationship into a marriage face particularly high odds of experiencing physical assault by their husbands. Again, this points to some limitation on the relationship choices made by these women.

A partner's social learning is another variable linked to higher odds of overall violence for PC marrieds. The analyses of each component of violence show that the importance of partner's social learning for PC marrieds relative to the other marital status groups persists in terms of verbal abuse, psychological aggression, and minor physical assault. A partner's social learning also has a strong impact on severe physical assault for PC marrieds, though not nearly as strong as for non-PC marrieds. In general, men married to women who cohabited with someone else and who learned violence from their fathers appear less inhibited from engaging in these acts of violence.

The importance of jealousy identified in the overall analysis also persists on all but one of the components of violence. PC married women with a jealous partner are particularly likely to report experiencing verbal abuse, psychological aggression, minor physical assault, and severe physical assault. Jealous men married to women who previously cohabited seem less inhibited to vent their insecurity across the range of violent possibilities. The importance of the limiting contact variable for PC marrieds relative to the other groups, on the other hand, is restricted to the physical assault variables. It appears that for husbands of women who have previously cohabited jealousy leads to an array of behaviors, but those who translate jealousy into attempts to socially isolate their partner are also more likely to focus on physical violence.

Overall, while the analysis of each component of violence has provided some nuances of understanding the experiences of PC married women, the general impression from the analysis of lifetime prevalence of violence persists. The importance of the female having more educational resources, any age heterogamy, having been previously married, in addition to violence in the relationship while dating, the male partner having grown up in a violent home, and the importance of sexual propriety all point to the greater social marginality of these couples. Thus, there may be a greater social marginality among PC married couples that affects their relationship choices and renders men in these unions less inhibited from being violent.

Violence among Non-PC Marrieds

Recall that the logistic regressions on lifetime prevalence of violence indicated that having a domineering partner who prevents access to family income is particularly likely to lead to reports of violence for non-PC married women. The analyses for each component of violence, however, show that it is only on minor physical assault where non-PC married women with such a partner stand out as having particularly high odds relative to the other marital status groups. This is initially surprising given the importance of dominance for non-PC marrieds in the overall analysis. A possible explanation for this, however, is that, in addition to being an important predictor of minor physical assault, dominance among non-PC marrieds is also a particularly important predictor of sexual coercion. Recall from the descriptive analysis that there are so few cases of sexual coercion among cohabitors and PC marrieds that their respective rates cannot be reported. As well, in the separate logistic regressions for marital status groups there are too few cases for cohabitors and PC marrieds to allow the logistic regression procedure to find final solutions on the sexual coercion variable. The logistic regressions on sexual coercion for selection and relationship variables also indicated that non-PC marrieds face higher odds of sexual coercion than cohabitors and PC marrieds. Moreover, this analysis showed dominance through preventing access to family income to have a significant impact on the odds of sexual coercion. It may be that men married to more traditional women and who behave in a patriarchal manner are particularly likely to use minor physical assault and also to use sexual coercion to dominate their wives. This remains consistent with the conclusion of the overall analysis that these men may feel that they have the right to dominate their wives and/or that their more traditional wives will allow or cannot prevent these kinds of domination.

Theoretical Implications of Analyses on Separate Components of Violence

As with the typology of violent experiences for the three groups, it is also important to identify any further theoretical implications of the logistic regression analyses on each component of violence.

Feminist and Resource Theories

The overall analysis of lifetime prevalence of violence indicated that patriarchal cohabiting men are not as likely to be violent as their married counterparts. The analyses of each component of violence show this to be the case with the exception of verbal abuse and severe physical assault. While patriarchy does not account for cohabitors' higher levels of violence, it nevertheless has some role to play in violence perpetrated by all three marital status groups. With respect to resource theory, the overall analysis showed that education inconsistency favoring women actually reduced cohabitors' odds of experiencing violence. The logistic regressions for each component of violence indicate that cohabiting women having more education than their partner is linked to higher odds for moderate and severe physical assault. However, in both cases PC married women with more education than their partners have even higher odds of these forms of violence. Status inconsistency favoring women, therefore, does not provide a greater understanding of experiences of violence for cohabitors compared to marrieds. In general, based on these analyses it is evident that neither feminist nor resource theory account for the higher likelihood of violence among cohabitors.

Routine Activities Theory

As already discussed, the separate logistic regressions for each component of violence show that the youth of cohabitors is typically linked to increased odds of violence. As routine activities theory would predict, it is generally particularly young cohabiting women who are at the greatest risk of violence. Also in line with routine activities theory, the childlessness of cohabitors is consistently linked to higher odds of violence. While the results with respect to alcohol consumption are variable across the three marital status groups, contrary to the predictions of routine activities theory it is evident that alcohol consumption in general is not a factor in the differing experiences of violence for cohabitors. In terms of concern over separate activities, the analyses of the separate components of violence indicate that cohabiting men's concern about who their partner is with and where she is at all times contributes to their use of minor and severe physical assault. Cohabiting men who may be behaving in a proprietary way due to concern over more separate lifestyles seem to translate their concern into the most common and the most severe forms of violence. In general, the separate analyses do provide some further support for routine activities theory, though it is evident that this theory needs to be put to a much more specific and stringent test to further investigate its applicability to understanding martial status differences in violence.

Social Learning Theory

Consistent with the overall analysis of lifetime prevalence of violence, the results of the logistic regressions for each component of violence generally indicate that social learning has by far the greatest impact on odds of violence for marrieds. Even when one looks individually at the various forms of violence, it is apparent that cohabitors whose fathers were violent toward their mothers do not face a higher likelihood of violence than do marrieds who had such an upbringing. Clearly, social learning does not account for the higher prevalence of violence among cohabitors.

Sex-Role Theory

The analyses for each component of violence separately indicate that, with the exception of verbal abuse, cohabiting women who do not work face increased odds of violence. This supports the overall analysis such that cohabitors who behave in an egalitarian manner in terms of female employment face reduced likelihood of violence. Why, then, is female employment linked to increased odds of verbal abuse for cohabitors? It may be that, while men in these relationships are by definition less traditional, some may still hold very patriarchal attitudes and values. However, faced with the greater ease with which their cohabiting partner can leave, they vent their frustrations over their partner's employment with verbal attacks.

Social Isolation

The overall analysis of lifetime prevalence of violence has shown that having a socially isolating partner does not lead to appreciably higher odds of violence for cohabitors compared to marrieds. Separate logistic regressions for each marital status subgroup further support this finding. If anything, social isolation is linked to particularly high odds of physical assault for PC married women. Overall, it is evident that social isolation cannot account for the differing rates of violence among cohabitors.

The DAD Model

Consistent with the overall analysis, the analyses for each component of violence have shown that income dependency of cohabitors does not have any application for understanding marital status differences in violence. Though the analyses for individual components of violence do show that cohabiting men's dependency resulting from lower relative education resources has a positive impact on moderate and severe physical assault, overall the dependency of cohabiting men does not appear to play a large role in understanding their higher rates of violence. As well, the analyses on the subcomponents of violence reaffirm that alcohol dependency is not disproportionately linked to violence among cohabitors. Controlling for availability via duration, the results show that the only form of violence on which jealousy is linked to higher odds of violence for cohabitors is moderate physical assault. Contrary to the hypothesis of Ellis and DeKeseredy (1989), jealousy generally does not have a stronger impact on violence for cohabitors compared to other marital status groups. The individual analyses also reaffirm that social isolation and low income, factors posited to reduce deterrence, are not more important predictors of violence for cohabitors than marrieds. Consistent with the overall analysis, it is possible that the youthfulness of cohabitors is a factor leading to lower deterrence, overall the analyses of each component of violence confirm the earlier results, which suggest the inadequacy of the DAD model.

The Selection versus Relationship Dichotomy

With respect to the selection versus relationship dichotomy, it is evident from the logistic regressions on selection and relationship variables that selection variables have a larger overall impact on the odds for every component of violence. However, it is interesting to note that on verbal abuse, psychological aggression, moderate physical assault, and severe physical assault it is the combination of selection and relationship variables that lead to the greatest reduction in odds. While the type of people who cohabit may be more prone to violence, this selection into cohabitation does not fully explain the violence that occurs in these unions. Rather, there are also characteristics that result as a consequence of their union that provide the greatest explanation for the violence they experience in combination with their individual characteristics. As well, consistent with the analysis of lifetime prevalence of violence, logistic regressions for each marital status subgroup show that most of the relationship variables operate differently for different groups. This suggests that they play a unique role in distinguishing the violent experiences of different marital status groups. While selection variables do appear to be more important in comparison to relationship variables the separate analyses for each component of violence further indicate that the combination of both types of variables is crucial. Clearly, further research needs to be conducted to investigate the indirect effects between selection and relationship variables.

Summary

Based on the logistic multiple regressions it appears that the reasons for marital status differences in violence are not as clear-cut as previous explanations would have us believe. In addition to the preliminary results of the descriptive analyses, the results of the logistic regressions provide support for the hypothesis that cohabitors' and PC marrieds' differential selection and relationship characteristics are linked to their greater likelihood of violence. These results point to the prime importance of selection over relationship factors in understanding marital status differences in violence. Despite relationship variables typically having a significant impact on violence, it appears that marital status differences have the strongest link to the type of people who are selected into cohabitation. However, when the components of violence are examined separately it is evident that on several of these it is the combination of both selection and relationship variables that provides the greatest understanding of marital status differences in violence.

Aside from the theoretical synthesis in the present study, an evaluation of variables hypothesized to be linked to various explanatory frameworks for understanding marital status differences in violence shows little to no support for almost all of these theories, with the exception of Routine Activities theory. However, it is safe to state that Routine Activities theory needs a much more specific test to further investigate its applicability to marital status differences in violence. This lack of support for these explanatory frameworks also persists after investigating each of the components of violence separately.

As suggested by some of the findings in the descriptive analyses, the underlying dynamics of violence in different union types seems to be complex. Overcoming the tentativeness of the cross-tabulations through logistic regression, we are left with a portrait, perhaps more aptly a rough sketch, of three distinct groups.

For cohabitors the results demonstrate that young women, childless women, women who do not work, who have a history of being violently victimized, who are depressed, and who have a partner who keeps tabs on them are particularly likely to experience violence. It seems that there is a complex combination of factors linked to violence experienced by cohabiting women.

For PC marrieds the results show that women with more educational resources than their partner, who are different in age from their partner, who have been married previously, who were victimized while dating their partner, whose partners were exposed to violence as a child, and whose partners are jealous and socially isolating are particularly likely to experience violence. These factors point to a more general social marginality that may place limits on PC married women's relationship choices and render men in these relationships less inhibited from being violent.

While several variables have an effect on the odds of violence for non-PC marrieds, having a domineering partner who prevents access to family income is particularly likely to lead to reports of overall violence. Men married to more traditional women and who behave in a patriarchal manner through controlling family income are particularly likely to engage in minor physical assault and, quite probably, sexual coercion. This may be because these men feel that by virtue of their marriage license they have the right to be violent and because within marriage they can get away with it.

The fact that we are left with three rather distinct groups suggests that, as outlined in the theoretical synthesis, there are unique processes at work in these union types that lead to different forms of relationship nomos. It does appear that cohabitors and PC marrieds differential selection and relationship characteristics lead them to be more likely to establish a less stable nomos than non-PC marrieds, which, in turn, results in their higher likelihood of violence. That those who currently cohabit are different from those who have cohabited but are now married also provides some evidence for a carry-over effect. The past cohabitation experiences of PC marrieds does seem to make them different from non-PC marrieds. More research is needed to determine to what extent the nomos of PC marrieds' relationships is impacted by the subjective internalization of previous relationship nomos.

Notes

1. An examination of the correlation matrix showed that there may be a problem of multicolinearity between age and duration ($r = .87$). However, because these two variables are important and theoretically distinct, regressions were run with and without both variables to see how the inclusion of both changed the results. Since there were no substantive changes in the results, the decision was made to retain both variables in the model. As well, since the status consistency variables are ratios of respondent's and partner's income and education variables, it was decided that one partner's education and income should be left out to avoid redundancy. Models were run excluding partner's and respon-

dent's income and education in turn and there was no substantive change in results. Since there are far fewer missing cases on the respondent's education and income variables, it was decided to include respondent's education and income characteristics.

2. Selected results from this portion of the analysis were presented at the Sixth International Family Violence Research Conference, University of New Hampshire, Durham, NH, July 25-28, 1999.

3. Logistic regressions were also run on one-year prevalence of violence. These analyses did not add substantively to the discussion of lifetime prevalence. Given these results and the fact that lifetime prevalence is a more adequate account of all women in the sample who have experienced violence by their partner as well as the fact that both the selection and relationship models include risk markers that help account for the longer time frame (i.e., respondent's age and duration of relationship, respectively), the decision was made to only present the lifetime prevalence results.

4. Since Stets and Straus (1989) are also concerned with violence in dating couples, they limited their sample used in controlling for education to marrieds and cohabitors in the 18-24 age group. Thus, theirs is an incomplete test of the effect of education differentials on all marrieds and cohabitors in their sample.

5. Ellis (1989) reports this finding based on another study (Long, Tauchen, and Witte, 1983). To date this report has not been received by the author so it is not possible to comment on why there is a discrepancy between the findings of that study and the present one.

6. The logistic regression analyses for each marital status group separately are not reported because, due to the small number of cases of sexual coercion for cohabitors and PC marrieds, the regression procedure could not arrive at final solutions for these groups.

Chapter 8

A Post-Violence Comparison

To supplement the findings of the etiological analyses of marital status differences in violence, the present chapter examines marital status differences on four post-violence dimensions. These encompass the consequences of the violent incident, sources of help sought by the victims, their behavior in terms of leaving and returning to the relationship, and various aspects surrounding the police response to the incident.

Consequences

A recent publication from Statistics Canada reports that in 1997 some 77 percent of police-reported spousal[1] violence offenses involved either a weapon or physical force causing injury (Fitzgerald, 1999). Among women in the VAWS who experienced some form of violence[2] during their current marital or common-law union, 22.9 percent report that they had suffered physical injury. The disparity between these two figures is undoubtedly due to the fact that the cases of violence reported to the police tend to be those that are more severe. It is not surprising that many women who are victims of violence do not suffer physical injury, a point made by previous studies (e.g., Ratner, 1995). Of course, this is not to deny that victims who are not physically injured endure suffering. Indeed, research (Aguilar and Nightingale, 1994; Okun, 1986; Walker, 1984) suggests that the psychological consequences of violence may be

Table 8.1. *Consequences of Violence by Marital Status.*

Marital Status

Consequence	Non-PC Married %	n	PC Married %	n	Common-Law %	n
Physical Injury[a]						
Bruises	84.8	95	90.0	9	88.9	16
Cuts/scratches/burns	25.0	28	10.0	1	44.4	8
Fractures/broken bones	5.4	6	0.0	0	22.2*	4
Miscarriage/internal	4.5	5	20.0	2	11.1	2
Other[b]	14.3	16	10.0	1	11.1	2
Psychopathology[a]						
Depression/Anxiety attacks	12.5	61	8.3	3	13.0	9
Fearful	14.5	71	22.2	8	23.2	16
More cautious/aware	12.7	62	16.7	6	11.6	8
Sleep problems	1.6	8	2.8	1	2.9	2
Shock/disbelief	3.9	19	5.6	2	5.8	4
Hurt/disappointment	6.3	31	5.6	2	5.8	4
Upset/confused/frustrated	4.7	23	2.8	1	7.2	5
Altered Psyche[a]						
Ashamed/guilty	8.2	40	13.9	5	5.8	4
Lowered self-esteem	14.5	71	19.4	7	11.6	8
Problems relating to men	1.4	7	2.8	1	0.0	0
Increased self reliance	6.7	33	2.8	1	2.9	2
Anger	30.7	150	38.9	14	31.9	22
Alcohol/Drug Use						
Alcohol	4.7	24	18.9	7	8.5	6
Drugs/medication	5.3	27	5.4	2	2.8	2
Both alcohol and drugs	1.6	8	2.7	1	1.4*	1
Time Off Everyday Activities	12.0	61	24.3	9	12.7	9

* p ≤ 0.10

[a] Categories are not mutually exclusive. They therefore do not total 100 percent.

[b] Includes pulled hair, back injury, ear injury, concussion, sprain, dislocation, whiplash, mouth/teeth injury, other.

more devastating than the physical sequelae. Cantos, Neidig, and O'Leary (1994:123) conclude, "The additional psychological sequelae further reinforces the notion that any level of physical aggression is to be considered problematic and toxic."

Table 8.1 contains the results of the analyses by marital status on the consequences of violence. Among women who experienced physical injury as a consequence of their partner's violence, the most common type of injury in all marital status groups is bruising. This type of injury is reported at high levels for all three groups with a range of 84.8 to 90 percent. It appears that women who are victims of physical violence are likely to experience bruising, regardless of marital status. This is not the case, however, with respect to the other forms of injury. Cohabiting women who reported an injury are far more likely to indicate their partner's violence to have resulted in cuts, scratches and/or burns.[3] Nearly 45 percent of injured cohabiting women report these sequelae compared to 25 percent of injured non-PC married women and 10 percent of injured PC married women. Similarly, injured cohabiting women are far more likely to indicate that their partner fractured or broke one or more of their bones. PC married women, on the other hand, are nearly twice as likely as cohabitors to report a miscarriage or internal injuries. However, cohabitors are more than twice as likely as non-PC marrieds to report these injuries. Though non-PC marrieds are somewhat more likely to indicate suffering other injuries, it appears that there is a greater tendency for cohabitors to be more likely to report severe injuries. This finding buttresses the results of the descriptive analyses of this work that show that cohabiting women are more likely to experience more severe forms of violence.

While the differences between marital status groups are less dramatic in terms of the psychopathological consequences of violence, one can still note some interesting divergences. The most common psychopathological consequence of violence is fear. Though cohabitors and PC marrieds report being fearful at equal levels, both groups report somewhat higher levels of fear in comparison to non-PC marrieds. Again, this may serve as an indication of severity, or at least potential severity, of the violence experienced by cohabiting and PC married women. This may also be linked to the greater likelihood of problems with sleeping reported by cohabiting and PC married women. Finally, it is interesting to note that cohabiting women are most likely to report being upset, confused, and/or frustrated. It may be that the newness of such unions combined with an expectation of a more egalitarian, or at least liberated, ideology leads cohabiting women to be more likely to experience these sequelae when violence occurs.

Interestingly, it is PC married women who are most likely to report having their psyche altered by violence. Women who lived with someone other than their husbands before marriage are most likely to report that their experience of violence left them feeling ashamed and/or guilty. They are also more likely to report that their self-esteem has been lowered and that they have problems relating to men as a result of experiencing violence. In addition, PC married women are the most likely to report being angered by their partner's violence, and they are also far more likely to report having used alcohol to help them cope with their experience of violence. Nearly one in five PC married women use alcohol as a coping mechanism. As well, PC married women are nearly twice as likely to report that they needed to take time off from their everyday activities because of their experience of violence. These findings provide further evidence that PC married women are a distinct subgroup of marrieds. It appears possible that PC marrieds are a subgroup that is particularly psychologically affected by the violence they experience. Perhaps the greater social marginality of PC marrieds and their relationships also encompasses a more susceptible psyche.

While cohabitors are most likely to experience the most severe forms of violence, they are the least likely to report their psyche being altered by the violence. Indeed, not one cohabiting woman reports having problems relating to men as a result of experiencing violence. This may be due to their youth and perhaps less opportunity to have had poor relationships and repeated experiences with men who are violent. As a point of interest, cohabiting women are the least likely to report having taken drugs or medication to help them cope with their experience of violence. This suggests that the importance of the depression variable for cohabitors in the analyses in previous chapters of this work is not due to a greater likelihood of cohabiting women to take drugs or medication as a consequence of violence. Rather, based on this limited data, there would appear to be something else about depression that links it to particularly high odds of violence for cohabitors. It may be that depression is linked to violence for cohabitors through other variables on which they differ such as lack of relative resources or previous partner violence. This is an area of investigation that is certainly worthy of further attention in the future.

It is also interesting to note that non-PC married women are more than twice as likely as the other two groups to report that they increased their self-reliance as a result of being victimized by their partner. This may reflect the tendency of non-PC married women to be more dependent. For instance, the descriptive analyses show that non-PC married women are less likely than women in the other marital status groups to be employed. As one strategy for dealing with violence, these women increased their reliance on themselves. Without further information it is impossible to know exactly how they did this, but it is clear that for these women violence prompted them to attempt to become less dependent on their partner.

Help-Seeking

The results presented in table 8.2 suggest that cohabiting and PC married women are far more likely to report having visited a doctor or nurse for treatment as a result of experiencing violence. It is possible that more traditional non-PC married women are less likely to seek medical treatment for their injuries than are women in the other marital status groups. However, given several indications of the greater likelihood of severe violence in cohabiting and PC married unions, it is probable that the higher likelihood of these groups visiting a doctor or nurse is due to the severity of the violence they experience.

In terms of other help-seeking behaviors, it is interesting to note that cohabiting women are the most likely to report confiding in a family member and they, along with PC married women, are most likely to report confiding in a friend or neighbour. These results suggest that cohabiting women are not more socially isolated than other women, at least not in times of crisis. Cohabiting women are also by far the least likely to report having confided in a minister, priest, or clergyman. This is undoubtedly a reflection of the lower religiosity of cohabitors (Ward, 1998). This analysis suggests that even in times of crisis cohabiting women are unlikely to turn to the church for assistance.

A Statistics Canada snapshot taken of 422 shelters on April 20, 1998, found that 36 percent of women in shelters were victimized by their husbands and 32 percent were victimized by a common-law partner (Trainor, 1999). According to the results of the present study, relatively few women who are victimized contact a shelter. However, when PC marrieds are analyzed separately from non-PC marrieds, it is PC married women who are most likely to contact a shelter, followed by cohabiting women. Again, while this could be due to a hesitancy of non-PC married women to seek services, it seems more probable that this is due to the

Table 8.2. *Help-Seeking Behavior by Marital Status.*

Marital Status

Help-Seeking	Non-PC Married		PC Married		Common-Law	
	%	n	%	n	%	n
Visit Dr./Nurse for Treatment	24.1	27	50.0	5	42.1*	8
Confided in:[a]						
Family	35.3	179	32.4	12	39.4	28
Friend/neighbor	30.4	154	40.5	15	38.0	27
Doctor	15.0	76	16.2	6	12.7	9
Minister/priest/clergy	4.9	25	5.4	2	1.4	1
Services Contacted[a]						
Shelter/transition house	3.3	17	8.1	3	5.6	4
Crisis center/line	2.0	10	0.0	0	2.8	2
Another counselor	11.4	58	18.9	7	11.3	8
Women's center	2.7	14	5.4	2	2.8	2
Community/family center	2.5	13	5.4	2	1.4	1
Reasons Services Not Used[a]						
Did not know of services	6.6	27	8.0	2	0.0	0
None available	7.4	30	4.0	1	5.1	3
Incident too minor	42.5	173	32.0	8	47.5	28
Shame/embarrassment	3.7	15	4.0	1	1.7	1
Did not want/need help	47.7	194	48.0	12	50.8	30
Helped elsewhere	2.5	10	8.0	2	1.7	1
Other[b]	5.7	23	12.0	3	5.1	3

* $p \leq 0.10$

[a] Categories are not mutually exclusive. They therefore do not total 100 percent.

[b] Includes waiting list, would not be believed, he prevented her, distance, fear of losing financial support, fear of losing children, did not want relationship to end, fear of offender, keep incident private, didn't think service useful, other.

greater likelihood of severe violence in cohabiting and PC married unions. While, generally speaking, PC married women tend to be the most likely to use services, based on this analysis it appears that relatively few women who are victimized are using the services designed to help them.

The main reason for the women not using the services is that they did not want or need help. This is probably linked to the fact that many of the women felt the incident to be too minor to require the assistance of one or more services. Cohabiting women are both the most likely to find the incident too minor to want services and are also the most likely to report not wanting or needing help. As well, cohabiting women are less than half as likely to report not using services due to shame or embarrassment. Cohabiting women are not as likely as married women to find help elsewhere. This is despite the fact that all cohabiting women who are victims in the present study knew of one or more services at the time of the incident. Given that violence is more likely to be severe in cohabiting relationships, these findings suggest the possibility that cohabitors are more likely to perceive the violence as being minor. This may be due to some characteristic that selects them into cohabitation, such as the tendency to be young. To be sure, an underestimation of where "minor" violence can lead may be at cohabiting women's peril.

The VAWS also asked victims if their partner received counseling for their violent behavior. PC married victims are the most likely to report that their husbands received counseling. Nearly one-third (27.8 percent) of PC married victims report that their husbands received counseling. This is double the likelihood of non-PC married victim's husbands receiving counseling (14.3 percent) and nearly three times the likelihood of cohabiting victim's partner receiving counseling (10.0 percent). This appears to be yet another reflection of the qualitative differences between these types of unions. While the greatest likelihood of violence occurs in PC married and cohabiting unions, PC married men are the most likely to see a counselor and cohabiting men are least likely to do so. While more needs to be done to get all violent men to counseling,[4] this is particularly the case for those who are most likely to be severely violent; cohabiting men.

Leaving and Returning

The results of the marital status comparisons on leaving and returning to the relationship presented in table 8.3 indicate that, while the majority of victims do not leave, when one partner does leave it is typically the woman. Among those women who do leave, it is those who are PC married who are most likely to do so. Nearly one-third of PC married women leave compared to just under one-fifth of cohabiting and non-PC married women. Given that the subset of respondents in this study consists of women with a partner, it is not surprising that virtually all of the women

Table 8.3. *Leaving and Returning by Marital Status.*

Marital Status

Leaving and Returning	Non-PC Married %	n	PC Married %	n	Common-Law %	n
Ever leave/stay apart						
Yes, she left	17.6	90	29.7	11	18.3	13
Yes, he left	5.9	30	5.4	2	4.2	3
No	76.5	390	64.9	24	77.5	55
Where stay[a]						
Transition house/shelter	11.1	10	18.2	2	23.1	3
Nowhere	5.6	5	18.2	2	15.4	2
Friends/relatives	76.7	69	72.7	8	76.9	10
Hotel/motel	12.1	11	0.0	0	0.0	0
Hostel (salv. army/church)	0.0	0	0.0	0	0.0	0
Got her own place	11.1	10	18.2	2	7.7	1
Other[b]	2.2	2	0.0	0	0.0	0
Eventually Return	100.0	90	90.9	10	100.0	13
Main reason for returning						
Partner left	2.3	2	0.0	0	0.0	0
Partner promised to change	20.5	18	30.0	3	0.0	0
Resolved problems	8.0	7	20.0	2	8.3	1
No money	4.5	4	10.0	1	0.0	0
No where to go	3.4	3	10.0	1	0.0	0
Sake of children	26.1	23	10.0	1	33.3	4
Give rel. another try	30.7	27	10.0	1	50.0	6
Other[c]	4.5	4	10.0	1	8.3	1

[a] Categories are not mutually exclusive. They therefore do not total 100 percent.
[b] Specific meaning not provided.
[c] Other includes court ordered him away, shame of divorce, lack of housing, wanted to return home, threat from spouse, pressure from family, other.

in the sample who left their partner also eventually returned. One can deduce that the 0.1 percent of PC marrieds who did not return were living away from their husbands at the time of the survey.

While cohabiting women are less likely to contact a shelter than PC married women, table 8.3 shows that they are more likely to report having stayed in a shelter. According to this subsample, it is currently cohabiting women who are most likely to stay in a shelter. It seems probable that if Trainor's (1999) data were categorized in the same manner as the present study one would find currently cohabiting women to be the marital status group with the greatest representation in shelters.

By far the majority of women who leave a violent relationship stay with friends or relatives. As a further indication that cohabiting women who are victims of violence are not isolated from family and friends, the results of this study show that cohabiting women are no less likely to stay with friends and relatives compared to married women. While non-PC married women are most likely to report increased self-reliance as a consequence of experiencing violence, it is also interesting to note that they are not the most likely to get their own place when they leave a violent situation. Rather, PC married women seem to be the most likely to get their own place. This may be indicative of a greater tendency for these women to leave the situation for a long duration. The fact that only non-PC married women report staying in a hotel may be indicative of a tendency for these women to leave for a shorter period of time. Given the tendency for cohabitors to be young, it seems reasonable that they would be more likely to stay with people they know, particularly friends.

The most common reason cited for returning is to give the relationship another try. For PC married women in particular, this is because the partner promised to change. Interestingly, no cohabiting victims indicated that they returned to their victimizer due to a lack of money. This buttresses the findings of the multivariate analyses that suggest that income dependency of cohabiting women is not a problem. As well, it is also interesting to note that women who reported returning for the sake of the children are most likely to be living common-law. While the multivariate analyses suggest that the childlessness of cohabitors leads to increased odds of violence, this does not mean that cohabitors with children are free of victimization. That cohabiting women are most likely to return for the sake of the children is probably linked to their youth and, therefore, greater likelihood of having young children.

Police Response

Table 8.4 provides the marital status comparison of variables surrounding the police response to violence. The results of this analysis suggest that relatively few incidents of violence are reported to the police. The police are most likely to find out about violence experienced by PC mar-

Table 8.4. *Police Response by Marital Status.*

	Non-PC Married		PC Married		Common-Law	
Police Response	%	n	%	n	%	n
Police Found Out	8.1	41	32.4	12	15.5‡	11
Police Saw Respondent	85.4	35	91.7	11	81.8	9
Police Took Partner Away	29.3	12	41.7	5	36.4	4
Police Told About Services	26.8	11	50.0	6	18.2	2
Resp. Satisfaction w/ Police						
Very satisfied	17.5	7	16.7	2	27.3	3
Satisfied	50.0	20	58.3	7	36.4	4
Dissatisfied	12.5	5	16.7	2	18.2	2
Very dissatisfied	20.0	8	8.3	1	18.2	2
Police should have:[a]						
Done nothing else	59.5	22	66.7	8	54.5	6
Taken him out of home	13.5	5	8.3	1	9.1	1
Charged/arrested partner	18.9	7	0.0	0	0.0†	0
Responded more quickly	8.1	3	0.0	0	27.3*	3
Referred/took to service	10.8	4	8.3	1	0.0	0
Been more supportive	18.9	7	33.3	4	27.3	3
Other[a]	2.7	1	0.0	0	9.1	1
Post-Police Violence						
Increased	5.0	2	0.0	0	0.0	0
Decreased/stopped	70.0	28	75.0	9	81.8	9
Stayed the same	25.0	10	25.0	3	18.2	2
Reasons Police Not Contacted[b]						
Would not be believed	0.9	4	0.0	0	0.0	0
Thought could not help	4.4	20	12.5	3	3.4	2
Fear of offender	2.4	11	0.0	0	1.7	1
Too minor	73.4	331	83.3	20	75.9	44
Keep incident private	6.2	28	8.3	2	1.7	1
Shame/embarrassment	3.5	16	4.2	1	3.4	2
Didn't want police involved	5.5	25	8.3	2	3.4	2
Didn't want partner arrested	3.5	16	4.2	1	1.7	2
Did not want/need help	10.0	45	0.0	0	10.3	6
Other[c]	1.6	7	0.0	0	1.7	1

‡ p < 0.01; † p < 0.05; * p ≤ 0.10
[a] Includes relocated her, taken her to hospital, other.
[b] Categories are not mutually exclusive. They therefore do not total 100 percent.
[c] Includes used other channels, other.

ried victims. They are twice as likely to find out about violence experienced by PC married women compared to that experienced by cohabiting women. However, the police are also twice as likely to find out about violence experienced by cohabiting victims compared to non-PC married victims. This may be due to reluctance on the part of non-PC married victims to involve the police and/or this may be a reflection of a tendency for violence in non-PC married relationships to be less severe. The latter possibility is also supported by the fact that the police are most likely to remove a PC married or cohabiting victim's partner from the situation. Among victims about whom the police were aware, the vast majority were visited by the police regardless of marital status. In terms of satisfaction with the police, the majority of victims in each marital status group report being satisfied or very satisfied. The majority also feels that the police should have done nothing else.

While Statistics Canada (Trainor, 1999) reports that charges are laid in the majority of incidents reported to the police, nearly one in five non-PC married victims report that charges should have been laid. It appears that while the violence experienced by non-PC married women is less likely to be physically severe it is nevertheless serious enough for the victims to feel the need to have their husbands arrested.

Interestingly, cohabiting victims are far more likely than those in other marital status groups to report that the police should have responded more quickly. It is possible that this reflects a greater fear and therefore urgency on the part of cohabiting victims. However, when the victim was asked if she feared for her life, cohabiting and non-PC married victims are virtually equally likely to report this to be the case (9.9 and 9.8 percent, respectively). On the other hand, 27.8 percent of PC married victims report that they feared for their lives. Alternatively, then, this result may be due to a tendency for cohabitors to live in areas that are less easily accessible to the police.

The majority of the victims indicate that the violence either decreased or stopped after police intervention. Clearly, based on this analysis police involvement has an impact on the incidence of violence. Non-PC married women are the least likely to report this to be the case and they are the only marital status group in which some victims, albeit a small percentage, report violence increasing after police involvement. Moreover, one in four married victims and one in five cohabiting victims report no change in the level of violence after police involvement. More work certainly needs to be done in this area to end male partner violence against women.

Among victims who did not contact the police, regardless of marital status the majority did not do so because they felt that the incident was too minor to involve the police. However, there are some interesting marital status patterns among some of the other reasons for not contacting the police. PC married victims are nearly three times as likely to report that they thought the police could not help them. Though violence is more likely to be severe in PC married and common-law unions, it is non-PC married victims who are most likely not to contact the police due to fear of their husbands. While some victims in all three groups undoubtedly fear their partner, non-PC married victims are most likely to let their fear prevent them from involving the police. This may reflect the finding of the multivariate analysis that shows that dominance is particularly linked to violence for non-PC married women. If patriarchal dominance is a key factor in the violence experienced by these women, then some of them may be particularly likely to fear reporting to the police due to potential reprisal. As already discussed, this is also the group in which victims reported violence increasing after the involvement of police.

Finally, one can observe in table 8.4 that married victims, regardless of whether they are previously or nonpreviously cohabiting, are more likely than cohabiting victims to report that they did not contact the police to keep the incident private, because they did not want the police involved, and because they did not want their partner arrested. There does, therefore, appear to be a greater tendency on the part of married victims who do not involve the police to want to maintain their privacy and prevent an arrest. Since cohabitors are not married, it seems possible that they score lower on these measures because, consistent with the theoretical synthesis of the present study, their reality is less privatized.

Summary

The post-violence analysis provides an interesting context with which to supplement some of the etiological analysis. Based on the post-violence analysis there does appear to be some support for the sixth general hypothesis of the study. Consistent with past research on injury, cohabiting and PC marrieds in the present study generally seem to be more likely to experience injury than do non-PC marrieds. This is probably linked to the greater severity of violence hypothesized to exist in common-law than in marital relationships. In addition to the support for this hypothesis found in the descriptive and logistic regression analyses, there are several further indications in the present chapter that buttress this finding. Cohabiting and PC married women are more likely to report severe injuries, to visit a physician for their injuries, they are more likely to report being fearful and to have problems sleeping, to use a shelter, and to have their partner removed from the situation by the police.

There is also further evidence against the social isolation explanation. It is found that cohabitors are no less likely than marrieds to either confide in family or friends or to stay with friends and relatives when they leave their partner. This suggests that they are not more socially isolated than marrieds.

There are also some indications in the post-violence analysis of the distinctiveness of the three marital status groups. For example, PC marrieds' psyche seems to be more susceptible to the effects of violence. They are more likely to feel ashamed or guilty, to have lowered self-esteem and to have problems relating to men as a consequence of violence. It is possible that the greater psychological effect of violence for PC married women is linked to the greater likelihood of socially marginal people being in this type of union. A unique psychological profile may be linked to the social marginality of PC marrieds. In terms of cohabitors, the post-violence comparison finds that women in these unions are more likely to perceive themselves not to need help, and cohabiting men in these unions are the least likely to see a counselor. Both of these findings may be linked to cohabitors' tendency to be young. Young women may be less likely to recognize the danger they are in, and young men may be less willing to seek professional help for their problems. With respect to non-PC marrieds, the analysis in the present chapter found that women in these unions are the least likely to contact the police for help out of fear of their husbands. This is also the only group for which violence increased after police intervention. These findings suggest that adding a third party to the dyad via police intervention would aggravate their husbands who desire to dominate them.

The tentativeness of the analysis in the present chapter cannot be overemphasized. A much larger sample of victims of violence is required to make reliable inferences. Nevertheless, further investigation along these lines would be fruitful for placing causal analyses in context. The combination of both types of data would provide the greatest understanding of the underlying processes at work.

Notes

1. Includes current and former marital and common-law partners.
2. This excludes occurrences of verbal abuse.
3. Of course, as with the rate of violence, a higher likelihood of reporting injuries does not mean that more cohabiting women than non-PC married women experience these injuries. Rather, this suggests that a disproportionate number of cohabiting women experience these injuries.
4. Gondolf (1997), discussing comprehensive reviews of batterer programs, reports that batterer programs contribute to the cessation of violence in a substantial portion of men who complete them.

Chapter 9

Conclusion and Implications

The final chapter of this work discusses the central themes of this research enterprise, engages in a discussion of limitations of the study couched within a discussion of implications for future research, and ends with some concluding comments about the significance of the work.

Mixing Marital Status Groups and Mixing Messages

This journey into the relationship between marital status and violence against women began with the observation that most of the substantial body of research on violence against women subsumes cohabitors within marrieds. While DeKeseredy and Hinch (1991), whose argument for combining marrieds and cohabitors was outlined in chapter 1, should be commended for making a rare effort to justify combining marrieds and cohabitors into one group, the present work nevertheless takes issue with these and other researchers who would do the same. To treat marrieds and cohabitors as one for the sake of consistency with past studies is tantamount to arguing that researchers should not approach problems from different angles than their analytical predecessors. The justification of DeKeseredy and Hinch (1991) that the legal system treats certain cohabitors and marrieds equally places the proverbial cart before the horse. The institutions of society should look to social researchers for guidance in attempting to understand the underlying dynamics of social problems rather than vice versa. DeKeseredy and Hinch (1991) also argue that there are few differences between marrieds and cohabitors since cohabitors and marrieds report comparable levels of satisfaction and closeness and because these two groups report similar conflicts and problems. However, both the present study and past research have shown that there are several important differences between these two groups. Recent research regarding levels of satisfaction, closeness, and conflicts shows that cohabitors are less likely than marrieds to be happy (Boba, 1996; Stack and Eshleman, 1998), they are less committed to their relationships (Forste and Tanfer, 1996; Nock, 1995), they have differing expectations about the future (Bumpass, Sweet, and Cherlin, 1991; Waite, 1995), and they report both more trouble in their relationships and more disagreements (Boba, 1996).

The present work has taken great pains to identify whether or not cohabitors and marrieds should be combined in analyses of violence. Using a large-scale representative sample of Canada this study has demonstrated unequivocally that women who cohabit, and those who cohabited with someone other than their husbands prior to getting married, are more likely to experience violence than married women who have never cohabited with someone other than their husbands. While DeKeseredy and Hinch (1991:8-9) conclude, "it is difficult to differentiate between cohabitors and legally married women," the results of previous studies combined with the findings of the present investigation lead to the conclusion that mixing these two marital status groups in analyses results in mixed analytical messages that obscure our understanding of the causes of violence against women.

Different Processes

Past research showing that cohabitors have higher rates of violence than marrieds was taken as an indication in the present work that something different may be operating in the production of violence for cohabitors and marrieds. A number of different possible frameworks to explain this were articulated and tested in a holistic model. Following Nock's (1995) method, the analyses show that the difference between cohabitors and marrieds is not due to the status of the relationship per se. Since women who have a past cohabitation experience with someone other than their husbands but who are now married are more similar to cohabitors with respect to rates of violence than women without such a past experience, it is concluded that simply being married or cohabiting does not explain cohabitors' higher rate of violence.

A major gap in all research on cohabitation and marriage, as noted by Cunningham and Antill (1995), is the failure to understand the underlying processes at work in these types of unions. The present study synthesizes variables from past explanations in a context that attempts to understand the underlying processes that lead to differential experiences of violence for the different marital status groups. The descriptive analyses indicate that there may be many connections among variables in the model. Most of the general family violence literature that mentions higher rates of violence among cohabitors conjectures such tentative connections. However, the more sophisticated multivariate analysis, through taking into account the effects of all of the variables in the model, shows many of these tentative connections to be misleading. The multivariate analysis also finds virtually no support for the application of existing theoretical frameworks in the family violence literature to understanding marital status differences in violence. The one exception is an explanatory framework for which family violence researchers had, until now, deemed inapplicable to understanding "marital" violence. Based on the analysis in the present study, a number of hypothesized relationships of Routine Activities theory appear to hold true. However, this approach needs to be put to a much more stringent test rather than using proxies to evaluate its validity. The analyses in the present study also show that framing the discourse surrounding this issue in terms of the type of people who choose to cohabit *versus* the type of relationships characteristic of cohabitors and marrieds creates a false dichotomy. While the results do show that marital status differences have the strongest link to the type of people who are selected into cohabitation, it is also apparent that the most comprehensive understanding of marital status differences in violence is derived from the combination of both selection and relationship factors.

The most important general finding of the present study is that the selection and relationship variables do have some merit, but their value depends on which marital status group one is investigating. Something different does indeed seem to be operating in the production of violence across marital status groups. The theoretical synthesis in the present study points to different underlying processes at work in each of these union types. For cohabiting women it seems that violence is particularly linked to the selection factors of youth, unemployment, past partner violence, and the relationship factors of childlessness, having a cohabiting partner who keeps tabs on them, and depression. As already mentioned, the importance of some of these variables points to Routine Activities theory but, in addition, the theoretical synthesis of the present study suggests that underlying the importance of these selection and relationship characteristics is a less stable nomos. It seems that the type of people who choose to cohabit are less amenable to developing a stable nomos and the characteristics of their relationships, perhaps including their routine activities, both reflect and reinforce this state of affairs. It also appears that PC married women's selection and relationship characteristics lead them to be more likely to establish a less stable nomos than women who did not live with anyone other than their husbands before getting married. While some might expect cohabitors to be less conventional than PC marrieds since the latter have eventually chosen to abide by tradition and marry, multivariate analysis shows selection and relationship characteristics that point to a more general social marginality are particularly linked to violence for this group. PC married women who are previously married, who are married to a partner of a different age than they, who translated a violent dating relationship into a marriage, whose partners were exposed to violence as a child and are jealous and socially isolating are particularly likely to experience violence. In other words, it seems that these women have been limited to marginal relationship choices and are with men who may be less inhibited from being violent. These more socially marginal selection and relationship characteristics point to the development of a less stable relationship nomos. Different variables are linked to particularly high odds of violence for cohabitors and PC marrieds, and the descriptive analyses show these two groups to be different in terms of the types of violence that they are most likely to experience. This is indicative that the nomos they develop are unique. On the other hand, while cohabitors and PC marrieds may have a less stable nomos than non-PC marrieds, the characteristic of non-PC marrieds' that stands out as being particularly important relative to cohabitors and PC marrieds is dominance. To be sure, the stability of marriage that Berger and Kellner (1994) discuss is couched in a society with a patriarchal structure and ideology. One might say that the nomos to which they refer is a patriarchal nomos. The analysis in the present study further confirms the work of feminist researchers who find that "marital" violence is linked to patriarchy. Men married to more traditional women, that is those who have never cohabited, and who behave in a patriarchal manner through controlling family income, are particularly likely to commit the most common form of violence reported by Canadian women, minor physical assault. In addition, it appears that dominance by partners of non-PC married women may be linked to their higher relative probability of being forced into sexual activity.

Implications for Future Research

Having found that cohabitors, PC marrieds, and non-PC marrieds are three distinct groups with respect to violence, it would seem reasonable to conclude that for a greater understanding of the causes of partner violence against women, disaggregation by marital status is warranted in future research. To be sure, cohabitors and marrieds should not be combined simply to elevate marrieds' rates of violence or to increase the sub-sample of victims of violence in a given study. PC marrieds in particular, with their surprisingly higher rate of violence and unique characteristics, should be studied since we know even less about this group than we know about cohabitors.

There is also some indication in the present study that, depending on the purpose of one's study, researchers should also consider analyzing separate forms of violence in addition to overall violence. Most of the research on family violence simply investigates one violence variable that combines several different forms of violence. It is apparent from the analyses that the propensity to experience different forms of violence varies by marital status. PC marrieds are more likely to experience less physically consequential forms of violence, cohabitors are more likely to experience more physically severe violence, and non-PC marrieds are more likely to experience sexual coercion. As well, while the conclusions from the overall analysis remain the same, some selection and relationship variables operate differently across the marital status groups depending on which component of violence is being investigated. Analyzing each component of violence separately, then, can provide nuances of understanding that supplement analyses of variables that combine several different forms of violence. If it fits with the goals of their studies, future researchers should consider following such a method. At the very least, researchers should be sensitive to the components that comprise their violence variables and how the inclusion or lack of inclusion of certain components may affect their results.

Over the course of completing this work, many different hypotheses and branches for future research arose. The enormity of the task at hand meant that these research questions largely could not be pursued. Future research must address these issues. This section will conclude with a discussion of one such issue, but before doing so it is important to note a number of limitations of the present study that must be overcome in future research.

Future quantitative research in this area must be based on a survey designed from the outset to understand marital status differences in violence. Instead of using proxies to test theories, variables need to be tapped in the survey that more directly measure the concepts derived from theoretical explanations for marital status differences. The collection of data with variables that adequately measure theoretical concepts for understanding marital status differences would lend itself to more sophisticated methods of analysis such as LISREL. While the overall analysis of violence shows that variables that select individuals into cohabitation are of primordial importance relative to relationship variables, the examination of each component of violence separately shows that for most forms of violence it is the combination of both selection and relationship variables that offers the greatest understanding of the etiology of marital status differences in violence. This implies that further research is needed to identify the connections between selection and relationship variables. Better measures along with a structural equation modeling approach would allow one to identify specific connections between selection variables, relationship variables, and violence.

There are also a number of selection variables that persons may bring with them to their unions that may be included in future surveys. These include race and ethnicity. The only study that compares violence among cohabitors and marrieds in terms of race was conducted by Stets (1991). Stets (1991) reports that cohabitors are overrepresented among blacks. In a logistic regression analysis, Stets (1991) finds that being black, as opposed to white, has a statistically significant effect on marital status differences in violence. Research conducted by Turcotte and Bélanger (1997) points to the importance of collecting data on ethnicity in Canada. Using data from the 1995 General Social Survey, these researchers find that francophones are more likely than anglophones to form a common-law union as their first union. Interestingly, in addition to Quebec being a unique region culturally, it appears that the effects of culture in terms of cohabitation go beyond provincial borders. Defining those with a mother tongue of French as the measure of francophone status, Turcotte and Bélanger (1997) find that the relationship between francophone/anglophone status operates regardless of province of residence. That is, even francophones living outside Quebec are more likely to cohabit as a first union. As well as race and ethnicity, research indicates that parental divorce may make children skeptical of marriage and result in cohabitation. Several studies report a link between parental marital dissolution and cohabitation (Cunningham and Antill, 1995; Dumas, 1997; Thornton, 1991; Turcotte and Bélanger, 1997). Religiosity has also been identified as a correlate of cohabitation (Cunningham and Antill, 1995; Turcotte and Bélanger, 1997; Wu and Balakrishnan, 1992). Cunningham and Antill

(1995) have also identified a number of other selection variables that have been linked to cohabitation and that may be of interest to future researchers. The higher the number of sexual partners the more likely an individual is to cohabit. As well, the lower one's parental marital happiness, the poorer the quality of relationship with one's parents, and the lower the age at first sexual intercourse, the more likely an individual is to cohabit. Future researchers may want to investigate possible links between these selection variables and violence.

There is also one additional relationship variable that future researchers may want to explore. While the childlessness of cohabitors is linked to violence in the present study, future research should investigate possible linkages of step-children to violence. The presence of step-children is a risk marker of violence. Daly, Singh, and Wilson (1993) find an overrepresentation of women with children fathered by previous partners among shelter clients. Children in common-law unions are more likely to have been fathered by a previous partner than children in marital unions (Johnson, 1996; Wilson, Johnson, and Daly, 1995). It seems possible, then, that there may be a link between the presence of step-children and the development of a relationship nomos prone to violence. Though Ellis (1989) has also recognized the possibility of a connection between cohabitation, the presence of step-children and violence, this hypothesis remains to be tested.

In addition to collecting information on more selection and relationship variables, other questions must be included in surveys that allow further testing and development of the theoretical synthesis in the present study. Future studies must collect more detailed information on cohabitation. The best test of the theoretical synthesis in the present study necessitates collecting information that would allow marrieds to be divided into three groups: those who have never cohabited, those who cohabited with their current marital partner only, and those who cohabited with someone other than their current partner. In the language of the theoretical synthesis, studying those who cohabited only with someone other than their current partner, as has been done in the present work, allows one a glimpse into how cohabitation affects the subjective reality an individual brings to a new marital relationship. On the other hand, investigating those who cohabited with only their current marital partner will allow one to identify how the nomos the couple develops together carries over to their marital relationship. As well, it would be beneficial not only to have the cohabitation history of the female partner, as is the case in the present study, but also it is important to have data on the cohabitation history of the male partner. This would allow one to compare the effects of various combinations of past cohabitation experiences on relationship nomos and violence. Also with respect to gender specific data, another limitation of the present study is that no information is available on violence perpetrated by women. It was noted in chapter 2 that the rate of uxoricide perpetrated by women in common-law unions is even greater than that of men. As an aside, given the high rate of severe violence among PC marrieds, it would also be interesting to compare this group to cohabitors in terms of uxoricide in future research. As well, as is indicated in table A.1 of appendix A, studies that compare marital status groups on the perpetration of violence by women suggest that women in cohabiting unions are more likely to be violent than are women in marital relationships (Brinkerhoff and Lupri, 1988; Sommer, 1994). Given that cohabiting women in the present study are most likely to report severe violence, it may be that women in these relationships are more likely to use severe violence in self-defense. However, Stets and Straus's (1989) research suggests that cohabiting women may be more likely to be severely violent even when the male partner is not violent. These researchers found that 13.4 percent for cohabiting and 9.6 percent of married couples in their sample reported that the male was not violent and the female was severely violent. This suggests that severe violence among cohabiting women may not only be in self-defense and points to the development of a less stable and more violent relationship nomos. However, as noted at the beginning of this work there are many limitations to these studies and future research on marital status, gender, and violence is needed to provide accurate answers to these questions.

Aside from further quantitative testing of the theoretical synthesis in the present study, the results of this study also imply that qualitative analysis would be fruitful. Since it appears that there are unique experiences leading to violence in each marital status group, it would be interesting to generate grounded theoretical models of this process for each marital status group. This could be done à la the theoretical synthesis looking at the underlying processes and the role of selection and relationship variables. An approach grounded in the lived experiences of each group would provide insights needed to fully understand their differing experiences. As well, while it is useful to look at the context of the differing experiences of violence via post-violence comparisons, the extremely small post-violence subsample in the present study renders the findings extremely tentative. Future studies of victims only could also be conducted to provide a larger sample of respondents. However, the richest data about the context surrounding the violence experienced by different marital status groups would undoubtedly be collected through a qualitative approach.

One of the most interesting topics for future research arising from the present study concerns violence against women in Quebec. The results show that the prevalence of violence against women in Quebec is lower than in any other region of Canada. Not only is this the case for marrieds, but also for cohabitors. This is surprising since, as mentioned in chapter 2, Quebec has the highest rate of cohabitation in Canada. Given the higher rate of violence among cohabitors one might expect a higher rate of violence in Quebec. These results point to a cultural difference in Quebec. As hypothesized in the present study, the Quiet Revolution in Quebec has led to a less patriarchal culture and it seems possible that this explains both Quebec's higher rate of cohabitation and its lower rate of violence. In addition to this hypothesis, there are still many other questions that remain unanswered. Despite cohabitation being more normative in Quebec, the present study has shown that violence is still more prevalent among cohabitors than among marrieds in that region. This suggests that even in a less patriarchal culture and where cohabitation is more normative there is something about cohabitation that links it to higher odds of violence. The development of a less stable nomos may not be limited to societies in which cohabitation is not normative. Future research is needed to identify the role of culture on the development of relationship nomos in different marital status groups and the resultant impact on violence. A research study focusing specifically on Quebec would provide an excellent laboratory for answering these fascinating questions.

Concluding Comments

There remain many gaps in our knowledge of violence against women that need to be filled. Despite the fact that there have been hundreds of studies on the topic of violence against women since the 1970s, until now there has been a dearth of information, especially in Canada, on marital status differences in violence. On the basis of an exhaustive review of the literature, the present study has shown that there are only five studies in Canada that have included an investigation of variations in violence against women across marital status categories. With the exception of the VAWS, these studies are based on very small samples of less than fifty cohabitors and thus do not permit reliable generalizations. The only Canadian results based on large-scale data are descriptive in nature. This study represents the only in-depth analysis of the relationship between marital status and violence based on Canadian data at either the regional or national level. The importance of conducting research on Canadian data has been highlighted by a recent publication that shows partner violence, particularly severe violence, to be more common in the Canadian than in the American population (Grandin and Lupri, 1997). Analyzing the VAWS data has not only allowed an unequivocal investigation of differential rates of violence in marital and common-law unions in Canada, but it has also provided an opportunity to address previously unanswered theoretical questions through empirically testing a variety of potential explanatory frameworks for understanding marital status differences in violence.

The rubric of family violence has always been, and probably will always be, characterized by controversy. As the authors of a recent text on family violence have noted, "Much of the dispute has erupted over divergent views about the causes of family violence...and hence the most effective solutions" (Barnett, Miller-Perrin and Perrin, 1997:22). A deeper understanding of the etiology of family violence is thus needed. A number of researchers have also pointed to the unfortunate lack of research on the etiology of family violence (Avakame, 1993; DeKeseredy and MacLeod, 1997; Feldman and Ridley, 1995; Gelles, 1983; Hotaling and Sugarman, 1986; Lenton, 1995b; Smith, 1990b; Stith and Farley, 1993; Weis, 1989). Not only has there specifically been a relative lack of quantitative research in the field (Rosenbaum, 1988), but there has also been a corresponding deficit in multivariate analyses (Avakame, 1993; Herzberger, 1993; Hotaling and Sugarman, 1986; Howell and Pugliesi, 1988; Lenton, 1995b; Neff, Holamon, and Schluter, 1995; O'Leary, 1988; Ryan, 1995; Tontodonato and Crew, 1992).

This work has addressed these issues and filled a major gap in family violence research. We now know that an understanding of marital status differences in violence is a requisite for a complete understanding of the etiology of male partner violence against women. The methodological, theoretical, and substantive advances in this research represent a major contribution to our understanding of partner violence. It is our hope that through this effort we have moved one step closer to understanding and, ultimately, ending male partner violence against women.

Appendix A

Appendix table A.1 provides an exhaustive overview of studies that include a comparison of violence between marital and common-law relationships. The components of these studies identified in the table include when the field work was conducted, the size of the respective subsamples, the study design, the manner in which the data were collected, how violence and cohabitation were defined, the manner in which violence was measured, and the prevalence and incidence rates reported.

Table A.1. *Summary of Studies Comparing Differences in Violence Between Married and Common-law Unions.*

Scholars	Date of field work and sample	Design	Data Collection	Definition of Violence	Definition of Cohabitation	Measurement	Rates of Violence
Yllö and Straus (1981)	1976 National prob. n of couples. Total n 2,143 Marr. n 2,049 Coh. n 37	Telephone survey	Interviews	An act carried out with the intention of, or perceived as having the intention of, physically hurting another person (p.342).	A more or less permanent relationship in which two unmarried persons of the opposite sex share a living facility without legal contract (p.342).	CTS (physical violence items)	1 year prevalence of M-to-F *Overall:* Marr. 11.6 Coh. 32.4 1 year prevalence of M-to-F *Severe:* Marr. 3.6 Coh. 13.5 1 year prevalence of total couple *Overall:* Marr. 15.1 Coh. 37.8 1 year prevalence of total couple *Severe* Marr. 5.6 Coh. 27.0
Schulman (1981)	1979 Random x-section n of Kentucky women married or living with a male partner. Total n 1,793 Marr. n 1,733 Coh. n 20	Telephone survey	Telephone interviews	"Violence" refers to 8 acts included on the CTS (p.6). "Abuse" includes items which are more extreme and would result in greatest physical damage (p.6).	Any woman who, at the time of the survey, was presently living with a male partner (Appendix -C- p.1).	CTS	Total 1 year prevalence of acts of violence by male partner: Marr. 6.2 Coh. 9.4 Total 1 year prevalence of acts of abuse by male partner: Marr. 3.3 Coh. 2.0

Table A.1 continued.

Scholars	Date of field work and sample	Design	Data Collection	Definition of Violence	Definition of Cohabitation	Measurement	Rates of Violence
Lane and Gwartney-Gibbs (1985)	1982 Random n of undergraduates at a large university in the Northwest. Total n 325 Marr. n 31 Coh. n 11	Survey	Self-administered mail questionnaires	*Conflict:* During disagreement: discussed issue heatedly; sulked/ refused to talk; got drunk; cried. *Abuse:* A deliberate act by 1 partner to hurt the other through words or symbolic actions. *Violence:* One partner attempting to hurt or maim the other through physical force. *Assault:* The most extreme violent acts (p.49).	Students cohabiting unmarried with a member of the opposite sex (p.52).	Modified version of the CTS.	Proportion that experienced some form of: *Conflict:* Marr. 97.9 Coh. 100.0 *Abuse:* Marr. 71.5 Coh. 91.2 *Violence:* Marr. 41.3 Coh. 83.3 *Assault:* Marr. 10.5 Coh. 8.3 Proportion that inflicted some form of: *Conflict:* Marr. 93.7 Coh. 100.0 *Abuse:* Marr. 62.9 Coh. 87.4 *Violence:* Marr. 38.8 Coh. 70.7 *Assault:* Marr. 5.2 Coh. 15.3

Table A.1 continued.

Scholars	Date of field work and sample	Design	Data Collection	Definition of Violence	Definition of Cohabitation	Measurement	Rates of Violence	
Smith (1986)	1985 Probability n of adult women in Toronto. Total n 315 Marr. n 192 Coh. n 47	Telephone Survey	Telephone Interviews	Any physical assault on a woman by a man with whom the woman has, or has had, a romantic relationship (1987, p.179).	N.A.	Slightly re-worded ren-dition of the CTS.	Lifetime prevalence of abuse by intimates: Marr. Coh.	14.1 34.0
Brinkerhoff and Lupri (1988)	1981 Systematic random n of of Calgary couples. Total n 562 Marr. n 518 Coh. n 43	Survey	Interviews and self-administered questionnaires	*Normal Violence:* An "act carried out with the intention, or per-ceived intention, of causing physical pain or injury to another person. *Abusive Violence:* An "act which has the potential for injuring the person being hit" (p.415).	A heterosexual couple who indicated that they were living common-law at the time of the study (p.413).	CTS Present data only on overall violence which includes both "normal" and "abusive" violence (p.415).	1 year prevalence of overall violence by either partner: Marr. Coh. 1 year prevalence of M-F violence: Marr. Coh. 1 year prevalence of F-M violence: Marr. Coh.	13.1 27.9 10.2 11.6 12.7 20.9

Table A.1 continued.

Scholars	Date of field work and sample	Design	Data Collection	Definition of Violence	Definition of Cohabitation	Measurement	Rates of Violence
Stets and Straus (1989)	a) 1985 National (US) probability n. Total n 5,242 b) 1987 Random n of university students. Total n 526 Total n 5,768 Marr. n 5,005 Coh. n 237	a) Telephone survey b) Survey	a) Telephone interviews b) N.A.	An act carried out with the intention or perceived intention of causing physical pain or injury (p.162). Eight items of the CTS divided into minor and severe violence (both together equal Assault rate).	A currently cohabiting heterosexual couple (p.166).	CTS	*Assault rate* by either partner during past year: Marr. 15.0 Coh. 35.0
Kennedy and Dutton (1989)	1987 Probability n of Alberta. Total n 1,045 Marr. n 631 Coh. n 48	Survey	Fact-to-face and telephone interviews	Any act carried out with the intention or perceived intention of causing physical pain or injury to another person (p.41).	Single, separated and divorced people who have lived in a marriage-like relationship in the previous year (p.672).	CTS	Husband-wife violence during the past year: Marr. 8.7 Coh. 24.4

Table A.1 continued.

Scholars	Date of field work and sample	Design	Data Collection	Definition of Violence	Definition of Cohabitation	Measurement	Rates of Violence	
Stets (1991)	1988 National (US) probability n. Total n 13,017 Marr. n approx. 5,000 Coh. n approx. 500	Survey	Interviews	An act that causes harm to another (p.669).	An individual living with another as a couple in a household without being married (p.672).	How often, during the past year, fights with a spouse or a partner resulted in their hitting, shoving, or throw-ing things at their spouse or partner.	Hit, shoved or thrown things during past year: Marr. Coh.	5.0 14.0
Statistics Canada (1993)	1993 Random n of Canadian women. Total n 12,300 Marr. n 7,396 Coh. n 1,022	Telephone survey	Telephone interviews	Questions designed on legal definitions of physical and sexual assault as contained in the Canadian *Criminal Code* (Johnson, 1995a: 129).	Partners living together as husband and wife without being legally married (Statistics Canada, 1994:30).	"Wife Assault": derived from the CTS with the addition of sexual attack. Respon-dents asked a series of quest-ions describing violent actions their spouses may have taken against them (Statistics Canada, 1993:5).	a) Lifetime prevalence of violence (current partner): Marr. Coh. b) 1 year prevalence of violence (current partner): Marr. Coh.	15.0 18.0 2.0 9.0

Table A.1 continued.

Scholars	Date of field work and sample	Design	Data Collection	Definition of Violence	Definition of Cohabitation	Measurement	Rates of Violence
Sommer (1994)	1991-1992 Probability n of Winnipeg (Wave 2) Total n 369 Marr. n 334 Coh. n 27	Survey	Interviews and self-administered questionnaires.	An act (or acts) carried out with the intention, or perceived intention of causing physical pain or injury to another person (p.4).	Derived from marital status category "living with partner" (p.220).	Abridged version of CTS (six "physical force" items) (p.85).	1 year prevalence of male perp.: Marr. 5.1 Coh. 22.2 1 year prevalence of female perp.: Marr. 5.1 Coh. 27.3
Jackson (1996)	1985 National (US) probability n. of couples. Total n 5,159 Marr. n 4,910 Coh. n 249	Telephone survey	Telephone interviews	N.A.	Non-married subjects living together as an unmarried couple at the time of the survey.	CTS	Cohabitors have higher 1 year prevalence of violence than marrieds at all levels of severity.
Boba (1996)	1987 National (US) probability n. of couples Total n 6,166 Marr. n 5,811 Coh. n 355	Survey	Interviews and self-administered questionnaires	Physical violence that occurs between intimates (p.3).	N.A.	Respondents asked if partner became physical in an argument (p.38).	1 year prevalence of physical violence: Marr. 9.6 Coh. 26.5

Table A.1 continued.

Scholars	Date of field work and sample	Design	Data Collection	Definition of Violence	Definition of Cohabitation	Measurement	Rates of Violence
Anderson (1997)	1987 National (US) probability n. of couples Total n 4,948 Marr. n. N.A. Coh. n N.A.	Survey	Interviews and self-administered questionnaires.	Physical violence.	N.A.	Respondents asked if any argument became physical. If so, asked how many arguments resulted in the respondent, or the respondent's partner "hitting, shoving, or throwing something" (p.661).	Cohabitors more likely to engage in physical violence in previous year.
Magdol et al. (1998)	1993-1994 Representative n of young adults age 21. Longitudinal study of complete birth cohort in Dunedin, New Zealand. Total n 777 Marr. n 27 Coh. N 219	Survey	Interview with responses re-corded on a private answer sheet by the interviewee.	Physical violence.	Living together as a couple (p.47).	Respondents asked if had performed behaviors toward current or most recent partner in Past 12 months. Constructed dichotomous measure of any physical violence based on the CTS items plus 4 additional items (p.47).	1 year prevalence of physical violence: Marr. 41.0 Coh. 48.0

Appendix B

Appendix figures B.1 and B.2 provide a graphical representation of the one-year and lifetime prevalence rates by age controlling for duration of relationship. These figures suggest that the key variable for understanding the difference between lifetime and one-year prevalence rates by age is duration of relationship. As one would expect, the percentage of respondents reporting violence is higher in the lifetime than in the one-year time frame. Also, as one would expect, with the one-year prevalence rate there is a negative relationship between duration and violence. With the lifetime time frame the relationship is positive. What is striking, however, is the similarity between the one-year and lifetime prevalence rates in terms of their operation within the duration categories. The relationship between violence and age is the same within the duration categories for both one-year and lifetime time frames. This suggests that, all other things being equal, if one controls for duration of relationship prevalence rates with a lifetime and one-year time frame should operate in the same manner.

Figure B.1. *One-Year Prevalence of Violence by Respondent's Age Controlling for Duration of Relationship.*

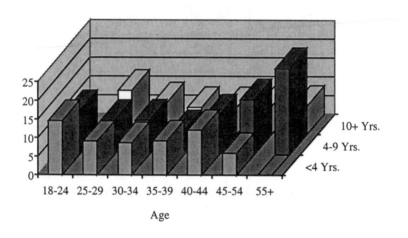

Age

Figure B.2. *Lifetime Prevalence of Violence by Respondent's Age Controlling for Duration of Relationship.*

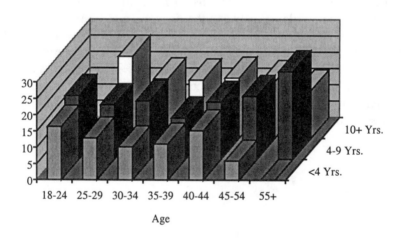

Age

Bibliography

Adams, Bert N. *The Family: A sociological Interpretation.* Toronto: Harcourt Brace Jovanovich, 1986.

Aguilar, Rudy J., and Narina N. Nightingale. "The Impact of Specific Battering Experiences on the Self-Esteem of Abused Women." *Journal of Family Violence* 9(1994):35-45.

Aldarondo, Etiony. "Cessation and Persistence of Wife Assault: A Longitudinal Analysis." *American Journal of Orthospsychiatry* 66(1996):141-151.

Anderson, Kristin L. "Gender, Status, and Domestic Violence: An Integration of Feminist and Family Violence Approaches." *Journal of Marriage and the Family* 59(1997):655-669.

Avakame, Edem Frank. "Explaining Domestic Violence." Doctoral Dissertation, Department of Sociology, University of Alberta, Edmonton, 1993.

Baer, Douglas E., Edward Grabb, and William A. Johnston. "The Values of Canadians and Americans: A Critical Analysis and Reassessment." *Social Forces* 68(1990):693-713.

Bandura, Albert. *Social Learning Theory.* Morristown, N.J.: General Learning, 1971.

Barnett, Ola W., Cindy L. Miller-Perrin, and Robin D. Perrin. *Family Violence across the Lifespan: An Introduction.* Thousand Oaks, Calif.: Sage, 1997.

Bennett, Larry W. "Substance Abuse and the Domestic Assault of Women." *Social Work* 40(1995):760-771.

Berger, Peter, and Hansfried Kellner. "Marriage and the Construction of Reality: An Exercise in the Microsociology of Knowledge." Pp. 3-17 in *The Psychosocial Interior of the Family*, edited by G. Handel and G. G. Whitchurch. New York: Aldine de Gruyter, 1994.

Bernard, Jessie. *The Future of Marriage.* New Haven: Yale University Press, 1982.

Bersani, Carl, and Huey-Tsyh Chen. "Sociological Perspectives in Family Violence." Pp. 57-86 in *Handbook of Family Violence*, edited by V. V. Hasselt, R. Morrison, and A. Bellack. New York: Plenum Press, 1988.

Blood, Robert O., and Donald M. Wolfe. *Husband and Wives: The Dynamics of Married Living.* Glencoe, Ill.: Free Press, 1960.

Boba, Rachel Louise. "Violence Between Married and Unmarried Cohabiting Partners: An Analysis Using Couple-Level Data." Doctoral Dissertation, Arizona State University, Phoenix, 1996.

Booth, Alan, and David Johnson. "Premarital Cohabitation and Marital Success." *Journal of Family Issues* 9(1988):255-272.

Bowker, Lee H. *Beating Wife-Beating.* Lexington, Mass.: D. C. Heath, 1983.

Brinkerhoff, Merlin B., and Eugen Lupri. "Interspousal Violence." *Canadian Journal of Sociology* 13(1988):407-434.

Brownridge, Douglas A., and Shiva S. Halli. "Measuring Family Violence: The Conceptualization and Utilization of Prevalence and Incidence Rates." *Journal of Family Violence* 14(1999):333-350.

____. "'Living in Sin' and Sinful Living: Toward Filling a Gap in the Explanation of Violence against Women." *Aggression and Violent Behavior* 5/6(2000):forthcoming.

Brush, Lisa D. "Violent Acts and Injurious Outcomes in Married Couples: Methodological Issues in the National Survey of Families and Households." *Gender and Society* 4(1990):56-67.

Bumpass, Larry L, James A. Sweet, and Andrew Cherlin. "The Role of Cohabitation in Declining Rates of Marriage." *Journal of Marriage and the Family* 53(1991):913-927.

Burch, Thomas K., and A. K. Madan. "Union Formation and Dissolution: Results from the 1984 Family History Survey." Statistics Canada, Housing, Family and Social Statistical Division, Ottawa, 1986.

Bushman, Brad J., and Harris M. Cooper. "Effects of Alcohol on Human Aggression: An Integrative Research Review." *Psychological Bulletin* 107(1990):341-354.

Call, Vaughn, Susan Sprecher, and Pepper Schwartz. "The Incidence and Frequency of Marital Sex in a National Sample." *Journal of Marriage and the Family* 57(1995):639-652.

Canadian Centre for Justice Statistics. "Family Violence in Canada." Statistics Canada, Ottawa, 1994.

Cantos, Arthur L., Peter H. Neidig, and K. Daniel O'Leary. "Injuries of Women and Men in a Treatment Program for Domestic Violence." *Journal of Family Violence* 9(1994):113-124.

Cazenave, Noel A., and Murray A. Straus. "Race, Class, Network Embeddedness and Family Violence: A Search for Potent Support Systems." *Journal of Comparative Family Studies* 10(1979):281-300.

Che-Alford, Janet, Catherine Allan, and George Butlin. "Focus on Canada: Families in Canada." Statistics Canada, Ottawa, 1994.

Crawford, Maria, and Rosemary Gartner. "Woman Killing: Intimate Femicide in Ontario 1974-1990." Women We Honour Action Committee, Toronto, 1992.

Cunningham, John D., and John K. Antill. "Current Trends in Nonmarital Cohabitation: In Search of the POSSLQ." Pp. 148-172 in *Under-Studied Relationships: Off the Beaten Track*, vol. 6, *Understanding Relationship Processes Series*, edited by J. T. Wood and S. Duck. Thousand Oaks, Calif.: Sage, 1995.

Daly, Martin, Lisa Singh, and Margo Wilson. "Children Fathered by Previous Partners: A Risk Factor for Violence Against Women." *Canadian Journal of Public Health* 84(1993):209-210.

DeKeseredy, Walter, and Katherine Kelly. "Woman Abuse in University and College Dating Relationships: The Contribution of the Ideology of Familial Patriarchy." *Journal of Human Justice* 4(1993):25-52.

_____. "Sexual Abuse in Canadian University and College Dating Relationships: The Contribution of Male Peer Support." *Journal of Family Violence* 10(1995):41-53.

DeKeseredy, Walter S., and Ronald Hinch. *Woman Abuse: Sociological Perspectives*. Toronto: Thompson Educational Publishing, 1991.

DeKeseredy, Walter S., and Linda MacLeod. *Woman Abuse: A Sociological Story*. Toronto: Harcourt Brace and Company, 1997.

Dobash, Emerson R., and Russel P. Dobash. *Violence against Wives: A Case against the Patriarchy*. New York: Free Press, 1979.

Dobash, Russell P., and R. Emerson Dobash. "Reflections on Findings from the Violence against Women Survey." *Canadian Journal of Criminology* 37(1995):457-484.

Dobash, Russell, R. Emerson Dobash, Margo Wilson, and Martin Daly. "The Myth of Sexual Symmetry in Marital Violence." *Social Problems* 39(1992):71-91.

Doob, Anthony N. "Understanding the Attacks on Statistics Canada's Violence against Women Survey." Pp. 157-165 in *Wife Assault and the Canadian Criminal Justice System*, edited by M. Valverde, L. MacLeod, and K. Johnson. Toronto: Centre of Criminology, University of Toronto, 1995.

Duffy, Ann, and Julianne Momirov. *Family Violence: A Canadian Introduction.* Toronto: James Lorimer and Company, 1997.

Dumas, Jean. *Report on the Demographic Situation in Canada 1996.* Ottawa: Statistics Canada, 1997.

Dutton, Donald G. "Profiling of Wife Assaulters: Preliminary Evidence for a Trimodal Analysis." *Violence and Victims* 3(1988):5-29.

Ellis, Desmond. "Male Abuse of a Married or Cohabiting Female Partner: The Application of Sociological Theory to Research Findings." *Violence and Victims* 4(1989):235-255.

Ellis, Desmond, and Walter S. DeKeseredy. "Marital Status and Woman Abuse: The DAD Model." *International Journal of Sociology of the Family* 19(1989):67-87.

Eshleman, J. Ross, and Susannah J. Wilson. *The Family.* Scarborough: Allyn and Bacon, 1998.

Fekete, John. *Moral Panic: Biopolitics Rising.* Montreal: Robert Davies, 1994.

Feldman, Clyde M., and Carl A. Ridley. "The Etiology and Treatment of Domestic Violence Between Adult Partners." *Clinical Psychology: Science and Practice* 2(1995):317-348.

Felson, Richard B. "Routine Activities and Involvement in Violence as Actor, Witness, or Target." *Violence and Victims* 12(1997):209-221.

Fitzgerald, Robin. "Family Violence in Canada: A Statistical Profile 1999." Statistics Canada, Canadian Centre for Justice Statistics, Ottawa, 1999.

Follingstad, Diane R., Larry L. Rutledge, Barbara J. Berg, Elizabeth S. Hause, and Darlene S. Polek. "The Role of Emotional Abuse in Physically Abusive Relationships." *Journal of Family Violence* 5(1990):107-120.

Forste, Renata, and Koray Tanfer. "Sexual Exclusivity Among Dating, Cohabiting, and Married Women." *Journal of Marriage and the Family* 58(1996):33-47.

Freeman, Michael D. A., and Christina M. Lyon. *Cohabitation without Marriage.* Aldershot: Gower Publishing, 1983.

Funk and Wagnalls. *Standard College Dictionary.* Winnipeg: Funk and Wagnalls Publishing Company, 1982.

Gelles, Richard J. "Toward a Theory of Intra-Familial Violence: An Exchange/Social Control Theory." Pp. 151-165 in *The Dark Side of Families: Current Family Violence Research*, edited by D. Finkelhor, R. J. Gelles, G. T. Hotaling, and M. A. Straus. Beverly Hills, Calif.: Sage, 1983.

Gondolf, Edward W. "Batterer Programs: What We Know and Need to Know." *Journal of Interpersonal Violence* 12(1997):83-98.

Goode, William J. "Force and Violence in the Family." *Journal of Marriage and the Family* 33(1971):624-636.

Grandin, Elaine, and Eugen Lupri. "Intimate Violence in Canada and the United States: A Cross-National Comparison." *Journal of Family Violence* 12(1997):417-443.

Halli, Shiva S., and Zachary Zimmer. "Common Law Union as a Differentiating Factor in the Failure of Marriage in Canada, 1984." *Social Indicators Research* 24(1991):329-345.

Hamberger, Kevin L. "Introduction—Domestic Partner Abuse: Expanding Paradigms for Understanding and Intervention." *Violence and Victims* 9(1994):91-94.

Handel, Gerald, and Gail G. Whitchurch. *The Psychosocial Interior of the Family* (4th Ed.). New York: Aldine De Gruyter, 1994.

Herzberger, Sharon D. "The Cyclical Pattern of Child Abuse: A Study of Research Methodology." Pp. 33-51 in *Researching Sensitive Topics*, edited by C. M. Renzetti and R. M. Lee. Newbury Park: Sage Publications, 1993.

Hilton, N. Zoe, Grant T. Harris, and Marnie E. Rice. "On the Validity of Self-Reported Rates of Interpersonal Violence." *Journal of Interpersonal Violence* 13(1998):58-72.

Hobart, Charles, and Frank Grigel. "Cohabitation among Canadian Students at the End of the Eighties." *Journal of Comparative Family Studies* 23(1992):311-337.

Hoglund, Collete L., and Karen B. Nicholas. "Shame, Guilt, and Anger in College Students Exposed to Abusive Family Environments." *Journal of Family Violence* 10(1995):141-157.

Holland, Winnifred. "Introduction." Pp. 1-62 in *Cohabitation: The Law in Canada*, edited by W. H. Holland and B. E. Stalbecker-Pountney. Toronto: Carswell, 1995.

Hornung, Carlton A., B. Claire McCullough, and Taichi Sugimoto. "Status Relationships in Marriage: Risk Factors in Spouse Abuse." *Journal of Marriage and the Family* 43(1981):675-692.

Horwitz, Allan V., and Helene Raskin White. "The Relationship of Cohabitation and Mental Health: A Study of a Young Adult Cohort." *Journal of Marriage and the Family* 60(1998):505-514.

Hotaling, Gerald T., and David B. Sugarman. "An Analysis of Risk Markers in Husband to Wife Violence: The Current State of Knowledge." *Violence and Victims* 1(1986):101-124.

Howell, Marilyn J., and Karen L. Pugliesi. "Husbands Who Harm: Predicting Spousal Violence by Men." *Journal of Family Violence* 3(1988):15-27.

Jackson, Nicky Ali. "Observational Experiences of Intrapersonal Conflict and Teenage Victimization: A Comparative Study among Spouses and Cohabitors." *Journal of Family Violence* 11(1996):191-203.

Johnson, Holly. "Response to Allegations about the Violence against Women Survey." Pp. 148-156 in *Wife Assault and the Canadian Criminal Justice System*, edited by M. Valverde, L. MacLeod, and K.

Johnson. Toronto: Centre of Criminology, University of Toronto, 1995a.

____. "Seriousness, Type and Frequency of Violence against Wives." Pp. 125-147 in *Wife Assault and the Canadian Criminal Justice System*, edited by M. Valverde, L. MacLeod, and K. Johnson. Toronto: Centre of Criminology, University of Toronto, 1995b.

____. *Dangerous Domains: Violence against Women in Canada*. Scarborough: Nelson Canada, 1996.

Johnson, Michael P. "Patriarchal Terrorism and Common Couple Violence: Two Forms of Violence against Women." *Journal of Marriage and the Family* 57(1995):283-294.

Kantor, Glenda Kaufman, and Jana L. Jasinski. "Dynamics and Risk Factors in Partner Violence." Pp. 1-43 in *Partner Violence: A Comprehensive Review of 20 Years of Research*, edited by J. L. Jasinski and L. M. Williams. Thousand Oaks, Calif.: Sage, 1998.

Kasian, Marilyn, and Susan L. Painter. "Frequency and Severity of Psychological Abuse in a Dating Population." *Journal of Interpersonal Violence* 7(1992):350-364.

Kaufman, Joan, and Edward Zigler. "Do Abused Children Become Abusive Parents?" *American Journal of Orthopsychiatry* 57(1987):186-192.

Kennedy, Leslie W., and Donald G. Dutton. "The Incidence of Wife Assault in Alberta." *Canadian Journal of Behavioural Science* 21(1989):41-54.

Koss, Mary P. "The Underdetection of Rape: Methodological Choices Influence Incidence Estimates." *Journal of Social Issues* 48(1992):61-75.

Kurz, Demie. "Physical Assaults by Husbands: A Major Social Problem." Pp. 88-103 in *Current Controversies on Family Violence*, edited by R. J. Gelles and D. R. Loseke. Newbury Park, Calif.: Sage, 1993a.

Mihalic, Sharon Wofford, and Delbert Elliott. "A Social Learning Theory Model of Marital Violence." *Journal of Family Violence* 12(1997):21-47.

Miller, JoAnn L., and Amy C. Krull. "Controlling Domestic Violence: Victim Resources and Police Intervention." Pp. 235-254 in *Out of the Darkness: Contemporary Perspectives on Family Violence*, edited by G. K. Kantor and J. L. Jasinski. Thousand Oaks, Calif.: Sage, 1997.

Neff, James A., Bruce Holamon, and Tracy D. Schluter. "Spousal Violence among Anglos, Blacks, and Mexican Americans: The Role of Demographic Variables, Psychosocial Predictors, and Alcohol Consumption." *Journal of Family Violence* 10(1995):1-21.

Newcomb, Michael D. "Sexual Behavior of Cohabitors: A Comparison of Three Independent Samples." *Journal of Sex Research* 22(1986):492-513.

ock, Steven L. "A Comparison of Marriages and Cohabiting Relationships." *Journal of Family Issues* 16(1995):53-76.

un, Lewis. *Woman Abuse: Facts Replacing Myths*. Albany, N.Y.: State University of New York Press, 1986.

eary, K. Daniel. "Physical Aggression Between Spouses: A Social Learning Theory Perspective." Pp. 31-55 in *Handbook of Family Violence*, edited by V. B. V. Hasselt, R. L. Morrison, A. S. Bellack, nd M. Hersen. New York: Plenum Press, 1988.

on, Patricia. *When She Was Bad: Violent Women and the Myth of nocence*. Toronto: Random House, 1997.

d, Michael S., and Zheng Wu. "The Divergence of Quebec/Nonebec Marriage Patterns." *Population and Development Review* (1998):329-365.

Pamela A. "Societal Responses as Moderators of the Health Conuences of Wife Abuse." Doctoral Dissertation, Department of sing, University of Alberta, Edmonton, 1995.

____. "Social Science Perspectives on Wife Abuse: Current Debates a
Future Directions." Pp. 252-269 in *Violence against Women:*
Bloody Footprints, edited by P. B. Bart and E. G. Moran. Newl
Park, Calif.: Sage, 1993b.

Lane, Katherine E., and Patricia A. Gwartney-Gibbs. "Violence
Context of Dating and Sex." *Journal of Family Issues* 6(1985):

Larrivée, Daniel, and Pierre Parent. "For More and More Car
Common-Law Unions Make Good Sense." Statistics Can;
tawa, 1993.

Lenton, Rhonda L. "Feminist Versus Interpersonal Power TI
Wife Abuse Revisited." *Canadian Journal of Ci*
37(1995a):567-574.

____. "Power Versus Feminist Theories of Wife Abuse.'
Journal of Criminology 37(1995b):305-330.

Long, S. K., H. V. Tauchen, and A. Witte. "Violence an
Within Male-Female Relationships: An Empirical St
Institute of Mental Health, Washington, D.C., 1983.

Lupri, Eugen. "Male Violence in the Home." *Canadia*
14(1989):19-21.

Lupri, Eugen, Elaine Grandin, and Merlin B. Brinke
nomic Status and Male Violence in the Canadia
amination." *Canadian Journal of Sociology* 19(19'

Magdol, Lynn, Terrie E. Moffitt, Avshalom Caspi.
"Hitting without a License: Testing Explanatior
Partner Abuse between Young Adult Daters ar
nal of Marriage and the Family 60(1998):41-5!

Martin-Matthews, Anne. "Change and Diversity
Intergenerational Relations." Pp. 323-360 in (
versity, Conflict, and Change, edited by N.
Toronto: Harcourt Brace, 2000.

_____. "Modeling Acts of Aggression and Dominance as Wife Abuse and Exploring Their Adverse Health Effects." *Journal of Marriage and the Family* 60(1998):453-465.

Richardson, C. James. "Divorce and Remarriage in Families." Pp. 215-248 in *Changing Trends in Canada*, edited by M. Baker. Toronto: McGraw-Hill Ryerson, 1996.

Ritzer, George. *Contemporary Sociological Theory*. New York: Alfred A. Knopf, 1988.

Rodgers, Karen. "Wife Assault in Canada." *Canadian Social Trends*, 34(1994a):3-8.

_____. "Wife Assault: The Findings of a National Survey." *Juristat* 14(1994b):1-21.

Rodgers, Karen, and Georgia Roberts. "Women's Non-Spousal Multiple Victimization: A Test of the Routine Activities Theory." *Canadian Journal of Criminology* 37(1995):363-391.

Rosenbaum, Alan. "Methodological Issues in Marital Violence Research." *Journal of Family Violence* 3(1988):91-104.

Ryan, Kathryn M. "Do Courtship-Violent Men Have Characteristics Associated with a 'Battering Personality'?" *Journal of Family Violence* 10(1995):99-120.

Safilios-Rothschild, Constantina. "Family Sociology or Wives' Family Sociology? A Cross-Cultural Examination of Decision-Making." *Journal of Marriage and the Family* 31(1969):290-301.

Satzewich, Vic. "Race and Ethnic Relations." Pp. 215-239 in *New Society: Sociology for the 21st Century*, edited by R. J. Brym. Toronto: Harcourt Brace, 1998.

Schulman, Mark A. *A Survey of Spousal Violence against Women in Kentucky*, vol. 96. New York: Garland Publishing, 1981.

Sherman, Lawrence W. *Policing Domestic Violence: Experiments and Dilemmas*. New York: Free Press, 1992.

Smith, Michael D. *Woman Abuse: The Case for Surveys by Telephone.* LaMarsh Research Program on Violence and Conflict Resolution, Report No. 12. York University, North York, Ontario, 1985.

_____. "Effects of Question Format on the Reporting of Woman Abuse: A Telephone Survey Experiment." *Victimology* 11(1986):430-438.

_____. "The Incidence and Prevalence of Woman Abuse in Toronto." *Violence and Victims* 2(1987):173-187.

_____. "Woman Abuse: The Case for Surveys by Telephone." *Journal of Interpersonal Violence* 4(1989):308-324.

_____. "Patriarchal Ideology and Wife Beating: A Test of a Feminist Hypothesis." *Violence and Victims* 5(1990a):257-273.

_____. "Sociodemographic Risk Factors in Wife Abuse: Results from a Survey of Toronto Women." *Canadian Journal of Sociology* 15(1990b):39-58.

_____. "Enhancing the Quality of Survey Data on Violence against Women: A Feminist Approach." *Gender and Society* 8(1994):109-127.

Sommer, Reena. "Male and Female Perpetrated Partner Abuse: Testing a Diathesis-Stress Model." Doctoral Dissertation, Department of Family Studies, University of Manitoba, Winnipeg, 1994.

Spanier, Graham B. "Married and Unmarried Cohabitation in the United States: 1980." *Journal of Marriage and the Family* 45(1983):277-288.

Stack, Steven, and J. Ross Eshleman. "Marital Status and Happiness: A 17-Nation Study." *Journal of Marriage and the Family* 60(1998):527-536.

Statistics Canada. "Families: Number, Type and Structure." Minister of Industry, Science and Technology, Ottawa, 1992.

_____. "The Violence against Women Survey." *The Daily,* November 18(1993):1-9.

____. "Violence against Women Survey: Public Use Microdata File Documentation and User's Guide." Canadian Centre for Justice Statistics, Ottawa, 1994.

____. "1996 Census: Marital Status, Common-Law Unions and Families." *The Daily* October 14(1997):1-13.

Stets, Jan E. "Cohabiting and Marital Aggression: The Role of Social Isolation." *Journal of Marriage and the Family* 53(1991):669-680.

Stets, Jan E., and Murray A. Straus. "The Marriage License as a Hitting License: A Comparison of Assaults in Dating, Cohabiting, and Married Couples." *Journal of Family Violence* 4(1989):161-180.

Stith, Sandra M., and Sarah C. Farley. "A Predictive Model of Male Spousal Violence." *Journal of Family Violence* 8(1993):183-201.

Stout, Cam. "Common-Law: A Growing Alternative." *Canadian Social Trends* 23(1991):18-20.

Straus, Murray A. "Measuring Intrafamily Conflict and Violence: The Conflict Tactics (CT) Scales." *Journal of Marriage and the Family* 41(1979):75-88.

____. "New Scoring Methods for Violence and New Norms for the Conflict Tactics Scales." Pp. 535-559 in *Physical Violence in American Families: Risk Factors and Adaptations to Violence in 8,145 Families*, edited by M. A. Straus and R. J. Gelles. New Brunswick, N.J.: Transaction, 1990.

____. "Physical Assaults by Wives: A Major Social Problem." Pp. 67-87 in *Current Controversies on Family Violence*, edited by R. J. Gelles and D. R. Loseke. Newbury Park, Calif.: Sage, 1993.

Straus, Murray A., and Richard J. Gelles. "Societal Change and Change in Family Violence from 1975 to 1985 as Revealed by Two National Surveys." *Journal of Marriage and the Family* 48(1986):465-479.

Straus, Murray A., Richard J. Gelles, and Suzanne K. Steinmetz. *Behind Closed Doors: Violence in the American Family*. Garden City: Anchor Press/Doubleday, 1980.

Straus, Murray A., Sherry L. Hamby, Sue Boney-McCoy, and David B. Sugarman. "The Revised Conflict Tactics Scales (CTS2): Development and Preliminary Psychometric Data." *Journal of Family Issues* 17(1996):283-316.

Thornton, Arland. "Influence of the Marital History of Parents on the Marital and Cohabitational Experiences of Children." *American Journal of Sociology* 96(1991):868-894.

Thornton, Arland, William G. Axinn, and Jay D. Teachman. "The Influence of School Enrollment and Accumulation on Cohabitation and Marriage in Early Adulthood." *American Sociological Review* 60(1995):762-774.

Tolman, Richard M., and Larry W. Bennett. "A Review of Quantitative Research on Men Who Batter." *Journal of Interpersonal Violence* 5(1990):87-118.

Tontodonato, Pamela, and B. Keith Crew. "Dating Violence, Social Learning Theory, and Gender: A Multivariate Analysis." *Violence and Victims* 7(1992):3-14.

Trainor, Cathy. "Canada's Shelters for Abused Women." *Juristat* 19(1999):1-10.

Trussell, James, and Vaninadha K. Rao. "Premarital Cohabitation and Marital Stability: A Reassessment of the Canadian Evidence." *Journal of Marriage and the Family* 51(1989):535-540.

Turcotte, Pierre. "Common-Law Unions: Nearly Half a Million in 1986." *Canadian Social Trends* 10(1988):35-39.

Turcotte, Pierre, and Alain Bélanger. "Moving in Together: The Formation of First Common-law Unions." *Canadian Social Trends* Winter(1997):7-10.

Ursel, Jane. "The Winnipeg Family Violence Court." Pp. 169-182 in *Wife Assault and the Canadian Criminal Justice System*, edited by M. Valverde, L. MacLeod, and K. Johnson. Toronto: Centre of Criminology, University of Toronto, 1995.

Verburg, Peter. "Is it Statscan—or Propcan?" *Alberta Report* 20(1993): 36-39.

Waite, Linda J. "Does Marriage Matter?" *Demography* 32(1995):483-507.

Walker, Lenore E. *The Battered Woman Syndrome*. New York: Springer, 1984.

Ward, Margaret. *The Family Dynamic: A Canadian Perspective*. Toronto: ITP Nelson, 1998.

Weis, Joseph G. "Family Violence Research Methodology and Design." Pp. 117-162 in *Family Violence*, edited by L. Ohlin and M. Tonry. Chicago: University of Chicago Press, 1989.

Wilson, Margo, Martin Daly, and Christine Wright. "Uxoricide in Canada: Demographic Risk Patterns." *Canadian Journal of Criminology* 35(1993):263-291.

Wilson, Margo, and Martin Daly. "Spousal Homicide." *Juristat* 14(1994):1-15.

Wilson, Margo, Holly Johnson, and Martin Daly. "Lethal and Nonlethal Violence against Wives." *Canadian Journal of Criminology* 37(1995):331-361.

Wolfgang, Marvin E., and Franco Ferracuti. *The Subculture of Violence*. New York: Barnes and Noble, 1967.

Wu, Zheng. "Premarital Cohabitation and the Timing of First Marriage." *Canadian Review of Sociology and Anthropology* 36(1999):109-127.

Wu, Zheng, and Douglas E. Baer. "Attitudes Toward Family and Gender Roles: A Comparison of English and French Canadian Women." *Journal of Comparative Family Studies* 27(1996):437-452.

Wu, Zheng, and T. R. Balakrishnan. "Attitudes towards Cohabitation and Marriage in Canada." *Journal of Comparative Family Studies* 23(1992):1-12.

_____. *Nonmarital Union Dissolution in Canada.* Population Studies Centre, University of Western Ontario, London, 1995.

Yelsma, Paul. "Marriage vs. Cohabitation: Couples' Communication Practices and Satisfaction." *Journal of Communication* 36(1986):94-107.

Yllö, Kersti, and Murray A. Straus. "Interpersonal Violence among Married and Cohabiting Couples." *Family Relations* 30(1981):339-347.

_____. "Patriarchy and Violence against Wives: The Impact of Structural and Normative Factors." Pp. 383-399 in *Physical Violence in American Families: Risk Factors and Adaptations to Violence in 8,145 Families*, edited by M. A. Straus and R. J. Gelles. New Brunswick, N.J.: Transaction, 1990.

Index

About the Authors

Douglas A. Brownridge is assistant professor of family studies at the University of Manitoba. His teaching interests include family violence, family relationships, theory, and research methods. Much of his work has dealt with violence against women. His current research interests include violence against women in Québec and violence against immigrant women in Canada. He is also currently guest editor for a special issue of the *Journal of Comparative Family Studies* (with Shiva Halli) on violence against women in the family.

Shiva S. Halli is professor of sociology at the University of Manitoba. Over the past thirteen years he has published six books and more than thirty refereed articles in national and international journals. He has received many awards for his research. His book on minority status and fertility was chosen by *Choice Magazine* as the outstanding academic book for 1987. In 1990, he received the Rh Award from the University of Manitoba for his outstanding contributions to scholarship and research in the social sciences. His research is also regularly discussed in the national and local daily newspapers.